WITHDRAWN

The Spaces In Between

AN ARCHITECT'S JOURNEY

Also by Nathaniel Alexander Owings

The American Aesthetic

The Spaces In Between,

AN ARCHITECT'S JOURNEY

Nathaniel Alexander Owings

Houghton Mifflin Company Boston
1973

First Printing   w

ISBN: 0-395-15468-5
Library of Congress Catalog
Card Number: 72-9012
Printed in the United States
of America

To all the unnamed people
of SOM who shaped
the experience

Foreword

SOMEONE ELSE will have to write an objective history of Skidmore, Owings and Merrill. What follows is a very personal recording. I have selected only things that made me laugh or swear or cry.

Believing that the printed word is the most lasting form of human effort, I first wanted to set out my basic feeling about the American aesthetic — how our ecological and structural urges meshed — and this I did in collaboration with Bill Garnett in *The American Aesthetic* (Harper and Row, 1969).

For three years I have been trying to write my own version of the growth of the tiny organism that Louis Skidmore and I started in 1936, now an organization proliferating all over. It began as a personal thing between the two of us, and has never developed into a corporation as most architectural firms have. It is not a product of a conglomeration or a computer.

As my younger partners created their own legends about SOM, coming up with startling statements as to why Skidmore and I did thus and so, it became clear to me that there would be legends, so I might as well have a hand in their creation.

It has been difficult to explain what I have been a part of for these past forty years. Architects are involved primarily with themselves and need only explain their own personal work. My contributions have been — and still are — in the preparation of an environment within which others might create, and operate fully within the structure, framework or armature of SOM. This is the entity which Louis Skidmore and I initiated.

I as an individual cannot point to any major building for which I am solely responsible. But I can point to individual, brilliant architects like Gordon Bunshaft, Charles Bassett and Walter Netsch who are products of this entity. I can claim a major role in planning projects like Pennsylvania Avenue in Washington, D.C. This kind of thing architects just didn't used to do, and still don't.

SOM is a phenomenon. Architects, engineers, politicians, sociologists and psychiatrists have tried to figure out what makes SOM tick. My book is supposed to give a few clues as to its nature. The claim I make for SOM is that we have established a framework by which major urban centers can be shaped and formed to the new requirements of this population-exploding age — ground rules for the development of cities with proper open spaces around them and their high-density, low-rise complexes separated properly into natural ecosystems. I feel that the hope for the future lies in planning, where man can live in harmony with nature, contributing his own natural system of habitat building, just as the beavers create their own form.

I believe that man must develop a humility toward nature. Thus he can produce the necessary habitat in *harmony* with nature. There has been more building done in the United States since 1929 than there was between 1802 and 1929. During these years our environment, our habitat, was largely controlled by the architecturally unconcerned. To use these energies in the proper direction was part of the job Skidmore and I needed to do. We also needed a new kind of "man for all seasons" to help

viii

us do it, one who would be at home in all walks of life, to sit at a conference table with a client to help decide in the formative stages what was to be built. In earlier days, the architect was called in at the end of the decision-making process and told what to build, was treated as an artist too dumb to know the facts of the profit-making system. The decisions were often wrong.

Even the location of the project on the ground, or the use to which it would be put, was almost always decided before the architect got into the act. These predecisions cut off most of the areas of creativity. SOM had to earn a place as equal with these decision-makers. To gain the respect of the client, SOM had to be powerful, had to have national coverage.

In almost any major city in the United States you will find principal buildings done by SOM. To accomplish this coverage we used a very old ethic: the master builder system based on the anonymous Gothic builders of the Middle Ages.

When the White House Conference on the Industrial World Ahead: A Look at Business in 1990 was held in Washington last year I tried to prove that there was no such thing as good planning or economic stability without beauty. This shook up a good many people — it was supposed to. I was looked upon as a radical, but a captive radical, with SOM involved in such huge projects as the John Hancock Center in Chicago.

We deal with the oldest forms of man's concern: his shelter, and, even more, his need for beauty and personal expression. I feel that if we can satisfy the need for personal expression by building a habitat in cooperation with nature — not against it — then our philosophy in SOM can have long-term relevance. We can continue to renew creative ideas which may flower in structure and habitat. Nonarchitecture — open spaces — will be the objective, and the buildings will simply frame them. We can use the oldest of all forms, yet one which is considered new today: we can reintroduce into our crowded cities the open space — the plaza — where man can dance, celebrate and experience the joy of living in *the spaces in between.*

Contents

xi

CONTENTS

BOOK II — FOUR MIRACLES

Illustrations

following page 146

Chicago: "Big John" and the little Victorian water tower
Indianapolis: Soldiers and Sailors Monument
N.A.O. — Eagle Scout on Jamboree
Nat watches Rufus Dawes sign contract for the Sky Ride, Chi-
    cago 1933 World's Fair
Louis Skidmore, 1937
Skid and Eloise bound for Bermuda, 1945
Chicago: the riveted edge of Lake Michigan
Six early partners: N.A.O., John Merrill, Louis Skidmore, Wal-
    ter Severinghaus, Gordon Bunshaft, Bill Hartmann
New York: Lever House
San Francisco: Crown Zellerbach in its plaza
Under the banyan tree, 1957
New York, where the sun rises on the Chase Manhattan Bank
    building
Plaza, Chase Manhattan Bank
Bassett, Kraft and Dunlap at a partners' meeting in Luxor, Egypt
Hawaii: the corridorless interior courts of Mauna Kea Hotel
Air Force Academy against the Rampart Range
Air Force chapel

BOOK I

Compost

1

Black Dirt and River Water

IN THE DARKNESS of that Fourth of July night the pinwheel nailed to our big maple quivered and hit its stride, chattering into a gyroscope spin sending forth glowing structures, a clutch of shafts: glass, metal, fused into shapes — the slim, cool shaft of our "first tall office building," Park Avenue's twenty-one-story Lever House; in the heart of Wall Street another tower sixty stories high, Number One Chase Plaza, the Chase Manhattan Bank; a pueblo-like cluster of glass and aluminum shapes shining on a mesa, the United States Air Force Academy standing against the Rampart Range in Colorado; and on the Kauna coast of the island of Hawaii, a giant fragment gleaming against the sea, a resort hotel; another in Australia; and the green glass shaft of the Crown Zellerbach Building in its own plaza at the foot of San Francisco's Embarcadero — all these and more the designs of Skidmore, Owings and Merrill, architects, planners and engineers; all of these tumbling from the charring pinwheel spokes in a rush of terrifying violence.

And then I woke up, dazed, this miscellany of twentieth-century architecture still falling around me. Was this evidence of forty years of designing constructs simply detritus? What parts were relevant? What was their place? For me, these designs were intended to be "form givers," for purposes deeper than mere shelter — but had they turned out that way? Were they any better than what had gone before? If the images I had seen in my nightmare dream reflected in any way a social implication, then I had to ask: where were we headed?

Architecture has been my way but I have never been satisfied. I have persistent visions, out of which have come some ideas. The most persistent is the central theme of bringing man back to the seat of the will, the plaza, the core, where space and architecture began. The plaza and the kiva are the seeds, the kernels, where man, since prerecorded history, has carried out his functions — his trade, his festival, his worship. Since then, buildings have become more complex, but, as efficiency has gained, the joie de vivre has shrunk. I ask, can't we reach back to the beginnings, can't we reach back to the human element?

Perhaps I have been lucky. I have been able to stimulate this concept because, it seems, things are always happening to me. The desire lines of other people's lives suddenly flash out of nowhere and intercept or cross my own. Events unknown to me consistently match my own conspectus, fitting, expanding and strengthening an invisible collaborator's plans with my own. A stranger sits next to me on the plane. I may hold the key to his unsolved problem and an exciting building can result. Or I meet an old friend or fellow architect, and we discover parallel dreams which our chance meeting can turn into reality. So many happenings turn miracle that I have come to believe, as Flammarion did, "there exists in nature in myriad activity a psychic element, the essential nature of which is still hidden to us."

A chance idea expressed years earlier rests latent until it is mysteriously conjoined with others, and all form a powerful compost. Gardeners, amateur or professional, know about compost. Judged as waste in one context, things can, taken together, react to create fertile soil for growth toward ends directed by

4

mysterious forces beyond our vision. There is an excitement and a hope in the knowledge that there need be no waste.

The New Yorker magazine said it cheerfully: "Composting is an exciting way of changing otherwise worthless leaves, grass cuttings, coffee grounds and other organic stuff (but nothing mailable second class) into a heady, chocolate-colored mold that drives whatever it touches into a frenzy of growth. As a matter of fact we know a gardener in Larchmont who is so enthusiastic about his compost that he will take guests out to it in the middle of winter and invite them to feel of its ferment by sinking their arms in it up to the elbow — a reportedly ineffable sensation."

My own original compost was the rich black sod of a heartland that measures its topsoil in feet, not inches. I was born in Indianapolis, Indiana, on February 5, 1903, delivered on our dining room table by our family physician, Dr. Kimberlin, and was already vocally seeking public approval.

An Owings had had a hand in the city's shape from the very beginning. In 1816, two years after the British burned Washington, the state of Indiana was carved out of the public domain and admitted to the Union. This was done by the Congress of the United States. In 1820 a commission was appointed to select the site for the state capitol. In their wisdom these gentlemen placed this site almost exactly at the geographic center of the new state: the cabin of John McCormick, on the unnavigable White River in a dense forest, without means of communication. A town of sorts was laid out in 1821 within the original site. Some land speculation followed, but when the state government actually moved there in 1825, the town had but a single street. The archives listed among the six hundred inhabitants the name of my grandfather: Nathaniel Bond Owings.

At about this time the city fathers adopted a L'Enfant-inspired plan and followed it with remarkable integrity. The plan imposed a geometry pleasing to the eye, drawing city traffic into the central core, profoundly affecting the movement of people.

"The utility of the cart," we are reminded by Lao Tzu, "depends on the hollow center in which the axle turns." The city's four avenues radiate from this hollow center, confirming the dignity of the monument to the four corners of the city. The central shaft rises to a height of two hundred forty-eight and a half feet above the street, surmounted, of course, by a figure called Miss Indiana, where a balcony commands a panoramic view of the flat prairie city.

The ghost-white Indiana limestone shaft rises out of a cluster of William Blake angels. The guidebook reports that water can flow through the fountains at their base at the rate of twenty thousand gallons per minute. This central tower of my boyhood world was completed in 1902 and cost six hundred thousand dollars. The focal point of Indianapolis, it is baroque and self-conscious, located east of the true prairie and west of the true East. This monument to war is like a giant confection molded from dough, baked in some great oven and overlaid with pale, enameled icing.

For Indianapolis, this "Victorian puffery" is the Eiffel Tower, the Boston Common, the Statue of Liberty. It is a symbol of urban identity that its early citizens thought necessary, discounting their own setting: a limitless ocean of tall corn and golden wheat.

Yes, Indianapolis shaped my point of view for life. Tree-lined vistas, broad boulevards and solid buildings with granite, marble and stone, bronze and copper, confirmed from birth my instinct for permanence and a predilection for style.

Turning the leaves of our early family album . . . my father: Nathaniel Fleming Owings, of Welsh and pixie extraction, seated proud and straight, with handlebar mustachios, hat and stick on table, mocking dark eyes glinting with a sense of humor that was impossible to hide even in that stiff pose.

Standing beside him, almost in his shadow, is Mother: graceful, lithe, slender, with charming, appealing dark eyes that

6

snapped a little, handsome, stylish rather than pretty, her submissive pose not quite hiding a thoroughly independent spirit. Her mother, Mima Murray Alexander, was the youngest of thirteen girls, which explains why my mother was an only child. Mother was very young when her parents died and she was brought up the ward of many aunts and cousins, the recipient of hand-me-down dresses until, on her eighteenth birthday, she got her first new one.

Father seemed unconcerned as to life's outcome. Mother's enigmatic smile expressed some doubt. She looked capable of taking over if necessary. In front my sister and I stand, both apple-cheeked, hand in hand, starched and stiff, she with white bows standing straight out and I, three years older and acting it, exuding confidence in what few angles my plump body could muster.

My father's love of textured, aromatic woods skillfully cut, exposing grain and color, provided a continuity of interest that held us all together. His pursuit of these exotic veneers to be incorporated in fine furniture became the family business. Absent for long periods, upon his return he told us of his journeys into the interior of Old Mexico and South America. There he sought out the single tree in remote jungles. He told us shadowy stories of dense, creeper-draped pools writhing with crocodiles; and, such a veteran of the jungle, he said that the mosquitoes had lost their taste for his blood.

He brought back an ancient robe, an artifact made from the feathers of a thousand tiny birds, and a narrow strip of board with a long sequence of the episodes of a Mexican cockfight also depicted in feathers. My father sailed the seven seas with Sir Francis Drake. He was a conquistador with Cortez in Mexico, interchangeable as redskin or backwoodsman in James Fenimore Cooper's tales, equally effective as the wielder of the deadly longbow in Sherwood Forest. He brought far-off peoples of strange worlds home to us, sharing each high adventure. We were Ulysses' children, but we liked home best with Father there.

I made trips to Father's mill in his bright red 1910 Stutz roadster, an early model high above the ground. I remember being rescued, caught by his strong arm as I lunged over the low door while we sped along Park Avenue at twenty miles an hour with the pavement rushing by below.

Father's arrival at the mill transformed it into a theater. With the dramatic flare of a Lord Duveen exhibiting a rare Correggio, he would point to the rich burl of a matched flitch of veneer skillfully cut from a black walnut stump, his long-fingered hands moving the folded strips of veneer: ruby teak, amber-and-gold-patterned white oak, cherry and red mahogany, from one high stack to another. A film of pungent sawdust covered every surface, giving off a rich bouquet and creating a patina. Those smells and textures return to memory at unexpected moments, providing for me the taste of the tea biscuit of Marcel Proust.

Our neighborhood had two churches, a grocery store, barber shop, drugstore, the Morton Place Livery Stable — named after Indiana's Civil War governor — and Public School No. 45, all within easy walking distance. The vacant lot where our gang built shacks and held secret club meetings was our equivalent of an urban park, essential to any modern neighborhood development plan.

Edward Hall, George Sidensticker and Bruz Ruckelhaus alternated in monitoring our neighborhood gang in those devilish divertissements which often aroused the ire of mothers. Cherries, illicitly garnered from the top of Mrs. Hall's cherry tree, tasted best even when that name rang out: "Nathaniel! What are you doing in that tree?" I must say it seemed obvious.

A dozen and a half houses very much like our own on both sides formed the nucleus of a family life revolving around the customs of our German and Irish neighbors. The Germans, with names like Slotzhauer, Sahm and Haerle, more than outbalanced

8

the Irish Catholic Kellys, O'Rileys and Maddens, and their pre-dominance explains why both English and German were taught in our school until World War I. Memorial Day, Fourth of July and Christmas were the important festivals. Memorial Day meant iris, peonies and flags. The Fourth of July meant fire-crackers and flags. Christmas was a German festival, with St. Nicholas and his reindeer far outweighing the Biblical images of the manger and the three wise men.

Our two-story house was of white clapboard, with kitchen and combination living and dining room divided by an arch. A stair hall led to the basement — where there were shadowy places for hiding — a facility mostly missing from modern houses. Largely because Welsh, Scottish and Irish blood lines are pixie, we lived among a galaxy of imaginary things which included a colony of fairies in the furnace room. They were well concealed, never sending out a trace. But in the evenings Eloise and I would listen over the hot air register in the living room — with Father strangely absent — and with encouragement from Mother would cautiously lower an exploratory bent pin tied to a long piece of grocery string through the grill. Often a tug on our line would reward us and we would carefully draw up a caramel candy hooked to the pin. Once I drew up a small penknife.

My outrage persists over the senseless destruction of the attic brought on by so-called contemporary architecture. The reasons, whether economic or aesthetic, do not justify the loss. It is too late to question whether this cultural genocide should be laid at the door of the architect or the contractor, or fashion or mobility. With the house pared down to bare bones, we have discarded the storeroom of sentiment and lost a good many potentially valuable antiques in the process.

On rainy days when there were costumes to search out, we made for the attic. Our attic, like those of our neighbors, was a treasure house. I remember the eerie feeling as the faint light glimmered through the two dormer windows, and the cobwebs attached from the rafters to the pregnant steamer trunks. The anteroom of the tomb of King Tutankhamen had no more to offer in the way of cultural symbols than was to be found in our attic.

The remembered musty smell of the attic revives a remembered sound: the purring of the family sewing machine as our itinerant seamstress pedaled her way through endless blouses, dickies, skirts for Eloise, shirts and pants for me, and more elaborate creations copied out of the pattern book for Mother. In black alpaca, looking like a daguerreotype of herself, this shadowy creature lived with us for a week each year. As a seamstress she was essential, but in her masterly distribution of the county gossip, indispensable.

There is the smell of the thick heat of an Indiana summer night, when fireflies flashed like tiny Christmas tree lights suspended by invisible wires from the heavy maple leaf canopy; when porches were emptied by common consent and rockers sank into the damp, thick turf amidst the din of crickets and katydids.

Our living room walls were lined with golden oak sectional bookcases filled with matched volumes of Scott, Eliot, Thackeray, Dickens. I suspect that Father bought the books for their bindings and Mother read the volumes for their content. I read Conan Doyle's *Sir Nigel*, the story of a young boy winning knighthood; Robert Louis Stevenson's *The Black Arrow*, with old Appleyard, an arrow between his shoulders, and Dick Shelton, Joanna and Sir Daniel; *Little Smoke*, about a white boy captured by the Indians; and the elegantly illustrated volume *The Capture of Montezuma by Cortez*.

Beyond the city, the prairies. Indianapolis was nothing without those endless oceans of windswept grain surrounding it, marked only by dark patches of farm buildings nestled in clusters of hardwoods, hickory and maple. One of those dark patches was my mother's Cousin Will Alexander's farm, and the combination of farm and city automatically and forever burned into my heart a love for both. The central core city and the endless open space of the American scene were inseparable, and in October, when the frost was on the pumpkin, that farm had no equal.

So far as I could tell in all the years we visited my Cousin Will's farm near Rushville, his good wife, India Alexander, never sat down. While we three and the four male Alexanders (Cousin Will and sons Donald, Russell and Ivan) and the farm hands, at harvest time, tucked into plates heaped with fried chicken, mashed potatoes and gravy, cold pickled beets, slabs of baked ham, baked beans, buttermilk with real butter floating, apple pie covered with cream so thick it could barely flow from the big pitcher, and peach ice cream from the hand freezer, Cousin India seemed to hover a foot or two above the wide board floor somewhere between the great black wood-burning stove and the oilcloth-covered dinner table, always on the alert to correct the slightest threat of short supply in any item on that groaning board. Cousin India stoked those threshers — sons, husband, farm hands and us — with the same vigor, the same skill, the same commitment that they, the threshers, showed in stoking their threshing machines or corn husking devices.

But we weren't eating all the time. Within that kitchen, redolent of bulging loaves of newly baked bread, square yards of browning cinnamon-covered cookies and gingerbread and chocolate devil's-food cake and angel food cake and raisin and spice and burnt sugar cake, Cousin India, her flushed face conditioned by the chemistry of a kind of perpetual country sauna, directed traffic with her dishwater-chapped hands and held absolute sway over her dynasty of men. Within the kitchen we were enjoying the benefits of a matriarchy. But once outside that kitchen, with heavy boots and thick denim jackets back in place,

Cousin Will and the three boys and the farm hands regained their manhood. Armed with shovel or pitchfork, harness or saddle, they took over and it became a man's world.

Most machines were essentially two- or four-legged and the prime fuel was corn or wheat, oats or hay. Mechanization had not taken over and kerosene and simple combustion engines did little to lessen the work. It was a bone-tiring, ten- or twelve-hour, dawn to dusk day for the men and women and animals alike.

This was flat black dirt, corn and hog country where forty inches of rain fell almost every year. Crops could be depended upon. Walnut snake fences still enclosed the north forty with its grove of hard maple. The frost and the sap produced maple syrup and the appetite for it. The barns bulged with rows of blimp-shaped cows steaming in the evening air. The sour-sweet acrid smell of urine, sweat and milk stung the nostrils at milking time. *Swish, swish, swish,* the warm milk foamed against the side of the pail each time one of my cousins, with an admonitory "Whoa, Bessie," released another stream and eased the tension of the swollen udder.

Cousin Will was aggressively proud. This was a marked characteristic of an Alexander and one example of it was his prize-winning strain of hybrid seed corn much valued in Rush County, predictably named "Alexander's Blue Ribbon Seed Corn." This crowning achievement ranked in his order of priorities with wife, family, home and mother.

For Cousin Will, his occupation was an art. This confidence in the order of things made him prosperous. The foursquare yellow brick structure boldly profiled on a treeless prominence said so. English basement, first and second floors and attic, fronted by a huge porch and flanked by a porte-cochère embraced four rooms and a central hall on each floor. The demands of World War I for corn, hogs and cereals were reflected in this splendid house. But prosperity hadn't changed the Alexanders. They lived in the kitchen and the sitting room facing the barn. The only time I was ever allowed in the two front rooms was for Ivan's wedding and Cousin Will's funeral. The golden oak front stairs seemed to have known only the stocking-footed steps of the wielder of dust mops.

In this man's world, this daughterless, sisterless duchy of Rush County, my little sister, Eloise, was the princess. The Alexanders gave her her own pony, spoiled her rotten. They made me sick. Through no fault of my own as far as I could see, I was a boy and as welcome and necessary around that farm as a sixth finger on a third hand. My lack of talent for farm skills was no secret. Day's end would usually bring anguished cries across the fields from my cousins in hot pursuit of loose animals or fowl from the barnyard. Nathaniel had left the gate open.

In those days it was easier to get from Indianapolis to Rushville and back than it is today. When I mentioned the interurban system as it existed in 1914 between Indianapolis and Rushville, my wife protested: "Oh, come now! Stop using the term 'interurban' in such simple rural places as Rushville and Indianapolis fifty years ago!" But in those days there was an electric railroad, a network covering the central area of Indiana which, if it were operating today, would solve most of those transportation problems considered beyond our reach in this wealthiest of countries.

There were two more Alexanders in Indianapolis: sisters, old maids. My Cousin Georgia Alexander — masculine, angular, large boned — arrogated to herself the direction of my education. She had the advantage on two fronts, both as a close relative and as the superintendent of the Indianapolis public schools. Cousin Georgia could bring her influence to bear at home and at school — and did. Progressive in her views, Cousin Georgia had written the officially adopted *Alexander Speller,* and her standing in the school system was comparable to Cousin Will Alexander's standing in the seed corn industry.

I suspect that, underneath, Cousin Georgia wasn't all that

gruff. Her sister Grace, the tiny, wispish, feminine half, was probably the stronger willed. Cousin Grace kept house and found time to be an executive editor for Bobbs-Merrill, publishers. She also wrote two novels, one called *Prince Cinderella*. Staying in the background, she pushed her sister forward. Together they were startling: the tall, lumpy one in shapeless black, hair gathered in a loose knot; the tiny one in a gray flowing gown.

Cousin Georgia didn't enter a room — she charged. I resisted containment by a halfhearted show of independence. Somehow I sensed that this childless spinster had tacitly adopted me, giving me an advantage. As a school officer she had reason enough to avoid any outward show of favoritism, but she overdid it to the point of near persecution. This treatment stimulated rather than crushed me.

Despite or because of the *Alexander Speller,* I never learned to spell. I blamed Cousin Georgia for my ignorance. She had discarded the disciplines of spelling and drilling in the three R's, replacing the birch rod with the laxity of sweet reason. Latin, which can turn language from a clumsy sword into a fine rapier, was another omission in my education. And so it is today that my friends preserve my letters as curiosities of spelling and grammar.

Religion was one area from which Cousin Georgia was excluded. That was strictly Mother's area. A disembodied spirit, Cousin Georgia apparently didn't need religion. We did, because Mother did. How Mother discovered Unitarianism in the first place I do not know.

For different reasons, both sides of our family looked upon us as barbarians. My father's sister, Aunt Jo, and her husband and five children were devout Catholics. My mother's relations, the Pruitts and the Mathewses and the Murrays, were Methodists and Congregationalists. Both sides agreed on one thing only: our prospects in the next world.

Dr. Frank Scott Cory Wicks, our Unitarian minister, was a

man from England by way of Boston, a whole man whose spirit and intellect must have found scant response in Indianapolis. But I suspect he took advantage of this intellectual malnutrition and puckishly accented the unconventional: the baseball game Sunday afternoon, the red necktie worn with episcopal gray, his sporty handlebar mustaches beneath his expressive, amused eyes — in all, a most uncleric manner. In appearance and general mien he suggested my father. Certainly a strong current flowed as I sat at the feet of Dr. Wicks. He stoked my mind in small doses, offering as a privilege things that are so often presented in school as a chore. He allowed me to discover his book-lined library and made the Saturday afternoons spent there an exciting adventure. He fed my unsuspecting mind on a carefully designed program of reading that under other circumstances would have been called lessons. Balzac and Anatole France were more alive than most people I knew; at the age of fourteen I raised some eyebrows when I read France's *The Red Lily* in a minister's library.

The year: 1913. Indiana was not yet stripped of her dense forests. Fine hardwoods such as white oak, black walnut, hickory, ash, beech and maple remained. This, plus the central location of Indianapolis as an important railroad center, had been reason enough for my father to place his mill and lumberyard just southeast of the city. That the spur track serving his mill ran parallel to White River was purely an accident of geography. The shallow, placid, meandering stream had no commercial use, nor any record as a potential source of flood.

One day this placid river turned into a swollen, writhing torrent. Old newspaper files for the fall of 1913 confirm my boyhood impressions. There really was a deluge, a month-long unending downpour, causing White River to do the impossible.

I remember standing close to my father, braced against the wind on the flat roof of his mill, watching the roiling waters of the flood beneath us tear away the precious logs. One by one they pitched down that torrent and disappeared. I understood the value he placed on those logs. His whole scheme of things was tearing apart. Hurting like the day at the mill when a band saw severed a man's hand, I watched him suffer, his capital, spiritual and financial, vanishing in the foaming maelstrom. His wry expression as he watched, seemingly exhilarated, was a brave gesture. Whipped by the wind above the roaring water, I heard him cry out, making one last show of defiance — but the river won. The flood that washed away those precious logs also washed away the solid ground around my father's root structure. He began to drift, moving from New Albany to Crawfordsville and back again to Indianapolis.

Suddenly, as suddenly as the flood had come and gone, my father was gone. The burden of the family's support was on Mother. The net effect of the death of my father seemed to have been to strip down to its bare essentials the business of living. Mother at thirty-seven and I at eleven sharply reoriented our minds toward income-producing occupations and I began to make choices between things to do slanted toward those that could best help pay the bills. Mother assumed my father's debts and a part of every cent I made went into their liquidation. I remember sharing the sense of relief and freedom from a load when the last note was paid.

Our Uncle John offered Mother a job in his furniture factory as a bookkeeper. Apparently unaware of Women's Lib, he paid her just one half of what he would have had to pay a man to fill the same job. At night she took correspondence courses to learn public accounting. With a C.P.A. after her name, she finally escaped to a command post on the balcony of W. K. Stewart's bookstore as credit manager and bookkeeper. Authors, educators and ordinary book lovers got into the habit of drifting into Stewart's (an affiliate of Bobbs-Merrill Publishing Company), which served as a downtown intellectual center, for a bit of gossip with Mother. Routinely George Ade, Meredith Nicholson and Booth

16

Tarkington dropped by; and sometimes not so routinely there was an exciting invasion through the back shipping entrance by James Whitcomb Riley, in his cups, declaiming at the top of his voice one of his lesser-known odes, such as "The Outhouse Built for Two."

These were the war years, with the guns of August 1914, Germany moving into Belgium, the teaching of German banned from the schools, the Turnverein renamed the Atheneum, my Uncle Albert Sahm taking down the Kaiser's picture from his parlor wall, war bond posters — "That Liberty Shall Not Perish from the Earth — Buy Liberty Bonds" — the flu epidemic and wearing a mask in the streetcars, where everybody else wore one too. Then the Armistice, a parade, and it was over. Most of this passed over my head and my own concerns swung in a wide circle around my center: Mother's balcony.

Some boys are committed to the church and are sent early to a seminary, or enrolled in St. Paul's or Groton at birth. Instead, my family chose scouting and my ordainment was assured through another cousin, Scoutmaster Rexford Pruitt, who saw to it that scouting was not a passing phase, as it seemed to be in many families. For me it held the authority of a monastic rule: voluntary, self-imposed and fun.

Induction as a Tenderfoot Scout on my twelfth birthday in 1915 was neither casual nor accidental. There was the phenomenon of a new kind of youth movement behind it. Throughout history certain ethical cults have caught hold of the minds or hearts of men and spread over whole continents like wildfire. Scouting did just that in a very short time without the benefit of fire or sword. There were scouts in every part of the world — almost half a million in the United States by the time I was twelve. The Boy Scout movement had reached the status of a sect.

Like any viable way of life, the rule included ritual and rewards for the attainment of its goals. Besides the ethical experi-

17

ences of the oath and the good turn and the scout law, we learned to be at home in the woods, to tie a square knot, to know the constellation Orion, to save a life on land or water, to survive in the wilderness, to spot a kingfisher's nest and find the first snow lily. There were meetings each week in the church basement and camping on White River on weekends. The boys in our troop, passing through the ranks from Tenderfoot to First Class, or the coveted Life, Star and Eagle, were held fascinated, mystically bound by marvelously combined ancient devices from many cultures, proven through millenniums to motivate man. The system was as simple as that indigestible staple of a campfire supper, "twist on a stick," or a cold dip at sunrise in camp, while rivaling in complexity the feathered headpiece of a Gambel quail. From reveille to taps, between the ages of twelve and seventeen, I shared scouting's secrets, quite unaware of the part they would later play.

Added to the ritual of church, school and scouting was a diversity of jobs. Delivering groceries on the handlebars of my bicycle was a job filled with hazards even for a careful, organized boy — and I was neither. That job ended abruptly one Saturday night when a clutch of freshly baked pumpkin pies crashed to the pavement.

One summer job I had at an amusement park consisted primarily of beheading chickens and making the cones for ice cream. I had to pour just the right amount of thick batter onto a waffle iron, which was in turn supported on a portable open-flame gasoline stove. The gasoline stove was a most dangerous combustible item in any case. The large coffee pot in which the batter was held, unwieldy in itself, became thoroughly covered with batter on the sides and bottom early in the process. When the pot inevitably stuck to the gasoline stove, the entire contrivance upset. The stove exploded and the ensuing conflagration enveloped the flimsy buildings, showering sparks and flames on the adjacent chicken yard. In my effort to escape I fell and cut a long gash in my leg. Bleeding freely, by reflex I released the hundreds of chickens in the coops, and they and I fled. On the streetcar headed for home, a fellow passenger spotted my open wound, extracted a wad of chewing tobacco from his bulging cheek and slapped it over the gash — a homely but effective remedy.

At sixteen, stage-struck, I adopted Stuart Walker and his stock company when they came to the Murat Theater and for three summers I served as a kind of "roustabout" in old-fashioned stock, eighteenth-century drama, Restoration, Classic and Modern productions. We had varied excitement, two premières — *The Book of Job* and Booth Tarkington's *Seventeen* — then *School for Scandal, The Rivals* and *The Country Wife.*

Like a starry-eyed puppy I wandered around, behind and in front of the stage, and shadowed actors and actresses: Tom Powers, George Soames, Ruth Gordon, Judith Lowrey, Gregory Kelly, Wallace Ford. But it was George Gaul, whether playing in *Grand Hotel* or *The Book of Job,* whether crook, villain or saint, it was George Gaul for whom I risked truancy and family discipline rather than miss one of his performances. Years later, after a successful presentation to a client where I had staged the basic architectural idea in a particularly dramatic setting, I would have reason to remember Stuart Walker and my introduction through him to great theater.

While not necessarily great theater but ranking well above Commencement, the significant yearly event of the graduating class at Arsenal Technical High School was the senior play, traditionally staged in that same fifteen-hundred-seat Murat Theater. In 1920 our play was to be Sir James Barrie's successful comedy, *The Admirable Crichton,* a choice strangely prophetic of the reversal of roles of Labor and Establishment to come in the 1970s. Jobs, scouts and dates had affected my grades to an alarming degree — alarming, that is, to my teachers — and for permission to take part in the play my class adviser had to be

19

lulled into a vague understanding that I was doing little more than walking on stage carrying a spear.

They seemed to think that I fitted the minor part of The Honorable Ernest Woolley, who answered to the description: ". . . a happy smile on his pleasant, insignificant face . . . this man about town . . . was not without a sense of humor . . . saved by carrying a smile . . . in his spats, shall we say."

When the great evening came, backstage was chaos as our directress collapsed at the sight of the newly shorn Admirable Crichton, Kenneth Dynes, whose mother had just given him a fresh haircut. The nervous cast twitched in the wings while the curtain rose. On the otherwise empty stage, there was I, seated on a papier-mâché rock in a stand of potted funeral palms, clad in flannel pajamas with a silk hat cockily placed on the head and a monocle at the eye. I can still recall my opening lines: "Wrecked, wrecked, wrecked on an island . . . the sole survivor of the steam yacht *Bluebell* sunk in a frightful gale . . . assailed by . . . wildcats and . . . snakes which terrifies us extremely."

There was an instant audience response. My spine tingling, I savored that moment and have never ceased to try to arrange things so that it would happen again and again.

2

I Discover the Cathedrals

I was totally unprepared for the miracle of the cathedrals. No one had taught me really to look at the façade of a building. Not even Cousin Georgia.

Sometimes it takes a miracle to make a miracle. It seemed miracle enough to be one of 304 Boy Scouts from all over the United States aboard the S.S. *Pocahontas,* bound for the first world Boy Scout Jamboree, to be held in London. The date was July 20, 1920. I was there representing Indianapolis, having won out in a heated competition among long-time scouting pals which had suddenly pitted us against each other — a strange sensation.

We found ourselves in a huge tent encampment with boys from around the world, our every move under scrutiny as we performed our functions in the Jamboree. Then after our job was done, the second miracle happened: I rounded a critical bend — I experienced the confrontation of the cathedrals.

Our American contingent visited the sites of the very recent battles in France, including Château-Thierry and the Marne. Taller than most, and bareheaded — my hat had been blown overboard crossing the Atlantic — I stood in the front rank and laid wreaths before plain white crosses on those battlefields throughout France. And then I discovered the cathedrals.

At the western portal of Notre Dame de Paris, as I entered the rich, dark canyons of the interior, a flood of music rolled out and over me. A wedding Mass for some high personage and the resulting stately procession was in progress. The imposing Mass diverted me to a side aisle and, as I reached the crossing of the transept and passed into the Lady Chapel, I found there a different, somber congregation and heard the muted tones of a funeral Mass. Within a few moments of entering the Virgin's great church I had experienced the gamut of life through death.

Outside the church again, in the brilliant Paris sunshine I stared upward at the masculine broad-stroked tiers of living stone and shadow, the stark white towers turned to the copper bronze of the western façade. That image of Notre Dame on that late afternoon of August 1920 still remains my most important architectural vision. I knew, even before I read *The Education of Henry Adams,* that this was the Virgin's work, not man's.

Mont-Saint-Michel was a clustered mountain of stone climaxed in a beautiful, graceful spire, built for no other reason than the glory of God. The miracle lay in the whole. A toy castle floating on a cloud surrounded by water.

Finally there was the approach across the plains of Beauce and my first sighting of the slim whiffs of spire suspended above the plain as I discovered for myself the feminine masterpiece of all, the Cathedral of Chartres — finding the potency of the *Tree of Jesse,* "Milton in burning glass," and the glory of the medallions in the Charlemagne windows, contributed, I will always remember, by the Merchants, Tailors and Furriers Guild. It was years before I understood the technical aspects of the miracle of Chartres. I appreciated then the varying shades of blue in those tenth-, eleventh- and twelfth-century windows simply because they were there and the light was streaming through them.

The miracle lay in grasping the truth that a structure, or a group of structures, is an orchestration controlled by one great idea amplified in a thousand ways, but always one great idea which must spring from the basic needs and usages of the people at a given time. These miracles occur from instinctive drives which originate in emotional rather than intellectual impulses — never the reverse. Louis Henri Sullivan sums up his *Autobiography of an Idea* with these words: ". . . the initial instinct of the child as set forth is the basis of all fruitful ideas, and that the growth in power of such ideas is in itself a work of instinct, that, if it has been convincingly shown that instinct is primary and intellect secondary in all the great works of man, this portrayal is justified."

Returning home I was surprised to find the routine unchanged. I felt that everything should be different. I was.

There was the flat prairie campus of the University of Illinois in Urbana. I had gone there to enroll in the College of Architecture, armed with nine hundred dollars from my mother's savings, a bid from the Sigma Chi fraternity and a resolve to fulfill my Cousin Georgia's faith in me.

As I passed beneath the baroque portals of the school I was struck by an enormous plan drawing, called an *envoi*, of the École des Beaux Arts. If this complex product was to be the object of my education, I knew that it was more than I could ever handle. With the blurred images of Chartres and Notre Dame whirling in my brain, I modified my major to something simpler: architectural engineering.

Straight into the Sigma Chi fraternity house I went, and once past the door, I learned how the Brothers made the decisions and processed the raw freshmen. I watched the system as each of that year's classes — sophomore, junior and senior — distilled and molded each other until nine months and nine hundred dollars were gone. My table manners were improved and I had mastered the Sigma Chi grip. I was not only broke, but disenchanted. I chose to try for the United States Military Academy at West

Point where pay, as well as education, was offered. I was eighteen, and my architectural dream could wait.

Suddenly an involuntary passenger on a mental roller coaster, I shot to the top on learning that I had passed the entrance examination, and plummeted to the bottom when the physical examiner reported that I had nephritis — Bright's disease — "with but six months to a year to live."

Lying flat on my back, dazed, I became a ward of the neighborhood. Then, of course, Cousin Georgia appeared carrying six thick volumes of Gibbon's *The Decline and Fall of the Roman Empire*. I kept my sanity by moving everything but my body into another era, another age, another character, as each book I read opened up another door, another role to play. Almost all the time my bed and the body on it were far, far away, filled with the excitement, danger and risk found in those books.

Mother kept her sanity with the minutiae of the credit risks at the bookstore and the supervision of my sister's education.

In 1970, Ben Duvall, who had been a fellow freshman and Sigma Chi at Illinois, wrote from Winnetka, Illinois:

Because you were my best friend in our class, I went over to visit you between semesters in February 1922. The note on the door said COME RIGHT IN. I suppose your mother was at work and your sister probably in school. I was very distressed to find you upstairs in bed. You didn't even know for sure when your health would enable you to go back to college. There wasn't even TV or radio in those days to help pass the time. We reminisced about the "old days" of just a year or less before, and we were only nineteen and a half years old.

Time passes swiftly when there are no events to mark its passage. And so it was with me — flat on my back on doctor's orders for eighteen months. When it became clear that his conventional treatment was failing, Georgia Alexander introduced a strange, withdrawn doctor considered queer by most. Queer he may have been, but I reacted favorably to his many electrical devices — short wave, high frequency — tucked away in unexpected corners of his dark, many-gabled, high-ceilinged Victorian house. He looked upon me as a human guinea pig. Pleased with my progress, he made no charge to Mother for his services, urged a hot, dry climate and a strict diet for a while. Cousins living in Tulsa, Oklahoma, promised me a safe, inside, white collar job as clerk in the hot, dry climate of Claremore, Oklahoma. I boarded a coach train west.

Oklahoma unrolled outside my train window: arid wastes of red gumbo, considered by the white man so worthless as never to have been taken from the Indians. When oil spurted in those regions in the 1920s the Indians, wrapped in new store-bought blankets, bogged down in new Cadillacs in red mud ruts so deep that even a Model T Ford could hardly make it. In 1923 the main street of Claremore, Oklahoma, was a ghost town, each rickety structure unpainted, bleached by sun, rain and wind, standing in starved emptiness. Inside the ticket office beside a water tower and a single railroad semaphore, a man wearing a green eyeshade, dead cigar stub clamped in his stiff and miserable mouth, watched with clammy eye the pale-faced youth in dusty city clothes, carrying a city suitcase, standing uncertainly in the middle of the single track. He pointed to a tin sign on a company shack: LOCK JOINT PIPE COMPANY — HELP WANTED.

A whistle blew and a stream of men flowed from a long, low hall. The ghost town came to life. I asked about a timekeeper clerk job. The red-faced man inside the company shack said there was no such job. I could work outside, at thirty-five cents an hour unrolling steel wire, or else.

My job, along with Mike Perez and Buck Riley, was to unroll rusty coils of reinforcing wire needed for the core of the concrete pipe. We weren't exactly mechanized. Stripped to the waist, we had nothing but gloves and wire clippers and sheer brute force to fashion the hot, angry wire. With heads down, shoulders

25

braced against its spring, we unrolled that wire to the required length — cutting, clipping, snipping, tying — and pushed again and again all day long. My weakness from the start was apparent, and Mike and Buck made up for the strength I lacked, no questions asked. These interstate vagabonds were a separate stratum of society, conforming to strict, self-imposed codes — African Masai wanderers scorning possessions, living from day to day. I was flattered to be accepted as one of them. Exposed to oven heat, coarse food and work-deadened nights, I flourished.

I tried to glamorize this bringing of water to Tulsa, Oklahoma. Great aqueducts had always been treated with respect, as fitting monuments to the dignity and importance of the culture they served. Some of the ancient ones are still standing, arching their way across the Campagna paralleling the Via Aurelia, carrying water to Rome; or serving the principal Roman seaport of Tripolitania, Sabratha. Marching with powerful rhythms, constructed of sandstone or granite or marble, their graceful shapes, elegant materials and permanence of construction reflect their importance to a culture. The best we could claim for our Claremore-Tulsa aqueduct, made of reinforced concrete pipe locked together by a patented device, rising from a dam at Silver Springs, was that it didn't leak.

My reading was done on the sly. Buck and Mike were suspicious of book learning. Sneaking a rare moment alone I was lying on my cot reading the *Rubáiyát* of Omar Khayyám one Sunday afternoon when a grinning face thrust through the narrow bunkhouse window, and a voice exclaimed, "Just what in hell are you doing in there reading that stuff?" A junior engineer, fresh out of Yale and on his first job, he turned out to be a kindred spirit — but my cover was blown. Suddenly the heretofore oblivious top brass of the Lock Joint Pipe Company became "concerned" about my condition, which by now was much better than theirs.

A dull, safe job resulted and my relationship with Buck and

Mike deteriorated; they no longer trusted me. But I met a Mrs. Churchyard, still passionate about her alma mater, Cornell University. She found me an eager listener and easily persuaded me to try for an eastern education, which she brought nearer by a promised job of waiting tables at Cornell's Baker Cafeteria in Ithaca, New York. With next fall's meal ticket at Cornell safe, I returned to Indianapolis. There I found a summer job as Boy Scout counselor on Les Cheneaux Island in Lake Huron, sole mentor for two dozen sons of the very rich, which would take care of my tuition.

For two months I negotiated with that aggregation of hard-eyed teen-age youngsters to whom hiking with packs on their backs seemed sheer nonsense when their power boats were lying idle at the dock. But finally, somehow, studying birds and trees, with overnight camping trips, barriers between fathers and sons broke down, tensions eased and communication grew — and so did my honorarium, unsolicited but not unearned.

Off hours, there was the gentle luxury of the Nicholas H. Noyes home, where I met boys and girls my own age. I even dreamed of that coveted college education at Cornell, almost within my grasp. But a letter from Cornell's dread registrar rudely shattered that dream. Architecture required two years of a foreign language and I had only one. Then one of those mysterious events occultly triggered happened. My host, Nicholas Noyes, was also Cornell Trustee Noyes. Straightaway the trustee sent off cryptic messages. That fall I entered the College of Agriculture, which welcomed me and where foreign language didn't seem important.

From the Lehigh Valley Railroad sleeping car my first stop in Ithaca was the old converted World War I barracks, Baker Cafeteria, ruled by Mrs. Grace, who loved it and would admit of no defects. She even denied the presence of cockroaches, some so large that they were capable of carrying a loaf of bread on each shoulder — or so we claimed. She labeled me her "social butterfly" and sent me each Sunday morning to my rooming house across the street, a bag of crushed ice — assuming I would need it for a hangover.

Students working their way through college did not need to be pale, gray and subdued. I saw to it that life on training table became interesting by devising a routine in which the team could participate in the serving and clearing of tables. After the heavy plates of steak and eggs had made their rounds up and down the long tables, the sixty huskies, their long hours of grueling practice in the racing shells on Lake Cayuga capped with the heavy meal, would shoot their plates and cups and saucers down the length of each table into great baskets held by each of us waiters. The trainees loved it. Not many dishes were broken and it saved a lot of time. There was studying, or a party at the end of training when the waited upon and the waiters would meet again in sweaters and slacks or black ties; it made no difference.

My partner on the training tables at Baker Cafeteria, Arthur Winkler, wasn't pale, gray or subdued. His mother, who spoke no English, had been born in Poland, lived in Paterson, New Jersey, and operated a knitting machine in one of the grimmest ghetto sweatshops in America. Winkler, on a partial athletic scholarship, seemed to be a mathematical genius. When time was of the essence he was apt to cut corners in class. Once he went into the final examination in calculus without preparation, deriving the formulas right in class, then using them to solve the problem posed. When he received the highest mark in the class on one examination, the professor refused to validate his performance on the grounds that it could not be done. Winkler was required to take a special examination under supervision, and he came out with an even higher grade.

But, although he was superendowed in both mind and body, he fell apart when it came to the social and spiritual areas of human relations. Painfully aware of his ghetto background, in his imagination he exaggerated the division that might exist between him and those more gently reared. We operated pretty much in tandem. Cafeteria, Architectural College and play — he and I did all three hard, plotting to open our own offices after a reasonable postgraduate course in one of the big New York architectural firms. Those were our dreams.

Equally important to my education were status and comfort. As manager of Willard Straight Hall, a promotion I received when Mrs. Grace moved there, I could afford both, happily offered by Cornell's Sigma Chi House on an estate complete with swimming pool, formerly occupied by the late Irene Castle. I straightaway moved into what I thought was her boudoir — but, as the lingering odor indicated, it was her aviary. In those surroundings I fell under the spell of an itinerant Jewish tailor. Lured by the piles of shirts and neckties, bolts of tweed and pinstriped wool, I remained in debt to that tailor for the next three years.

Ithaca and the rugged, glaciated Finger Lake region of west central New York State got into one's blood. Paired town and college clung to the hills of variegated blue stone overlooking the foot of Lake Cayuga, with rushing waterfalls over the exposed fissures, deep canyons and heavy slopes of hardwood, broadleaf and fir on the surrounding hills — breathtaking scenery in the spring, a spectacular display of color in the fall, heavy snows serene and glistening in the winter sun. There was the city of Elmira for those seeking a taste of the world's oldest profession, and Wells College for those who were content with less.

In post–Civil War red brick Victorian and early New York State blue stone buildings, indigenous, high-ceilinged, charming New York State primitive, we students of architecture engaged, surrounded, involved and loved our rare and wonderfully diverse professors. One, famous for winning competitions, was Professor Seymour, whom we called Uncle Joe. He commuted from New York to give us our architectural design criticism and called us a "self-satisfied group of rustics up there in the woods pinning medals on each other." Perhaps we were, but perhaps such isolation wasn't a bad idea. We came out of Cornell more inclined toward independence in our point of view and less bound by conventions — a good foundation for sturdy, independent thought.

Our 1927 senior class at Cornell numbered twelve. This meant a close-knit life for those of us who had survived the five-year course.

The attic of White Hall, an acre of drawing boards and stools, the rafters hung with discarded paraphernalia of bygone projects, was the common room for all members of the College of Architecture. It was open twenty-four hours a day. It was there that we lived. During the six-week duration of a problem in design, any time spent away from the attic was considered a total loss.

At certain times there would be a silence in the attic. That was when the big German shepherd dog stood perfectly still, tongue dripping slightly, ignoring his surroundings while his master, that short-bodied, great-nosed, leonine-headed man with the grizzled hair, studied a project, quizzical eyes sparkling with restrained merriment behind his tiny gold-rimmed pince-nez. Our beloved Dean Franke Bosworth was making his biweekly senior design critique. Like one of the half-man, half-animal gods of the ancient Egyptians, master and mascot symbolized and embodied the mystique of the indescribable, the indefinable, the aesthetic of design.

Excitement intensified and the competitive tensions reached their highest pitch as Dean Bosworth moved from desk to desk, managing with some special magic to bring to life latent design ideas hidden and unsuspected within us. I remember him balancing himself precariously on the edge of my three-legged stool, peering down at my carefully drawn design, his glasses perched on the end of his great nose, his fat graphite pencil stub slithering over a half-unrolled tracing paper intended to protect my study beneath. The resulting abstraction from his hand was provocative, undecipherable, fascinating. One felt a marvelous design solution there — now almost clear, now half-lost in mist — seen again only to be lost, a not-quite-defined mirage. Then, as I stood poised, a question ready, with a deep-voiced "Bully! Bully!" and a slap on my smocked shoulder, he would be off chuckling to himself, leaving me in a suspended state associated with just having seen a supernatural vision.

Dean Bosworth was our Delphic oracle. He avoided giving specific solutions. He simply stimulated every creative instinct in us. He made us think. As a practicing architect he had done little of note. As a critic and a teacher he did more for the students than all of the other professors and critics and architects I have known. From him I learned that teaching architecture and practicing architecture are two entirely different professions, the teaching being the rarest and most elusive.

As Professor Seymour explained and demonstrated his theories of living the life of an architect, he confused us in the process — which is probably what he intended to do anyway. He made us think. He told us of a competition he had won by putting five columns in plan and four in elevation. He said it made the solution more interesting.

I took my engineering under one Professor Urquart, in Cornell's Professional Civil Engineering College, who was alleged to "know all about concrete" from the days of the Romans to the modern thin-shelled, hydraulic, coffer dams, and pre- and post-tension systems. Ancient aqueducts, Roman baths, clear, clean-spanned Swiss bridges all interested me. Concrete was something

I wanted to know more about. I journeyed to the College of Civil Engineering and, with his famous textbook in hand, confronted the man himself.

The Architectural College faculty resented this. Biding their time, they gave me no quarter when I presented the thesis for my degree. "How," they asked, "do you plan to wash the fixed windows of your proposed library stack?" "The glass will be washed before we put it up!" Were the devices we finally developed to wash the fixed sash on Lever House my delayed answer? I hoped the faculty still alive will accept such as my apology.

Students of architecture were looked upon as the screwballs of the Cornell campus and were expected to cause excitement, provide entertainment and, hopefully, land in trouble. We did all three — thoroughly and with enthusiasm. Our leader was a beanstalk of a man, Hugh Troy, standing six foot five and a half. His exploits were famous throughout the university. He and I did what we could to shake things up from time to time. One spring we induced Cornell's leading professor of astronomy, world famed and respected for his contributions to the scientific world and for his conservatism, to write a letter to the *New York Times* stating that he had just discovered that, contrary to all he had learned before, the world was flat, not round; and that a certain cache of hiterto undiscovered and ancient papers proved beyond question that the business of the earth being round was simply a piece of fifteenth-century Madison Avenue promotion cooked up to help Isabella and Ferdinand finance their acquistion of the New World for Spain and gain. He said he wanted to get this word around as soon as possible so as to correct any misinformation he himself might have spread to the contrary at an earlier date about the world's being round.

Naturally this letter to the editor got a good bit of exposure, having been written by such a prominent scientist, and the students on campus took opposing sides. Two organizations were formed: the Rounds and the Flats. The Rounds wore hats of Columbus character; the Flats wore buttons. Troy was nearly suspended because of an article he wrote for the Cornell *Widow* about Mrs. Farand, the president's wife, "going ROUND with Davey Hoy," the much hated university registrar, while Dr. Farand "went FLAT."

3

Eloise Discovers Louis Skidmore

I AIMED FOR NEW YORK and a full-time job — a Steig-like dream of reflected glory in which my sister was to take up a career and my mother be released from one. Infrequent visits home (for Ithaca was remote), my self-centered drive and Mother's modesty had veiled from me her transition into a career woman. Her job on the Stewart bookshop's balcony had broadened into virtual management of the store, lacking only the title and the pay. The last thing Mother wanted was to drop the tools and become a lady of leisure. It was doubtful whether my sister really wanted a career. Was I, all unconsciously, bent on stripping my mother of her basic interests and imposing my own upon my sister? In the illusory role of a noble son and brother, did I wrongly change the course of all of our lives?

Dean Bosworth, knowing better than anyone my lack of education, offered me the rare privilege of studying with him for another full year, possibly to be followed by two more years at the American Academy in Rome. There was the slight matter of the competition, but with a twinkle in his eye he said this would be his year. Determined to support my mother and sister, I turned this tempting offer down. Mother quit her job and we each did what we thought the other wanted, and we were both wrong. What would three more years of pure design have done for me? What would a continuation of her career have meant to Mother — still young, handsome, healthy, doing her own thing instead of captive, dependent?

During the years Mother worked at Stewart's my sister, Eloise, had blossomed. Wise in the ways of my contemporaries when I was still in high school, I had exercised a certain amount of censorship as to who sat in the swing on the front porch with her after dark. Small-town institutions are designed primarily to promote the mating instinct. Sunday school, high school, dating, dancing, sororities at the local college — all ended up at the same point: boy and girl going steady, pinning one's girl, marriage, a family.

An excerpt from my sister's diary: "Brother graduated at the proper time in June. Cora [my mother] went to the graduation in Ithaca. I had to go to summer school to graduate because of the kind of courses my brother had made me take: a combination of art institute and Butler academic work for a degree in Fine Arts. This done, I went to New York at Brother's expense to enter either Pratt or Parsons. We favored Pratt but after an unsuccessful attempt to reach it by subway, involving an unplanned trip to Brooklyn which occurred by getting on the wrong express and took all day, I settled on Parsons which was in Manhattan. My interest was styling and dress designing, with a merchandising career in mind. Brother, working in New York, told Cora to stop work. Later Cora and I sailed for Europe on the one-class *American Banker* in the spring of 1928. The Paris branch of Parsons was in the Place des Vosges and we lived for this first summer at the Methodist Mission in the Rue de Rochefarad."

I enjoyed Eloise's and Mother's embarkation for Europe more than they did. Financing the European trip was a gamble and Mother proved her good sportsmanship by ignoring the slimness of the margin that stood between their expenses and my fifty dollars a week from York and Sawyer, plus another fifty dollars a week I earned designing tiles at night. The Businessmen's Exchange offered a standup luncheon: all the bread one could eat with a ten-cent bowl of bean soup. And there was nothing unusual about this. Most of us at York and Sawyer were in the same boat. We economized and we all moonlighted. In our exhausted state we alternated as watchmen to awaken each other if the boss strolled by.

Even then I found the workings of a big office obscure. My original assignment from the chief draftsman of York and Sawyer was to design for the Department of Commerce Building, a key structure in the Federal Triangle in Washington, D.C., an essential complex: the public washrooms and toilets.

I was content. York and Sawyer were the classicists of the day, humorless about their museum of plaster casts showing details of the great *palazzi* of Florence and Rome. They saw nothing ridiculous in their cavalier application of these choice masterpieces of the past to a miscellaneous banking room, a casual hotel lobby or an isolated hospital façade. We juniors did. After my initial stint at public washrooms, my selection to design the main entrance of the same building stirred some cynical comments, but at that age, toilets and entrances were all the same. I still have that great ink drawing, done with infinite pains on starched cloth, classic cornices rising above wrought-iron lamps straight from the Pitti Palace.

But at York and Sawyer I wasn't always drawing details. Framed by the great window beside my drawing board was the rising shaft of the new Empire State Building, until 1970 the world's tallest. As the tower grew I noticed that the heavy crosshatching of jet black scaffolding marked an ever-changing pattern on its upper reaches. The infinite variety of shadow-shapes cast by the changing sun promised an excitement which the cold sterility of the finished tower denied. Why not find a design technique that would make permanent the excitement of anticipation?

Through the same great window, looking slightly downward to the apartment house across the street, promptly at ten o'clock each day we could perceive in the elegantly furnished rooms the nude figure of a richly endowed female who proceeded to execute an elaborate series of arabesques, leaps and spins in true Degas-like ballet rehearsal, all unconscious of her fascinated audience. With old-world gallantry we forbade research into the matter of her identity and speculated at length upon the likelihood of our ability to recognize her with her clothes on.

We of the Class of 1927 had migrated to New York en masse with Hugh Troy as our leader, and, in an effort to house a substantial number of willing victims in a one-room apartment, he promptly took over a huge converted brownstone basement with an areaway on the sidewalk for direct entry. The bathroom extended the full length of the back wall, and when its door was open, passers-by on the sidewalk could see a lively nude lady painted on the wall back of the tub, her arms raised, frightened by a large rat balanced on the edge of the tub holding a pince nez in one paw. When six-foot-five-and-a-half-inch Troy was also in the tub, the view was extraordinary. Our group split with the cop on the beat any tips picked up by showing our sidewalk viewers this phenomenon.

At that time architect Bertram Grosvenor Goodhue was my hero. To test the ambience of great Gothic spaces, when you are in New York City on Fifth Avenue and the five o'clock rush presses you unduly, slip gently into a pew near the crossing in Goodhue's Saint Thomas Church and let the organ waves of Vespers roll over you. After a few minutes you will understand about the architect Bertram Grosvenor Goodhue, and feel the life and truth this master draftsman and craftsman breathed into his designs, which seem inspired by the Virgin and conceived in the twelfth century. Stone on stone he built his structures, creating great works in a langauge I could relate to the mysteries of Chartres and Mont-Saint-Michel.

Bertram Grosvenor Goodhue died of a broken heart at fifty-five, and it was his Nebraska State Capitol design, his greatest creative work, that killed him. Having placed first in an international competition, his design revealed the nucleus of an indigenous American architecture, an answer to the tradition of the dome changed to a tower. But the protesting burghers of Nebraska, forced to accept the design since they had agreed to the competition in the first place, caused a series of acrimonious incidents, climaxed when the state condemned the natural encrustations of the imported veined verde antique marble slabs lining the lobby as being defective, saying that they must be replaced by sound material. The failure of these men to respond to beauty shattered him.

Off went a check each week to my mother and sister. Everything seemed to be going well at home and abroad until one drowsy afternoon in 1928. The mail had just been passed around and carefully read when suddenly I was brought back to life by a whoop from a colleague reading a letter from Paris. He gleefully related some choice gossip contained therein concerning one Louis Skidmore, architect and Paris denizen, and my sister, Eloise, fashion design student also in Paris. It seemed they were frequently observed together about the Deux Magots and other haunts of the Faubourg St. Germain. Skidmore's reputation as a gay blade, if not an outright rake, was well known; and my dear sister was, to my mind, not fitted to cope with such a past master in the art of seduction. Besides, she was over there at my expense.

The day after York and Sawyer raised my pay to seventy-five dollars a week and told me I had a future, I quit. Their affirmation of my solid worth in terms of hard cash seemed to me the equivalent of a postgraduate degree earned.

Winkler had nosed out a big job: a combination city hall, courthouse and jail all in one. These were still boom times, 1928, and Passaic County could still project such things for Paterson, New Jersey. The politically "in" architect, Henry Crosby, who held the commission, asked Winkler to take over. With Eloise and Mother still in Europe, I moved to Paterson; and while Crosby — a charming, most unlikely political type — lived the country life, Winkler and I made what must have been one of the most exhaustive studies of penology ever undertaken since de Tocqueville came to this country.

To us the job was a kind of abstract exercise, totally unrelated to the actual facts of crime, cruelty and human suffering. But without precedents for jails and prisons in combination with courthouses to hamper us, we worked furiously for eighteen hours a day, letting our imaginations soar. This was an architect's dream world: a challenging project of wide scope with freedom to design and no interference from Passaic County or the boss, Crosby. We finally arrived at our solution. It was to be a courthouse with a jail on top, the dimension of a pair of cell blocks determining the size of the shaft, producing an instant prisoner directly by elevator into the courtroom.

As our work proceeded I moved into a casual aggregation of semihabitable dwellings, long unused, in the charming tall-grass country of the Ramapo Mountains close to Tuxedo Park. I could already picture my mother and my sister, fresh from Paris, roaming our country estate. Small things like hot water and electricity could come later.

In accordance with schedule Eloise arrived home with Mother (no sign of Louis Skidmore) and for experience went to work as a comparison shopper for Lord and Taylor — an uncomfortable kind of spy job checking other stores for merchandise value and prices. This was followed by *the* job as stylist for accessories

39

and commentator for fashion shows, fulfilling every idea of grandeur for her that I had ever had. She was paid seventy-five dollars a week and the job was with Stewart and Company, an entirely new store, opening in June of 1929 and closing in bankruptcy in November the same year. When Stewart's closed forever, Eloise moved to Macy's as a glove salesgirl at twenty dollars a week.

Since the shift from Europe to Paterson to New York had seemed unreal anyway, when the balloon burst Eloise easily adjusted to Macy's and reported: "Walter Hoving, after interviewing me and learning of Paris school, Lord and Taylor and high style job at Stewart's, pronounced that I would not be successful at mechandising in New York because I was too well educated, too much of a lady, and could never learn to say 'goddamn' with conviction."

Eloise was well along in her career in the fashion world when one August day in 1929 Louis Skidmore landed at the Cunard dock on the Hudson River. Following Eloise's departure from Europe, he had stretched his fellowship through a commission for Samuel Chamberlain, preparing detailed plates of Tudor houses for a magnificent fee of five hundred dollars. But now, with Skidmore stony-broke, Eloise and I agreed that he could add the crowning glory to our nearly completed masterpiece: the developing courthouse and jail.

Skid was a third-generation Rhenish-Bavarian born of a Lawrenceburg family on the levee of the Ohio River. The war saw him in England, a ninety-nine-pound private in the fledgling Air Corps Construction Agency. When asked by an officer there what he was doing with the wheelbarrow he was pushing, he replied, "Trying to make the damn thing fly!"

Skid's commanding officer was an M.I.T. graduate, a practicing architect from Cincinnati, just twenty miles from Lawrenceburg. If those two allowed their joint interest in Tudor country houses of England to interfere with the due process of war, what they gained was an understanding of the elegant styles of that graceful, sixteenth-century period.

Discharged and unbemedaled, Skidmore had but one idea and that was to get right back again to where he had been and "damn the torpedoes." His old commanding officer, Captain Strong, backed him, pressing for loans, grants and scholarships for three years at M.I.T. In the 1920s only Boston's Rotch awarded a traveling fellowship for pure design talent and character alone; all others needed a college degree or two. What a searing set of competitive tests for the winning! But the winner's name joined a roster of the greatest contributors to architecture. Somehow the people who ran the Rotch were gifted with a sixth sense. Skid won on the second try.

Three years later, upon his disembarkation at the Cunard pier, his first request was for an American meal of corned beef hash with a poached egg on top — and while that hash with the egg was disappearing I studied this potential threat to the Owings trio. He was the image of a dazed expatriate, having lived for three years in the architectural history of England, France, Continential Europe and the Near East. There he sat, his battered hat beside him, two bright points of light flashing from wise, wide-set eyes balanced by a needle-sharp waxed mustache over a sensitive mouth and strong chin below. In his threadbare tweeds, worn with assurance over a slight frame, Louis Skidmore looked just as I had hoped he would, as I thought an architect should look: a sophisticated man of the world. After all, he had traveled far and wide, had mingled with the great and the near great and had sat at the tables in the Faubourg St. Germain with easy confidence. What else did the world have to offer?

Well, there were the courthouse and jail, and we could pay a hundred dollars a week. Skid stuffed each pocket of his ramshackle tweed suit with the crisp, new one-dollar bills. He could then be seen slyly extracting rolls of greenbacks and placing them in different pockets in different positions — apparently enjoying the sensation of the bulge.

We were a happy little community there in the Ramapos, with Mother in charge of the rambling headquarters and Eloise returning each night from her long New York commute. Winkler, Skid and I — and a distinguished Beaux Arts group of returnees whom Skid had attracted — worked hard and long until the weekend. Then, in the golden copper fall among the rolling hills of tall grass and surprise lakes, we would take off with a picnic lunch for a swim and a lazy afternoon.

Everything was moving smoothly, we thought, nearing the end of the job. Our plans were shaping up when one Sunday afternoon at Winkler's suggestion we all took off for the little lake nearby. It was deep, cold, crystal clear and spring fed, and its steep rocky shores plunged straight down. To start things off that day, Winkler was the first to profile against the sky beside our picnic spot. Waving his arms in challenge to us all, he sprang high in the air from his already high perch, arched his body and, thrusting down in a perfect dive, cut through the surface of the water with barely a perceptible splash. And then the moments passed. He did not come up. We thought he was proving his great lung capacity, but no. Finally we realized that he wasn't going to come up. Neither a good diver nor a hero, I plunged in and finally got him up. On-the-spot mouth-to-mouth resuscitation was of no avail. Apparently his head had struck a rock and dazed him, and he had drowned while unconscious. Just one year after we had joined together in what had seemed to be a perfect partnership, he was dead.

The depression's first wave, Black Friday, hit. Designs and models and drawings were nearly completed. We held a wake for the courthouse and jail which would never be built, our appreciation of the merits of our design growing with every toast to its demise.

Not very long afterward, holding a bunch of violets in one

hand, Eloise was married to Louis Skidmore in the chapel of Saint George's Church on Stuyvesant Square in New York City. As Otto Teegen spilled out heartbreakingly sweet music on his violin, Mother leaned over to me and said, "Why couldn't Eloise have married him instead?"

4

A Century of Progress, 1933

LOOKING UP rather than burrowing down for effective evidence of architectural compost, one may see an eleven-hundred-foot-tall steel and glass metronome jammed with technology standing on Chicago's Gold Coast. Commenced in 1964 and completed in 1970, the John Hancock Center is a living product of bits and pieces that fit, created by the co-triggering of parallel dreams — dreams of an unknown developer and the Chicago partners of SOM. But behind those dreams stands even more firmly a century's composting with heat and ferment and frenzy of growth which produced "Big John."

The one-hundred-story John Hancock Center was first called Big John by the taxi drivers. We had good reason to be concerned, since Big John was strictly our creation, and when taxi drivers chose a friendly nickname instead of "The Brute" or "The Monster," then we could relax a little. Big John encased a complete community, a kind of linear city thrusting skyward — a "cradle to the grave" building.

Big John casts a shadow long enough to strike the Chicago Water Tower, which has stood since 1867 in a little square two blocks to the southeast, said to be the sole survivor of the 1871 fire. Built to house a pump worked by a steam engine of twenty-five horsepower, it distributed water to the citizens through logs bored at "the works," five inches in diameter for the main line and three inches for the branches.

The hot disk of a July sun performed this miracle of moving shadow-shapes, bending the black-faced hundred-story giant over the squat landscape. As its shadow touched that foolish little Victorian water tower, which resembles nothing more than a toy castle in a goldfish bowl, I thought of the longer reach of history that lay between the two structures.

Between this Victorian collector's item and Big John lies raw industrialism: giant, passionate, undisciplined excess, but producing through heat and ferment the indigenous architecture of America. Louis Henri Sullivan, Dankmar Adler, John Wellborn Root, William Le Baron Jenney and Daniel H. Burnham — they reflect in mirror image the single-minded power of their almost legendary clients: merchant Marshall Field, packers Gustave Swift and Philip Armour, innkeeper Potter Palmer, railroad-car builder George Pullman, and the inventor of the reaper, Cyrus McCormick. The theme of their century was identified properly and celebrated in 1933 as "A Century of Progress," marking the end of an era accenting their personal power.

From a matched pair of horses in a rich man's stable to a pair of cars in every man's garage; from the rhymes of James Whitcomb Riley to the strong-shouldered Carl Sandburg; from the rope-suspended elevator cabs in the old Pullman Building to the half-a-mile-a-minute rise through the Empire State's one hundred stories, the theme of progress was pursued: a rhythm like the beating of Indian drums, persistent; an increasing crescendo and crash to its death in 1929. Then the long, slow rise.

But in 1929 Big John was far in the future and Skid and I were hungry. He soon sprang the first of those pieces of master strategy for which he was to become famous.

Seated at one of the marble-topped tables in the old Lafayette Hotel bar at Fourteenth and Fifth Avenue, just before taking off on his honeymoon with my sister, Eloise, Skid told me he had lined up a job while in Europe that would make all the difference to us both. He said he had put off telling me just in case the courthouse job had worked out. If it had, he might have stuck around and given up this plan he was about to outline. But the courthouse job had gone sour, and so he had an alternate for us. It had to do with the proposed Chicago World's Fair planned for 1933 to celebrate the "Century of Progress." He had a job there as chief of design.

There was a nine-man Architectural Commission already appointed and in Europe Skid had tracked down the key commission members, Raymond Hood and Paul Cret, separately convincing them that he was the man to reconcile such a group of egocentrics and get something built from their contrasting talents.

Hood, the genius behind the Rockefeller Center project then in progress, liked to paraphase Lincoln: "God must have loved the common man because He made so many of them." At three in the morning on an all-night charette he would call the charwoman away from her broom and dustpan and listen carefully to her first impressions of his latest design ideas. Intuitive, usually three-quarters full of apricot brandy, he was a designer whose instincts were sure.

Paul Cret, a remarkable Frenchman from Philadelphia, was a wise and great critic who was apt to advise already confused students that "ivy is the architect's best friend."

Even Hood and Cret had conflicting ideas for the fair design. Hood thought it should be a mountain three miles high in the lake, with the peak reached by elevators, and then the people could walk down and see exhibits on the way. Paul Cret had an idea just as wild, but it was symmetrical, as might be expected from a Frenchman. Skid got them to meet jointly and they agreed to make him chief of design of the fair.

This fair was planned during the stock market boom as an

46

extravaganza with unlimited funds, a fantasy. It was to be an enormous fair and the job of chief of design for such a fair would be a big job for an architect — in fact, the biggest job any young architect could hope for in the next three or four years.

Historically, world's fairs had significance. Landmarks had been produced and architectural development had been measured by them. London's Crystal Palace of five acres under glass, built by Paxton in 1851, was a legend still talked about and never equaled. The Eiffel Tower still dominates Paris, and Chicago's 1893 fair had produced Louis Sullivan's Transportation Building, which Europeans said was the only truly original structure there, carrying the seeds of an indigenous American style of architecture. Sprung from Chicago's South Side, famed as the "White City," that 1893 fair was more famous for what it had done badly than for what it had done well. The whole country was suffering aesthetically under the domes of pseudoclassic Rome. But the odds were that, good or bad, this new fair would be done in a big way and the chief of design of such a fair would share the glory.

In going after the job before anyone even realized there was one, in thinking things all out in advance, Louis Skidmore displayed early proof of the key role he would play. His friends called him a mystic. His competitors described him as a devious schemer. Actually, he was a combination of these traits and might be described as a long-range planner. But the job that Skid had landed from Hood and Cret was for a boom-time economy, now shattered. What about a fair in the depression? Skid said he thought that if there was any money at all — and he understood there was ten million dollars still salvageable — we would have a better chance to do a more important job; we could probably take over the fair completely, since the Architectural Commission wouldn't want to bother with it in a downgraded, makeshift form. Of course in 1930 we did not know that

47

the depression had only begun and would continue on a down-grade, but Louis Skidmore made that decision and asked me to join him as development supervisor.

In the profession the general comment was, "How the hell did Skid ever land that one?" Skid's job as the fair's chief of design was even more of a coup than it might have been in better times, because architects and draftsmen alike were out of work and getting hungry. Here was Louis Skidmore, holder of the Rotch Traveling Fellowship but otherwise unknown, without previous experience on any job, filling this most promising one, with an untried brother-in-law armed only with a bachelor's degree in architecture from Cornell to qualify him for what lay ahead.

First we took on each other, and then jointly we took on the design. From raw, man-made land on an alien strip of lakefront was to come a complete city — complete, that is, except for residential housing — with facilities big enough to serve the expected annual total of twenty-five or thirty million visitors (possibly more) with sewers, water, power, roads, walks, landscaping, exhibition buildings, restaurants, theaters and rapid mass transportation; and we would be ahead of our time in handling the people of core cities without automobiles. We could plan, build and study the import, impact and effect of our plans — *if* we were wise enough to know how to cope with the depression and the political implications, the time limit and no budget. With the risks so great, the odds so long, even a limited success could be spectacular. The fifty years of doom for American architecture that Louis Sullivan had predicted were coming to an end and we were right there on the lakefront in Chicago, ready to reverse the trend.

Chicago is said to breed its own genre and its own grim aesthetic. Confirming this, our first view of the fair site was forbidding. It was located on newly man-made land under the control of the Chicago Park District (an entity quite separate from Chicago's sinister political machine), on a desert of dredged-up mud; an island protected from the howling, wind-pushed waves and thrusting ice by jagged blocks of limestone floated across and dumped at random by barges the size of boxcars. At first huge rats, baring their double incisors, struck the right note. The atmosphere was emergency. It was cold out there.

In the boom times prior to 1929, General Charles G. Dawes, Coolidge's vice president, a pipe-smoking politician turned banker, had easily raised the first ten million dollars in pledges, with promises of much more to come. His brother, Rufus Dawes, was to be the president of the fair. Then the depression hit and the general's bank was closed. Almost all the money disappeared except for the ten million dollars, which miraculously remained. Rufus emerged, gained visibility and stature and took his place in the public eye slightly ahead of the famous general — and stayed there. He had probably belonged there all the time.

Rufus Cutler Dawes, whether sitting, standing, relaxed or at attention, always seemed to be presiding. A long catenary of black ribbon flowed from rimless pince-nez anchored on the upper reaches of his formidable nose to the white piping of his period waistcoat. Full of grace, he made us feel good — even important. Before state dinners (dry in 1933) the chairman of the board, Dr. William Allen Pusey, and the chief of protocol, the Honorable Ulysses Grant Smith, might be seen in the dusk slipping discreetly into my conveniently located outside office led by Rufus, an enormous silver cocktail shaker, its frosty surface glistening in the rays of the setting sun, half-hidden under the tails of his evening coat. These meetings, cloaked in secrecy, filled with Bible stories in baroque Alabama patoi, always left me a little tipsy, a lot wiser and much flattered to be a part of the conspiracy.

Brother Rufus served his purpose well, but scratching for money to build things like sewers, roads, water mains, public toilets, entrance gates, turnstiles, guard and police stations; trading world's fair bonds for a myriad of goods and services; and trying to mesmerize, beg, borrow and steal from corporation heads was not exactly his cup of tea. Add to these chores the selling of exhibit space and finding valid entertainment features, and it was a twenty-four-hour-a-day job, dominated by straight-laced, tight-minded, shell-hard World War I Corps of Engineers Major Lenox R. Lohr, with tiny Martha Magrew a prescient pilot fish to Lohr's predatory shark — a truly awesome combination.

The only reason why the fair was even possible was our political independence, further guaranteed by our imported management staff headed by General Manager Lohr, who moved from Washington and brought with him a tough cadre of retired Corps of Engineers colonels who, in true engineering fashion, were dedicated solely to the building of the fair, come what may.

Nothing ever happened twice the same way at the fair. Boredom was not our problem. There were rehearsals for productions that never came off. There were productions for which there had been no rehearsals. Everything changed all the time, and through such constant change often ended right side up after all. There was a rhythm to it, a pulsing regularity of inevitable change. I became an instant expert in a variety of fields, organized a drafting force for working drawings (having hardly ever drawn one myself), supervised construction, planned concessions, made up in enthusiasm for what I lacked in skill, and developed a swinging crew. If there were deviations from the original designs we were regretful but not surprised, sympathetic but intractable. It was always too late to go back.

We worked like quarter horses in short spurts, but the short spurts turned into 1440 days of preparation, and we into marathon performers for a fair that only lasted 153. We asked of ourselves and gave quite a lot, and got back more than we put in.

As chief of design Skid established his territory early, handily enough gaining prestige when he turned down the senior Heinz's request to build a 57 Varieties thousand-foot-long papier-mâché pickle, green and wrinkled, guaranteed (Mr. Heinz said) to look very much like the real thing. Even after the request was reinforced with a one-hundred-thousand-dollar cash offer, Skidmore turned him down.

Hard-line national corporations and basic industries across the continent were given concrete proof that the building dollar could also be an advertising dollar; that architecture could be idea expressive as well as weather protective. Skid ruled the world of signs and sounds and design quality, maintaining the high quality not only of these items but of his edicts as well. The list of chairmen of boards, presidents and executive vice presidents of nationally known companies calling on Skid lengthened, and his power to control their every move inside the world's fair fence solidified and became law. He played a role somewhere between a Cardinal Richelieu and a Falstaff. His waxed mustaches were no sharper than his wit, humor, patience and good judgment.

Superimposed on everybody's territory, I didn't have any of my own. I drifted into the role of a wide-ranging predator. While Skid presided over plans of hundreds of designs for exhibitors, I made forays into the sanctuaries of the great corporations. Prying and picking loose their idle resources, I gathered nuggets of pure gold in new forms, developing ways and means of getting a corporate contribution in kind: foundations, steel cables, elevators, glass, concrete, paint, light fixtures — anything movable, resulting in the fair's own shows: The Wings of a Century, the Enchanted Island and the monster Sky Ride. A wide variety of corporations participated, contributed in kind and shared in the profits. The Sky Ride made the most money. It was a monster straddling the fair grounds, two huge six-hundred-foot towers half a mile apart tied by heavy strands of wire, far-flung cables, and a suspension catenary system between them supporting a cable-car track on which pseudo-streamlined cable cars zoomed passengers at a snail's pace. At the top of each tower was a platform for visitor viewing. Although the ride was as aesthetically out of keeping for us as the Eiffel Tower must have been for Paris, its size and volume marked a presence for the fair, producing a kind of giant bracketing — ugly, big and popular. As a joint venture developed by a group of big corporations voluntarily joining together, was there a trend here for a future in private practice?

On the side I begged, borrowed and cajoled items like the largest locomotive and a lion and tiger act safe enough to provide Standard Oil with a live power show without bloodshed. "Controlled live power" with Clyde Beatty, lions and tigers, would cost too much. But controlled live power with an unknown — a man who said he had trained Beatty, strode into the cage and wasn't eaten by the nearest lion — was within our means.

It was any man's game: rich man, poor man, even a few beggar men and thieves. The amateur worked with the professional. The accidents of timing, luck and fortune smilingly favored some unlikely ones. Typical of these was Bob Sipchen, a pale, limp little fellow with sparse, faded straw-colored hair and red-lidded lashless eyes who affected the mien of an Oriental rug merchant eternally pleading for relief from bankruptcy. First as a shoestring contractor for the Fort Dearborn replica and later as owner-builder of the Black Forest Village with its open-air ice skating rink, heavily used in Chicago's hundred-and-two-degree August weather, he ended up with a cool million dollars' net profit. Chicago architects' local native humor, whimsy and creativity began to make themselves felt and found the climate sympathetic. Bored, Daniel Hudson Burnham's son, sitting nostalgically behind his father's desk and hitting his father's brass spittoon nine times out of ten, quit the fair and built an authentic section of a complete Belgian village.

Slowly the sleeping giant, Chicago, was stirring, becoming involved in the fair, where, on an uninhabited island, Skid and

I were doing strange things. Were we only the outskirts of Chicago, or were we perhaps the reality and old Chicago but a dream?

In 1932 an infectious air of carnival set in, and we found out. We were led by the explosively baroque, rich-blooded French-Italian, Andy Rebori. Prone to create a crisis under ordinary circumstances, he was Olympian in responding to a real one. He planned a gigantic Beaux Arts charity ball christened "The Streets of Paris" whereby largesse would flow into the coffers of our beleaguered and starving profession. Andy boldly rented most of the public rooms at the Drake Hotel without a sou to back him up.

The pre-ball promotion campaign turned into the social season of the year. The unemployed swarmed over the sedate, classic halls of the lower levels of the Drake, converting them into disquietingly convincing replicas of the demimondain haunts of the Left Bank. Materials charged to "The Committee" were converted into cafés, shops, bistros, ateliers — Deux Magots, Lipps, Montmartre, even bits of the Tuileries Gardens crept in — all arising while drafting rooms stood empty, the drafting boards stacked, bare of drawings. Principals and draftsmen alike shared the excitement. Andy Rebori, with spiked mustache, shared the chairmanship with schoolteacher-visaged John Root, son of John Wellborn Root. from some speakeasy in a dark alley, Root produced the incomparable Sally Rand, who agreed to a midnight ride on a great white Percheron through their Streets of Paris — bare-skinned and draped only in a flowing blond wig — her twenty-five-dollar fee to be paid upon completion of the contract. Sally had gone undiscovered for something better than the forty years she denied in age; her star began to rise that night.

I spent the night at the ball dressed as a concierge in a red nightcap. As the long night wore on it became clear that we should incorporate the essence of The Streets of Paris into a village concession at the approaching fair, and that Sally Rand might well become the 1933 equivalent of the 1893 Little Egypt. In an effort to find out, we met with Sally in Andy Rebori's architectural offices high above La Salle Street. In daylight she certainly looked like show business on its uppers. What could she do besides ride a white horse? She said she was a fan dancer. The group looked over the strawberry blonde. To prove it, she said, she needed some fans. Andy found a couple of ostrich fans. We all arranged ourselves for the impromptu show on the patio roof. Sally shucked her clothes in the ladies' room and then, shielded by ostrich plumes and to the rhythm of radio music, she did her dance. There was a high wind off the river that day and although Sally was the picture of grace, she hadn't the strength to hold those fans in place.

Old Chicago was unreal, somehow not with it. There were the great houses and the divided camps of the powerful families, still living like nineteenth-century Proustian characters frozen at the reception of the Prince de Guermantes in long, dark, richly furnished drawing rooms on the Faubourg St. Germain. My first dinner in Chicago was at the home of Michael Follensby, the general counsel to the Santa Fe Railroad. A massive man, his physique so arranged as to seem to be rising through a series of life zones toward the climax of glaciated shocks of snowy hair overhanging a sheer height of craggy brow, he lived in a venerable North Astor Street mansion surrounded by a variegated family resulting, no doubt, from his strange, wraithlike, wispy wife: a delicate son or two and a sturdy daughter named Susan. I remember the sherry served instead of cocktails before dinner in the huge dining room; the table set with deeply glowing silver and ambient china, snowy linen and rows of sparkling crystal like xylophones; wines, ladies, port, cigars and whiskey highballs and conversation; the unreal attitudes where only the past seemed credible.

There were weekends at Lake Geneva where Skid and Eloise

and I could savor another bit of the fabric of Old Chicago; where, in the style of Sackville-West Victorians, the tradition of the English houseparty was still maintained by such families as the Kellogg Fairbanks; where Janet Ayer Fairbank, author and politician, brought groups of twenty-five to thirty Chicagoans and their guests together at their Victorian mansion over most weekends, with pseudo-impromptu witty speeches at the long, noisy dinner table Saturday nights. There Skid and Eloise were fixtures of high visibility. One weekend, as dinner time approached and Skid's failure to appear from his bedroom became embarrassing, Eloise was forced to share with me their secret. She had forgotten his mustache wax. I found a can of Two-in-One shoe polish in the kitchen and soon Skid emerged, twirling a slightly darker but needle-pointed mustache.

One night at one of those dinners I met Emily Hunting Otis. Emily was nearing the dangerous area between fresh, marriageable girlhood and the clear-eyed candor of a youngish spinster. The family trees that bore her were of rare stock and, like the redwoods of California, boasted tree rings marking the year 1066 and the Battle of Hastings at a considerable distance from the center of the heart wood. The Websters on her mother's side and the Otises, true aristocrats, carried their impeccable lineage with certain, conscious ease. The thick tome of the Otis line even included (Emily was apt to boast) a colored branch of the family tree. The Chicago Latin School, Miss Porter's at Farmington, a formal debut with tea at the Casino, a ball at the Blackstone, and by Astor Street standards, her education was complete.

From the first impression her willowy graciousness, her heritage and her vague, generous nature attracted me. We met in March and in June I visited her family estate at Harbor Springs, Michigan — Victorian, not in architecture, but in its function in the social system.

A measured reproduction of a Georgian manor house in England, the mansion was all white, framed with a classic columned porch — two-storied, L-shaped — with the living room opening on the greensward and the dining room giving onto Mrs. Otis' rose garden beyond, the inspection of which was the last course of any Sunday noon eight-course dinner. In counterpoint, Auntie May, Mrs. Otis' poor sister, was the satellite who lived in a cottage nearby and was always there. At every function the background was white-shoed, white-dressed, white hair knotted on top of the heads, chokered ladies. The smiling, banker-shaped Mr. Otis shyly tried to hide his utter pleasure in this bit of northern Michigan beauty. A mile or two of virgin Lake Michigan meeting a virgin forest on its silver edge. A Michigan sky of Wedgwood blue and Jersey cream white. Birchwood fires and Indian rugs spread over spotless wide oak floors, a Redon still life in the round on every table. It was a mirror image of the Nicholas Noyes summerhouse.

In the limpid evening air, in the classic summerhouse secluded from the view of everyone but the entire family, what could be more likely than the marriage proposal and acceptance, the subsequent approval of father and mother and the immediate business closest to a woman's heart: a September wedding on the lawn at Harbor Springs — in fact, a production. In the fall of 1931 at Birchwood Farms in Harbor Springs, Michigan, we were married. Mrs. Otis presided. It was her wedding and the bedrooms were filled with incongruous offerings of tribute, just the kind of wedding gifts for a young couple starting out, made up of a substantial number of silver cocktail shakers.

On the Near North Side, the second floor of a remodeled frame house on Cedar Street (chosen for the huge elm dwarfing the entrance) became our nominal home. But all of us — Louis and Eloise, Emily and I — were running the rapids of an operating world's fair, sometimes around the clock, meeting people. Our life was a merging of work, play, socializing and business. For three years the north island on Chicago's lakefront was the eye of the storm.

The architectural design of the fair was functional in the extreme. Forced by economics to abandon the nit-picking, fussy scale of the Art Moderne designs proposed by the original Architectural Commission, we gained in simple building masses the lake's gigantic scale. We covered the raw wallboard surfaces with the cold water paint of penurious necessity and produced a masterpiece of contemporary art, topped off by millions of yards of blood red bunting splashed from slanting shafts pressed upon the throngs at the entry gate. We depended upon primitive devices: color, motion and light. Under the benign supervision of an inactive Architectural Commission — led by Raymond Hood, Paul Cret and John Holabird — Louis Skidmore, Joseph Urban and I, along with handlebar-mustachioed Vogelgesang and red-haired, toothbrush-mustached Otto Teegen, produced something absolutely new in the United States.

There was a certain eerie quality about the uncompromising huge, flat, windowless surfaces, strange in volume and shape, as they blazed in crude, primitive, startling color combinations. There were several variations of wine red and violet, umbers and ochers against the sky or each other; sometimes smoldering, sometimes blazing in the sun, etched against the enormous panorama of the lake.

Somehow the fund shortages and the dire need squeezed out and boiled off the fake, the false and the artificial and left pure Americana: brass bands, flags, dog and pony shows, color, music, noise. The Canadian Essex Scottish Regiment came down from Canada in 1933 in eight railroad cars, four of which were rumored to have carried exclusively Canadian Scotch. They performed Britain's greatest spectacle: the parade to the colors with shakos, kilts and bagpipes, the husky voices almost stilled by constant applications of that Canadian distilled Scotch — breathtaking, stirring, genuine, outstripping any professional entertainment in the world.

Special events were hourly events and world dignitaries sometimes came in bunches too large for even the efficient Ulysses Grant Smith to handle. At times like this I helped out, until I was declared untrustworthy. I lost my standing when, all the official cars and limousines being busy, there was still the Crown Prince of Siam in top hat and tailcoat to be transported from the Administration Building to the state luncheon at the United States Pavilion. My green Dodge convertible with the rumble seat open seemed perfect for the occasion, so I helped him in and, as he sat behind me in stately grandeur, arms crossed over his small medal-covered chest, I, acting as chauffeur, threw in the clutch and lurched into action — concentrating, as any good driver should, on the road. I was interested to find upon arrival that the rumble seat was closed (probably jolted shut en route). Inside was our Crown Prince, who, after the silk hat had been removed, made his way to his luncheon, his impassivity equaled only by my savoir-faire.

As director of special events that summer I pushed fireworks with sets of rockets and all the rest fired off at the finale each night. Rank amateur, and on my own, I called an actors' agency and hired what I thought was a professional parachute jumper. I had him dress in an Uncle Sam costume, arranged spotlights below, and planned that he drop from a plane over the grounds the night of the Fourth of July, 1933.

Everything went well: the final extra special burst of rockets, the blare of the band playing "The Star-Spangled Banner." The lights hit the plane, Uncle Sam tumbled out — and plunged to the ground to his death, his parachute unopened. But it was not an accident. There was a note on his body saying that he had wished to die in a blaze of glory and this had been his opportunity. He had never jumped before. The headlines the next morning were, I suppose, transmitted to the poor fellow in purgatory.

A strong man came in one day and wanted a job as a special event. Upon my suggestion that he prove his strength, he quickly grasped the thick Chicago telephone book and neatly tore it in half. Impressed, I offered to introduce him and his genius to the management, so office by office we went through the Administration Building until there wasn't a whole telephone book left in the place.

The turnstiles whirled — the best proof our bosses could ask as to the efficiency of our design. By the end of the 1933 fair on 12 November, 22,565,859 paying visitors had swarmed through the 344 acres of buildings and grounds, on foot and by Greyhound bus, where we had spent some twelve million dollars (today the equivalent of fifty million) on sewers, water, roads, grading. We were novices in entertainment, and our own amateur efforts, "The Wings of a Century" and the Sky Ride, had perhaps been awkward, ugly and angular; but they had lent fascination, been profitable and could, the management told us, be redesigned for another year. With this news some of the more successful concessionaires turned their minds — and perhaps their consciences — to contributing their 1933 profits to better things for 1934. Swift and Company asked how they could turn their hamburger and hot dog dollar surplus into an aesthetic gain. This was a question I had been waiting for. Let them give the public free concerts by the Chicago Symphony Orchestra, for example.

The final day of the fair came. On the flat, man-made island floating like a nibbled wafer on the skimmed milk surface of merged sky and water a blinding flash and a sharp explosion broke the crisp October air. It also broke the tension of a tightly drawn huddle of disparate human shapes clustered together, almost defensively, all eyes on the source of the flash and the sound. The two great steel towers of the Sky Ride, one standing at the Twenty-third Street entrance of the fair and the other a half mile away, shuddered, crumpled and fell one after the other as demolition experts burned lignite cartridges and felled the towers with precision.

The clutch of disparate watchers unraveled, revealing the Lincolnesque form of Rufus Dawes, the egg-shaped diminutive John Bull figure of William Allen Pusey, the autumn dry-leafed Martha Magrew and the hawk-nosed Major Lenox Lohr. Four years, forty-eight months, two summer seasons, 39,052,236 paying visitors had passed and we were all there to witness the ritual of final immolation.

As the towers fell, Chicagoans streamed through the gates, suddenly turned mob. The grounds were picked clean of every movable object. An old woman swept by, almost crushed by the weight of an entire floodlight assemblage. Trees, shrubs with wet dirt still clinging to their roots, benches, stools, doors, parts of signs were carried on the shoulders of a solid, milling mass.

The life cycle of the fair, "A Century of Progress, 1933," was complete. Under the swinging iron ball of the wrecker the island returned to the naked state from which it had been born.

5

A Modern "Gothic Builders Guild"

I TURNED FROM the naked grounds of an extinct fair. I pondered my qualifications for future employment and found myself eminently qualified as an itinerant hawker of snake-bite-cure medicine at a county fair. Any small success I might have enjoyed over the past four years was illusory; my sense of incompleteness was not. I had drifted so far from conventional architecture that an offer of a vaguely free-lance job with a Chicago meat packer didn't seem nearly as incongruous as it should have. The skills I had developed weren't identified with conventional architectural practice. For four years I had swung with the rhythm instinctive to the city editor on a big daily newspaper habitually concerned with deadlines, speed, snap decisions, the taking of calculated risks. This kind of thinking, I now knew, had become a part of my decision-making apparatus.

This was no accident. With industry off balance during those depression years, conventional procedures in the classic sense of the formal practice of architecture were dead. I launched big ideas because they were more easily launched than small ones. I worked my newly won status night and day — but I was unhappy at it, restless. The false stimulus of the fair was gone, and I was suffering from an acute attack of dualism. I remembered Mon-

61

taigne's sentence: "We are, I know not how, double in ourselves so that what we believe, we disbelieve, and cannot rid ourselves of what we condemn." How I regretted my failure to spend that extra year in design at Cornell with Bosworth, and the loss of the two-year fellowship at the American Academy in Rome. I did in fact still lack a primary education. How could I get control of my dualism? In-depth travel seemed at least a partial answer. There was money for this — a substantial windfall. The 20 per cent deduction taken out in World's Fair bonds from my salary for four years was paid off in full and in the bank, still intact. The Orient, with Peking, China, as the epicenter, would be my objective. I had had four years of exposure to the unmitigated snobbery of Francophile Skid and his fellow habitués of Parisian ateliers who never let me forget it for one moment. I was fed up with the École des Beaux Arts, Deux Magots, Lipps, their years of fellowship travel in Europe and the Near East. But what about the mysterious Orient? I had them there. Skid conceded that such a trip might add something of value to our plans. I would seek structures and their interchange with people, study old customs and artifacts in relation to twentieth-century problems in the United States. I was certain I would find parallels.

There were, even then, rumblings of Japanese aggression. We had better hurry. The United States was shipping scrap iron and student peace delegates, even-handed, to Japan. World War II would soon close Asia to travel.

Aboard the *Empress of Canada* out of Vancouver, Emily and I steamed across the Pacific, grimly cold in empty, threadbare elegance. In Tokyo a letter of introduction brought us into the courtly presence of Ambassador Grew, who confirmed the rumors and talked sadly of what lay ahead in 1942 and of the deaf ears of the diplomats in Washington.

We stayed at the famous Frank Lloyd Wright–designed Imperial Hotel, since destroyed, then in its prime, the lobby like the work of no man but rather nature's handiwork in some great cave where the surfaces mysteriously interchanged from flat to round to concave to volutes, cubes, stalactites. The infinite tracery of the Orient merging and blending with strong base structure. Intense delicacy overlaying and enhancing earth-sprung strength.

Pointing toward Peking, in a tiny steamer, we crossed the Japan Sea. Our fellow passengers were missionaries bound for northern China and Mongolia. In the Tientsin Harbor at dawn, tall, mustachioed Mongolian porters mobbed us and confiscated our luggage — forever, we thought. But out of that standard Oriental chaos came the order we learned to expect. The mob scene was repeated at the Peking station, where we were saved by the number-one boy of our hostess, Aunt Lucy Calhoun, widow of the first United States Minister to China, who welcomed us because of Emily's family, and her Chinese temple home became our refuge in Peking. We had our own rickshaws, with the wiry boys seemingly fixed between the shafts day and night, fueled by tiny bowls of rice mysteriously produced. We were told that a stroll on foot through old Peking was beneath the dignity of the white man.

The great tile and timber temples of the Far East were at once old, new — timeless architecture. We experienced the soon-to-die traditions of the International City, a highly sophisticated concentrate of European decadence gathered from world capitals and flavored with an Oriental spice. Here was the last gasp of the supreme English in the Far East. We could hear the gunboats firing up the river near Shanghai. Chiang Kai-shek was in his headquarters in the Summer Palace in Peking and he let Aunt Lucy Calhoun take me through the great treasure houses of the Imperial Palace, which we did for days at a time. It was none too soon. Within a year they were robbed of their ancient treasures.

The structures within the Forbidden City were of the grand scale, rich in ornament massed dramatically in an enormous plan hinged with long vistas, masses solidly contrasting with the fine veining of delicate marble balustrades. An ancient Chinese, contemplating his cricket in its tiny cage. A veil of mystery shrouds the architecture of Peking.

Aunt Lucy arranged the classic picnic in the northern hills, exactly as Pearl Buck said it should be — pure magic. With the wave of a hand, the white-coated Chinese servants produced a damask tablecloth, folded napkins, silver, iced drinks in sparkling crystal — softly, silently, deliciously, with the great sky overhead, the mystery and charm of the Orient confirmed.

For five days we sailed the China Sea in a Chinese rice boat complete with armed Indian Sikhs to protect us from Chinese pirates, slowly moving toward Saigon. The forward holds of the small steamer were jammed with milling sheep, Chinese deck passengers and cabbages, the three ingredients coalescing into a mixture producing their own special aroma, urged on by the searing sun and growing more potent each day as we steamed slowly across the placid waters.

Wherever the Frenchman goes he takes the Paris city plan with him, and Saigon was no exception. But not even the wide boulevards lined with lush, tropical foliage could hide the sloth and corruption which the French permitted to flourish here. We moved on to Angkor Wat, the monuments there almost consumed by the jungle, the huge piles of sculptured stone the records of a religious past. Then on through the endless dust of India, the temples, the burning ghats, the Ganges and the great yellow umbrellas along the river; the sixteenth-century red city of Fatehpur-Sikri, the unhinged Brahman cows eating in the marketplace while the people stood by, starving — all moving against rather than with each other. New Delhi, the British capital, with the red-turbaned, spit-and-polish magnificence of the horsemen in the guards, so unreal as to be incredible, a stage-set capital designed and built between 1912 and 1929 and existing rather as a matter of fantasy than fact; a stage set for great theater but terribly empty when the British left and the performance ended.

Aswan, Luxor, Memphis, Cairo, Alexandria, de rigueur for architects who could manage it. Even the desert fly and the Mohammedan dragoman could not detract from the architecture of the Valley of the Kings.

Just one year after the closing of the Chicago World's Fair, Emily and I met Skid and Eloise in London. There was no other course to take but architecture. We would discuss the pros and cons involved in our commitments to the future.

When the time of departure came the place was Paddington Station, London, the spans of its lacy Victorian ironwork almost obscured by the soot, smoke and steam of the murky interior. We four huddled together in the dismal atmosphere, perched on a pile of steamer trunks, suitcases and odd-shaped parcels wrapped up in butcher paper. Although the decision had been forming from the day six years before when Eloise and I had met Skid at the Cunard pier — perhaps even when he and Eloise Owings had talked about the future at the sidewalk table outside the Café Deux Magots in 1928 — the purpose of this meeting was to express out loud, in words, the final agreement creating the firm of Skidmore and Owings, put off by mutual consent until the last possible moment before sailing because Skid simply could not express in words that which moved him deeply.

The practice of architecture was not very old. It was formalized in the late 1800s by such strong personalities as Hunt and Richardson, when architects were a luxury in the precious atmosphere of building pseudo-European castles on Long Island or Manhattan for the very wealthy. Considered a partnership since 1931 by most everybody at the fair, Skid and I had been practicing under very different conditions. Partnerships among architects in the twentieth century were generally loosely made and easily broken. At the moment of our agreement in Paddington Station, dozens of architects were shaking hands and swearing undying loyalty to each other — and just as many were breaking up. To avoid this, we had a plan. Forty years later it is clear that this plan, largely unchanged, was a controlling factor in the continuity of our partnership.

Witnessed by Emily and Eloise, Skid and I pledged our lives to share and share alike — to offer a multidisciplined service competent to design and build the multiplicity of shelters needed for man's habitat. We would build only in the vernacular of our own age.

We could be ambitious; the scope in our field was unlimited. We would have to take responsibility to gain authority. We felt we knew how to build a modern "Gothic Builders Guild" practice and to apply the synergism of power thus created. We had witnessed the death of a century-long era in the 1929 crash and shared in the birth of a new one in 1930 of undetermined length. We felt we knew some of the pitfalls of the old and we planned a partnership refreshed by new talent to circumvent this.

We were not after jobs as such. We were after leverage to influence social and environmental conditions. To work, we must have volume. An efficient set of master builders can eat up a lot of work. Volume meant power. We would try to change men's minds. But the test would be: could we gain greater volume without supine order-taking sans ideas, ideals, innovation? We feared that idealism and order-taking didn't match. In his *Education* Henry Adams attempted to relate the eleventh and twelfth centuries' spiritual revival to twentieth-century dynamics. Through combining group practice and good design, social change, showmanship, we would marinate our architectural demands in sound economics to meet the criteria of our doubting critics — who didn't believe that one could have both economy and aesthetics — with proof that they were the same.

Prepared to prove these theories, Skidmore and Owings opened their first office in Chicago on January 1, 1936.

The type, size, location and general environment of our first

66

office were matters not to be taken lightly, but the restraint of virtual poverty would control the matter of rent. We found an attic meeting our several requirements standing two hundred and fifty feet above Michigan Avenue, with the open angle of its pitched ceiling framing a magnificent panorama of Lake Michigan. No ordinary landlord, Boston Brahmin Graham Aldis accepted our services as architects in residence — in other words, remodeling for tenants — in lieu of the fifty-dollar-a-month rent usually asked for this aerie. Our one secretary received sixty dollars a month and appeared greatly pleased.

We became three when our sometime Tavern Club drinking companion, architect-engineer John Ogden Merrill, a partner in the respected and conservative firm of Granger and Bolenbacher, sadly told us of the illness and death of both Granger and Bolenbacher within weeks of each other. By common consent on the spur of the moment, Skid and I asked John to join us in the only role we could afford: partner. The third name in SOM, John Ogden Merrill became our anchor man in Chicago. This inaugurated a kind of tradition of Merrills. His brother, Edward, and later his son John have furnished a powerful additive, contributing continuity, integrity and hardest of all to define, a kind of homely but indispensable dependability, unspectacular but irreplaceable.

In Chicago we had brilliant young designers — like Ambrose Richardson, Harry Weese, Charles Dornbusch — who came and went. It would be five years before Chicago had a third partner: William Hartmann, and another five before Walter Netsch, the first of the youngsters to stick, joined the partnership.

As if to test us, our old friend Rufus Dawes, ex–world's fair president then heading the Chicago Museum of Science and Industry, gave us our first job. We were asked to remodel and convert the Fine Arts Building in Jackson Park — the only temporary building remaining of the original World's Fair of 1893 — into a permanent museum of science and industry. This had been Burnham's apology to Greece and Rome, a huge structure containing practically every known motif of the Greek and Roman periods: Doric, Ionic and Corinthian columns were there by the dozens. The Parthenon was represented, the Erechtheum's porch of the caryatids, intact sections of the dome of the Pantheon — a selection too varied and too comprehensive to list. Into this compost of choice selections from the past we were asked to somehow implant modern science and industry. A devil's choice, it seemed, but we converted it into a useful if incongruous shell for an exhibition of our country's contemporary prowess in science and industry. We installed a mechanized coal mine to operate in a Roman temple, and designed the table of elements for the sacred cella of Athena. This was our first job in Chicago — acres and acres of it. We wondered what our rationale would be if we were asked to design a little something for the cella of the Parthenon.

Anyone who drops into the main drugstore in Petoskey, Michigan, today can probably find a brightly colored postcard displaying the American flag snapping out straight from a handsome flagpole, behind which is a red brick boxlike central pavilion standing foursquare upon the earth: a small hospital of one-hundred-bed capacity, designed by me in 1939, while a one-thousand-bed veterans' hospital was rising on Sandy Hook. And, on that same postal card, gracefully angling out from the main box structure is a wing standing on piloti, with slotted windows and limestone veneer. The central portion of this northern Michigan phenomenon, which might be described as American brewery style, is almost pure Owings; and anyone familiar with the contemporary architecture of the Bauhaus and the international style would know that the sloping wing was almost pure Bunshaft. Petoskey, Michigan, was Otis territory, and it was entirely through my father-in-law's influence that we had the job at all. While in the New York office, under Skid's direction, there were giant jobs, we in Chicago were content with small.

68

We bothered with trivia: small, fussy remodeling jobs, often the seedbed of later commissions. Our gestures of concern evoked surprised response from the laymen we helped. Architecture appears to be an occult art, frightening to the uninitiated, although touching every man. We found our proffered help most warmly received. Somehow we had struck a responsive chord. When told that no job was too small for us, William Patterson, president of United Air Lines, complained, "My staff says it will cost thirty thousand dollars to remodel my office so that I can have an escape exit." With the moving of one door, his secret exit problem was solved. Cost: thirty dollars. Reward: a long, warm relationship.

When Ed Wilson insisted, in lieu of my working for Wilson the packer permanently, I designed a visitors' route through the "assembly line" of their meat packing processing plant, dramatizing through lighting, color and graphics. Retainer: five hundred dollars a month.

But we needed solid capital. Our piecemeal efforts were not enough. A silent partner was the only solution, since we refused to become involved in debt. My father-in-law didn't spring at the opportunity and we had to omit Rufus Dawes since he was a client. Dr. William Allen Pusey was our man.

Dr. Pusey was an institution in Chicago and, next to Rufus, my best friend at the fair. For all his fame and prestige in civic and professional matters, he dispensed his wisdom from behind a nineteenth-century roll-top desk, the worse for wear and so crammed with stacks of papers and journals on dermatology as to remain unclosed all the years I knew him. He once asked me to remodel his smoke-blackened, golden oak private offices and I refused. No one should ever touch that museum piece. The radium was cached in what looked to me like an ancient Bull Durham box.

Dr. Pusey was a Scot and famed for his choleric irascibility, and I was flattered to be his friend. He quickly agreed to extend us credit of a thousand dollars a month up to a maximum of ten thousand dollars. In return for this we would pay him a percentage of the gross less a joint living expense of ten thousand dollars per annum, to be paid until his death — which act on his part was to end the obligation on our part. He loathed lawyers and wrote the agreement in his own handwriting. It was a temptation when we met to make discreet inquiry as to his health.

Our method of charging potential clients a modest monthly retainer instead of a percentage was a new angle on fees — life's blood to us and nominal to them — and a vital innovation in keeping us afloat. Basic to our long-term survival as a private partnership, where most other firms had flown to corporate cover, was a deferred-income method of accounts worked out by our legal counsel, Marshall Grosscup Sampsell.

Marshall Grosscup Sampsell folds his money flat with a silver clip, and all of the crisp bills held therein are new. Hipless, he too stands in neat, vertical folds. Peering out at you are his keen green New England eyes — piercing.

Gross is orderly where I am not, calm where I am not, cautious where I am not. Something like a satellite moon to Saturn, he is essentially a part of SOM, yet detached. Shy, retiring, he has been our legal mind since 1936, serving as confidant and confessor.

The overall partnership documents under which SOM operates were originally put together by Gross and are ever-changing, like the amorphous body of English law, which includes much that is not written down at all. In fact, Sampsell himself epitomizes that law, and our operating agreements, like a good many things about SOM, defy definition as soon as an attempt is made to write them down. Highly personal, Gross holds the many strands of concern for partner and partnership alike.

6

New York Partners

SEVEN MONTHS AFTER we had opened the Chicago office I suddenly found myself in New York City, facing the executive vice president of a toilet-manufacturing company. His suite was located on the top floor of a handsome black-shafted tower standing on the corner of Fortieth and Fifth Avenue, and from one of the great windows I could glimpse Bryant Park and the New York Public Library stretching out below. The executive vice president had plans to create sweeping interior changes in this, their home office building. He seemed to know a great deal about the work we had done and I was being queried as to our availability. I answered his questions carefully so as not to disclose the true extent of our rather extreme availability — which was much more than I wanted him to guess. He agreed that we could do the job, but then: ". . . and please, Mr. Owings, put that in writing in a letter to me, and upon receipt of it, I will call your New York office and give your resident partner the go-ahead."

Of course we didn't have an office in New York yet, nor did we have a resident partner. I didn't dare risk losing this chance for a critical commission by an explanation. So I replied: "Okay,

I will mail that letter to you this afternoon. You will have it not later than tomorrow morning."

In those days the Woolworth dime store offered almost every facility, including the instant printing of business stationery. A nearby telephone book provided a directory and, under ARCHITECTS in the classified section, I found the listing of two of my colleagues whose prime location suited me exactly. Those two friends were Joseph Urban and Otto Teegen, and the address of their office was 5 East Fifty-seventh Street. I only hoped they wouldn't mind too much.

Thirty minutes later the handsome new Woolworth letterhead of the New York office of Skidmore, Owings and Merrill emerged, complete with Teegen's telephone number — and, gratuitously, Louis Skidmore, A.I.A., as partner in charge. A visit to the public stenographer at the nearby Commodore Hotel completed the proceedings and, as the stamped envelope disappeared down the slot of the nearest United States mail box, our fate was sealed.

It would have made sense for me to stay in New York and design the job we had acquired, but my surface confidence covered a no-confidence feeling about carrying out the design decisions this commission would require, so Louis Skidmore moved East. It was a long six months of hard work and loneliness for Skid and Eloise before she joined him and the first two permanent headquarters were assured. As Skid put it, "Two guys like us need that much territory to operate in." Fortunately, the internal machinery of our operation was in good order. Dr. Pusey's new money gave us freedom of action, and Gross Sampsell's handling of the mechanics of law and accounting left our minds free to concentrate on architectural design.

Skid liked people and the intrigue and subtle maneuverings that he could carry on at the round table in the friendly, relaxed atmosphere of the Madison Bar or the Oak Room. But with his success the pressure mounted and he developed ulcers.

He could not sustain this pressure and the final push of the 1939 fair almost did him in. But out of that travail and to meet that crisis, Bob Cutler, Walter Severinghaus, Gordon Bunshaft and Bill Brown gained stature. Skid's boys, as he affectionately called them, molded and jostled and worked together among themselves and soon formed the nucleus of SOM's New York office.

In that cramped, cluttered space which we had pre-empted from Otto Teegen and Joseph Urban, these four men, without any discernible line of authority, somehow worked together. Coalescing in the early years into one united body when necessary, yet each performing his own independent function freely, for a long time they revolved around Louis Skidmore. During those years he exerted a powerful gravitational pull, but later they seemed to get along without that and presented a solid front, with dominant Gordon Bunshaft the master designer, Bill Brown the master builder, Bob Cutler the master manipulator and Walter Severinghaus the conscience and the worrier, the ultimate guarantor of credibility for all four.

I tried to help lighten the load during Skid's intermittent attacks of ulcers by spending considerable time in New York, working to help finish up the New York World's Fair; and this in turn helped me to pull this tightly knit, closely operating unit of the four New York partners into closer orbit with our Chicago operation.

Of the private lives of these four men I saw little, but they were easy enough to see together four or five days a week, nine or ten months out of the year, at the Brussels Restaurant. Heavy carpet underfoot, past square yards of the tortured geometry of glazed hors d'oeuvres and pastries, I'd often join them, following behind the bobbing coattails of the white-gloved waiter to a silver-china-glittering damask circle of light in the narrowest room.

I would take my seat among the New York SOM contingent of master builders, each twirling a tall-stemmed Beefeater's with a twist, shimmering beside the transparently thin smoked salmon slices on each plate.

But appearances were deceptive. SOM's fame for tailored excellence of building detail came from these four men who held an underlying fierce concern for those details; a tenacity, a solidarity and a consummate developing skill. In combination these four expensively educated, depression-stranded, casually assembled mid-continent–born men were producing, and would continue to produce, not only individually significant twentieth-century architecture but a remarkable volume as well. Each came to us fresh, only a few years out of college or fellowship travel, Walter Severinghaus having worked the longest — for Adams and Prentice, old friends of both his and Skid's — for three years. Each was totally committed to architecture as a professional career. Each remained with SOM throughout that career.

In my thirty-five-year exposure to Walter Severinghaus, the style of his signature, "J. Walter," was the only indication of some scant remnant of ego somewhere in that tall, dark, gravely soft and measured personality. He was deliberate of speech and action, considerate, compassionate, with a bachelor of arts from Ohio Wesleyan University and a bachelor of architecture from Ohio State University. In June 1970, he received the first honorary degree ever given by Ohio State to an architect: doctor of fine arts.

Walter Severinghaus meets the wildest of our ideas with a tempered logic and reason that drives me wild, as does his deliberate caution. Perhaps he has developed this patience required of him by spelling his name correctly to telephone operators. Or perhaps that patience was developed by being exposed to the coruscations of daily contact with his extraordinary associates in the New York office.

Gordon Bunshaft epitomizes in appearance and in his life style a baroque, nineteenth-century, individualized, temperamental artist. Fiercely intolerant and at times arrogant, always sincere in his commitment to his personal design ethic, Gordon can be as gentle as a dove when he chooses. Of the original nucleus, he was the acknowledged designer. Later others in the other offices challenged him, perhaps, but never in New York. Gordon held a then rare masters degree from M.I.T. and had won the Rotch Scholarship eight years after Skid; and, like the rest, he really never worked much for anyone but SOM. With his versatile, volatile brilliance streaming out from every crevice, it is not surprising that Bun was hot to handle, and that he strained the theory of anonymity for us all — especially his New York partners.

Gordon liked his New York setup. As he explained it, "The partners work as one big team. The others take care of all the headaches and I am in charge of design." Outside the office, in a civic sense he has done his bit, serving long and effectively on the National Fine Arts Commission.

Although Gordon Bunshaft has held the limelight I have always considered Bunshaft and William S. Brown as paired. Bill was, for thirty-five years until his retirement, the other half of an integrated whole. Brown and Bunshaft together carried out important industrial migrations to the suburbs, one of the first being Connecticut General, followed by the stunning Emhart corporate headquarters in the same town. In the city, Union Carbide, built over the tracks on Park Avenue at Forty-fourth, was a great solution jointly arrived at.

These jobs required collaboration between designers, engineers, metallurgists, chemists, manufacturers and material suppliers. The gleaming brilliance of a window wall where the stainless steel verticals between great panes of glass must run up without a joggle — sometimes as high as eight hundred feet straight, clear and clean — was their responsibility, to be accomplished at a reasonable price and within the competence of the construction industry. Inventions like the window-washing equipment of Lever House were developed under their aegis;

yet they were neither engineers nor constructors. Walter Severinghaus, Bill Brown, Bob Posey and their associates acted in the role of coordinating master builders, a job seldom filled because there are so few people to fill it — jobs anonymous even within our own family concept at SOM.

Robert Cutler is the opposite end of the spectrum from an identifiable architectural type. He has met, mingled with and largely contained the Rotarian Main Street Babbitt element among the clientele of commerce and industry, as well as those in the architectural profession who tend in that direction. This is Bob's natural métier. He has gained a large measure of professional acceptance for architects in general and SOM in particular by the hospital fraternity, and has maintained that acceptance and trained some important people within our firm to carry it on, led by Harold Olson. He has been rewarded, and has received credit for his work from those who appreciate it most. He has been president of the Building Congress and the Fifth Avenue Association and has held various offices in the American Institute of Architects.

But we are speaking now of the years of the 1939 World's Fair. Since 1936 this upcoming world's fair, to be held in New York, had been in the wind. Most of the prospects for it were Skid's old friends, and now that we had a New York office to handle them, these prospects materialized. Exhibitors interested in the fair gravitated to whichever round table Skid headed at the time for advice and counsel, and usually ended up paying a thousand dollars for a preliminary idea which he would suggest for their exhibit. The great industrial designers like Raymond Loewy were at their peak of popularity then and were preparing designs for everything from lipsticks to locomotives. An essential part of their success in gaining acceptance for these designs, it seemed to us, was based on their method of presenting them to the client. They used airbrush and produced fast, dreamlike visions turned out in slick spiral-bound volumes that could stir the coldest critic.

Suddenly Skid began to supply his clients with sleek brochures. This innovation followed closely the appearance in our New York office of Loewy's best delineator. Skid denied the rumor that this delineator had been stolen. Not true, said Skid — borrowed.

The ever-lengthening tendrils of SOM's roots pushed into new, unexpected fissures existing in the not-so-solid rock of Manhattan Island's monolithic professional field, reaching a climax when Robert Moses asked Skid to do the nearly impossible: design New York City's proposed exhibit for the Fair. It was to be a two-acre monster of a job, to be executed in too little time for too little money and, of course, with Moses as the client, in top-ranking quality. Under these restrictive covenants, anyone but Skid would have refused.

The in-depth exposure to Robert Moses that Skid gained through the acceptance of this job was the beginning of a thirty-year friendship fashioned from respect, and gave SOM a niche in the tight hierarchy which controlled architectural, planning, engineering and construction jobs in New York City. It was one thing to gain a niche; staying there was another. It all involved coping with Robert Moses and his associates. This was a rugged kind of life. At the time Skid seemed to depend on martinis, but he was never an alcoholic or even a bad drunk. I feel competent to judge, having been both. His martini-ulcer-milk diet routine was external evidence of his inner struggle with his shyness, over which somehow boiled an all-powerful urge for self-extension. The ulcer persisted and he was forced to share his mysticism enough at least to get the work done. Thus he built the kind of firm his spirit urged — group practice — through three building blocks forming a perfect arch: my sister Eloise, the four New York partners, and his persistent ulcer.

Yet, over and above it all, Skid was a mystic, and those who knew him best understood this.

Among Skid's papers I found this letter from Howard Heinz, founder of the famous 57 Varieties and the Heinz pickle, who was not given to writing sentimental notes or forgiving rebuffs (like having his thousand-foot papier-mâché pickle turned down for the 1933 fair) and was equally unaccustomed to providing deficit financing for architects:

> Dear Mr. Skidmore:
> I have awaited your recovery from your unfortunate illness to write. Our exhibit at the Fair is running successfully, thanks to you and your able staff. Now, having learned of the extra expense you and your associates have incurred, the enclosed check is extra remuneration. I have never worked with an architect who was more agreeable or fair in his dealings. My son joins me in this good wish and I hope that you will take such care of yourself that you will soon regain your normal health.

Howard Heinz's son Jack literally adopted Skid, Eloise and Gordon Bunshaft, playing the Medici to our Bernini, producing some of our best works.

From time to time I introduced a little variety into the New York practice — a Hugh Troy project, for example. Mr. Toffenetti (who composed his own menu notes and used prose for his spaghetti like "A hundred yards of happiness") seemed a logical target. I told Mr. Toffenetti that Troy was yearning to experiment with a combination of oil on canvas and blown-up photographs on a blank wall at one end of his new restaurant. With the help of a photographer, Troy promised to turn out a job that would set Salvador Dali back on his heels. The painted parts were done in pale greens and yellows and the photographs in sepia; the subject was to be madness. "Masses mold into each other," Troy said. Thus lambs turned eerily into peas, a bass violin into crockery, musical notations into baked potatoes, a parasol into the Winged Victory, melons into talking machines, a cow into a fish, a tree into fireworks. Troy had girls on beaches turning into baked potatoes, but Mr. Toffenetti said "No sex!"

With the close of the 1939 World's Fair, SOM had the problem of continuity of work. World War II was on full tilt. Hitler had marched the length and the breadth of Europe, and only the British Isles remained to be conquered. FDR had done what he could. Our country was in the war but didn't know it. But we knew it at SOM because we were asked to do supersecret preparatory defensive work starting in March 1940.

In 1940 Bob Cutler and I got involved in a job of gigantic proportions which stretched us like a very healthy rubber band until we had covered all the coasts of the United States. This task developed muscles SOM would use later. The job was to design and build seventy-two strange devices from a prototype imported from England, called information and filter centers, for the defense of our country. They were based upon the techniques used by Great Britain in its most critical hour, the Battle of Britain. Bob and I traveled from Maine to Florida, around the Gulf Coast of Baja California, to Victoria and Vancouver.

Like everybody else, I can recall December 7, 1941, even to the Sunday lunch we had in St. Charles, Illinois, with roast suckling pig. The seventy-two information and filter centers that we had installed successfully during that last eighteen months preceding December 7 and Pearl Harbor were never used, but they were designed to perform the functions described by Winston Churchill in his *Their Finest Hour.*

It was one of the decisive battles of the war, and like the Battle of Waterloo, it was on Sunday. I was at Checkers. All the ascendency of the Hurricanes and Spitfires would have been fruitless but for this system of underground control centers and telephone cables . . . built before the war by the Air Ministry. The . . .

operations room was like a small theater . . . Below us was the large scale map table around which were perhaps twenty highly trained young men and women with their telephone assistants . . .
. . . In a glass stage box were the four or five officers whose duty it was to watch and weigh information from our Observer Corps which numbered upwards of fifty thousand women, men and youths. Radar was still in its infancy but it gave warning of raids approaching our coast and the observers with field glasses and portable telephones were our main source of information about raiders flying overhead . . . The lower line of bulbs was out. There was not one squadron left in reserve. Conscious of the anxiety of the commander, [Churchill] asked, "What other reserves have we?" "There are none," said Vice Marshall Park.

Our four New York partners had received their educations during the depression period between 1929 and 1936. The utopia promised them had been the emergence of prefabrication as a solution to practically every problem of postdepression America. Among the clients of our dozens of New York World's Fair projects was a prefab addict, Joe O'Brien, who left Westinghouse to join the Pierce Foundation, a subsidiary of the American Radiator Company, with the sole intention of studying the science of prefabricated housing. This he did under the sobering influence of J. Walter Severinghaus. We agreed to serve as consultants and assigned Walter to the job, thus starting a chain reaction resulting in the joint development of a prefab of our own. The sponsor for this candidate for immortality in Prefab Heaven was the Celotex Corporation, and the product was christened Cemest-O-Board, of which the house principally consisted. A three-ply panel, the central core of Celotex, its exterior was soft gray in color, reasonably impervious to weather, easily erected and interchangeable. There were 13,826 design and engineering drawings prepared to produce this expandable, contractable, one-, two-, three- or four-bedroom house.

In 1930 F.D.R. had taken up the cause of the nation's ill housed, ill clad and ill nourished and had brought government into the mass-produced, factory-built house industry. In a nation slowed to a standstill, the building industry and the architectural profession turned to the prefab, not only for the ill housed but for the ill nourished and ill clothed too, because the prefabs would create new jobs, they thought. The return to prosperity was "right around the corner" and would be ushered in as soon as those pesky bugs in the production of housing could be worked out — which they never were.

Being pushed in South America, prefab was the thing — was on everybody's lips and was everybody's hope. It was the carrot at the end of the unemployment stick.

Everyone promised so much and delivered so little and met such resistance because of one important oversight: human nature. Man's adherence to custom and resistance to change was deep. Human nature resisted thinness, cheapness, ersatz materials. In a village of brick or stone houses, the intrusion of paper-thin, painted panel houses — usually with flat roofs — downgraded the surrounding property, reduced local labor input and violated local building and safety codes, usually written to protect labor input rather than in the interests of safety.

The hidden censorship of the Federal Housing Administration worked against modern houses and disapproved prefabs. There was virtually no contact between homebuilders and the architect. Architects had lost out to the building speculator and had no effective control over the design of housing in the United States. Suddenly the depression revived the architect's interest and it was fashionable to be involved in the designs of prefabs. The small architect was virtually dependent on prefabs as the only form of job-making available.

Buckminster Fuller demonstrated his prefabricated, all-in-one-piece factory-built bathroom to all who would look or listen, carting it around the country on a truck. One day in her fourteenth-floor apartment on upper Park Avenue, Clare Booth Luce got a telephone call. Bucky said, "Look out of the window and then come on downstairs." As the crowds gathered and stared, she did, and marveled at the new dymaxian bathroom she saw there. But the unions wouldn't let anyone install this threat to labor's future, and so in a depression where almost everyone was out of work, labor helped block the best promise of a building boom.

Sears Roebuck took up the cry, offering a variety of model prefab homes in their catalogue. Not to be outdone by Sears or the unions, Skid and I got together with a local Chicago builder and, in fair competition, produced a standard SOM-designed house at a lower cost, thereby reversing the position we would have been expected to take as enlightened modernists. We made the cover of *Better Homes and Gardens* magazine, an honor never listed in a prospectus.

But the word "prefab" held an evil connotation. Prefab would not fit the American idea of a proper house. Roadblocks stood in the way of enlightened solutions until this deadlock squeezed out from between the trailer and the house the worst of both — the mobile home. But it doesn't matter. The whole lot are temporary in terms of any continuum in society. Our great urban-destined populations will end up in beehive complexes: multilevel, stratified structures covering great areas as did the early tenth-century pueblos at Chaco Canyon in New Mexico. As serious architects and builders we must not ignore any avenue of approach to any technical area. One never knows from what small beginnings may come a big idea, or opportunity, or both.

Like the sower in *The Angelus,* only not so solemn, Joe O'Brien, director of the Pierce Foundation, seeded our lowly prefab on the wind by the thousands. Some of those seeds fell on a bit of rugged terrain near Knoxville, Tennessee.

7

Oak Ridge

"Which of you intending to build a tower sitteth not down first and counteth the cost whether he have sufficient to finish it?"

I T ISN'T EVERY DAY that someone drops into the office and orders a town. One fine December afternoon in 1942 two men in civilian clothes walked into our New York office unannounced and requested an interview with Louis Skidmore. These unknown men had to wait for quite a while because Skidmore was in a meeting. All efforts on the part of our receptionist to ferret out their interest in Skidmore were of no avail. Finally they were admitted and introduced themselves. Mr. Marshall casually stated without preliminaries that they were in need of a town and how long did we need to put one together? Mr. Block said nothing.

To answer intelligently, Skidmore thought a few simple questions might be in order. He inquired as to how large a town they needed, where it was to be located, and for what purpose it was intended. Met with frigid stares and frosty silences, and beginning to doubt his own sanity, Skidmore was about to tell these crackpots to get out. There was a war on and we were busy. Skid evidently made his point, and at this juncture the elder man produced his credentials. They appeared to be quite authentic: a colonel in the United States Army, Corps of Engineers, Manhattan District, and his younger assistant, a major. Having spent two years working with the Corps of Engineers on the installation of interceptor stations in seventy-two locations on the three coasts of the United States, Skid was pretty sure that the Manhattan District did not exist; but there was an aura of authenticity about this and he decided to take a chance. He quit asking questions and listened. There was one point on which these army officers posing as civilians were definite: speed. Whatever it was they were doing was of the greatest urgency. So, innocently enough, we became involved in a series of events that set off for us our own private chain reaction. We adjusted ourselves to the cloak and dagger aspects of the situation with relish. We were hooked, our curiosity standing triumphant over the prostrate figure of our reason.

Not until the atomic bomb was dropped over Hiroshima were two of the three questions we asked those gentlemen on that December afternoon answered: how big a town did they want and for what purpose was it being built? Then we could look back and examine how we provided first twelve thousand and then seventy-five thousand people with their morning paper over their morning coffee, with their classroom recitations, their church services, their bridge clubs, cribs for their ever-present infants, which always seemed to dominate the living area; and how those seventy-five thousand different individuals transplanted from every part of the country in an unbelievably short time (from December 28, 1942, until December 1945) took root and did their jobs.

Throughout the period of this development, secrecy reached the point of absolute negation. I suspect that they never quite forgave us for not figuring out a way of designing and building a town without a location. When things got dull — which they never did — we could always depend on the security officer to liven them up. One day Skidmore and I lunched together in New York and I casually mentioned having seen our Manhattan District friend, Colonel Marshall, in Chicago the preceding day.

That afternoon after our luncheon we had a visitation and were advised against mentioning any more names in public.

With nothing for the enemy more interesting than plans for houses, schools, restaurants, security required that our New York office be wired with an electric system so complex, so thorough, that to open a window or a door for ventilation sent bells ringing and detectives running. The difficulty about the Manhattan's special brand of security was that it kept us in a sort of vacuum. It would have been easy and fun if we could have mysteriously whispered into people's ears about secret jobs and secret missions, but we could not even admit that we had any mission or job at all.

Within our own organization on site, which at its peak reached six hundred and fifty technical personnel, speculation was rife as to the purpose of the production in the plants. I remember one day standing near a railroad siding on the site. There were several miles of railroad cars with construction shanties, size fifteen by twenty feet, lined up solidly almost as far as the eye could see, ready to be moved out to the hundreds of individual jobs already started. Someone suggested that we were probably there to build outhouses for the United Nations. During the 1944 Presidential campaign it was suggested that we were making fourth-term buttons for Roosevelt. There was another rumor that we were making certain parts of hobbyhorses that were to be sent to Washington for final assembly. But the one that appealed to me the most was that this was a giant spy trap, designed to attract and keep all foreign espionage agents in one safe place where they could be watched.

It is difficult for the normal, unregimented American to put superhuman effort into something unless he understands exactly what it is for. The morale of the individual is raised by being included. Eventually a different sort of fraternal spirit developed within this project: "Anything so damned secret must be damned important."

Over a billion dollars' worth of materials was shipped into the area in a short time. In an effort to obfuscate the enemy, this huge flow was funneled in staggered shipments to five little flag-stop towns surrounding our area. We objected to this method since even the Tennessee mountaineers could see that Elsa, Tennessee, for instance, with a population hovering at the top figure of 151, couldn't use fifteen thousand toilet fixtures. In fact, with the social standing of the privy being what it is in Tennessee, even one water closet started tongues wagging. We had difficulty convincing a Grand Rapids manufacturer that he should ship fifteen thousand mattresses to the town of Clinton, Tennessee, population 4820, where even beds unadorned were just coming into local acceptance. Several times in the early part of the project when we urgently needed specialized supplies and had them shipped from the East, we would find they had been returned to the shipper upon reaching Knoxville, Tennessee, because no one knew of a town called Oak Ridge.

The Knoxville area was chosen because of the ample supply of power furnished by the Tennessee Valley Authority. But it had other advantages, being remote and endowed with a native population whose bump of curiosity had happily remained underdeveloped. We were asked to program, prepare the site planning, design and supervise the construction of the housing and all the facilities required for a complete small city.

The design of Oak Ridge was a small part of the total responsibility of the Manhattan District Corps of Engineers (who also were charged with the building of the enormous plants). In General Leslie Groves' book *Now It Can Be Told,* Oak Ridge is listed as Appendix 5 and consumes two and one half pages. So we were left pretty much to our own devices. The extreme secrecy gave us no opportunity to check our decisions with others. We had been selected primarily because of our work for Joe O'Brien in prefabricated housing for the Pierce Foundation but, unbeknownst to them, our experience in building the

Chicago World's Fair in 1933 and our work on the 1939 fair in New York was what equipped us to accept the responsibility for a large-scale project on an emergency basis, where the givens were few and the unknowns were many. We played many roles, some of which were alarmingly all-inclusive, with which we had only a nodding acquaintance. Among such categories were psychology, sociology and geography; such things as town planning, airports, railroads and highway design — we had at least heard of them.

Our initial population target of 12,500 just matched Lawrenceburg, Indiana — the town in which Louis Skidmore had been born. We discovered that most stores and shops operate at about 51 per cent capacity and are marginal, but that people have to have a choice. When Mrs. Jones gets a bad piece of meat at Store A, she must be able to react by boycotting A for B — and, of course, later she will be back, furious at B and telling Butcher A all about it.

Skidmore remained in New York City in charge of programming. For security reasons, and to cope with the rugged terrain in which we were working, it was essential that the logistics of providing personnel and know-how be carried out on the site; in fact, we had to produce the entire design of the project on site. Thus we tackled everything and anything that came up even remotely connected with programming, planning, building, furnishing or equipment. We boned up at night so as to be able to proceed on the ensuing day and cope with the demands as they arose.

Skidmore, always reluctant to ask for fees, actually agreed to do the entire design for the first 12,500 population for a flat fee of 125,000 dollars. The final fee reached many millions, indicating simply how little any one of our colonels or ourselves understood the scope of our undertaking.

In order to fill many of the gaps in our experience we developed a strange assortment of imported talent. My old friends at the L. S. Ayers department store in Indianapolis loaned me the key merchandising manager of their home store. Skid borrowed from Robert Moses the chief engineer of the Triborough New York–New Jersey Bridge Authority to head our traffic and highway department. I hired a complete construction company, lock, stock and barrel, personnel and equipment, from Grand Rapids, Michigan, to fill out our construction division. John Merrill, Sr., moved to Oak Ridge and lived, breathed, slept, walked, climbed, crawled and chain-smoked there for three long years. Oak Ridge is a living mirror image of the love and care a new city in conception, gestation and birth should have. Merrill and two men, Jackson and Block, did the work.

Rigid secrecy eliminated interference from other government agencies, cut all red tape. Our Colonel Marshall or Major Block waved a magic wand. Our plans were approved, materials obtained, and the all-powerful War Production Board was bypassed, eliminated from interference — perhaps even ignorant of the operation.

A site plan is the basic blueprint of a community development. It is a fabric, the warp being the program requirements and the woof the natural characteristics of the terrain. To function effectively, the warp and the woof must be woven into a voluntary union of man's requirements with the natural characteristics inherent in the land; and thus a fabric is produced. As the project grew — and at no time did we ever know the exact size — the scope of our responsibilities mushroomed alarmingly and became all-inclusive. We met these demands by turning into a kind of stock company, donning the proper professional habiliments for a quick appearance as a sociologist; and then, without missing a cue, changing from mortarboard to stiff-brimmed hat and boots to hand out sound advice on the building of a railroad or the location for a highway. When asked by army experts if our surveyors were using the plane table or triangulation methods, I was only vaguely aware of what they were talking about but took the safe course and announced firmly that we used a little of each. This of course satisfied them completely. One day we got a directive to shoot Polaris. I put my foot down on this — no killing of wildlife here! — only to find out that this was engineering patois for reaffirming the true North by locating Polaris, the polestar.

Our responsibilities included the creation of a modern educational system in all of its complexities. We had to provide complete hospital facilities that did not exist. One unacquainted with the technical problems of laundries would have no idea of what is involved in keeping an ultimate 75,000 human beings all starched and spic and span. A site plan is something that you are foolish enough — when you draw it up in the ivory tower of a metropolitan architect's office — to think will look like that when it is built. But the carefully prepared fabric from the warp of the natural characteristics of the land and the woof of man's needs is subject to moths — and a strong-jawed variety at that. These moths are the countless natural enemies of an architect: money limitation, owners' prejudice, recurrent changes and requirements in conditions. We were, of course, subject to some of these, but not money and not owners' prejudices.

Our initial requirements were clear and definite: some 3000 specialists (income: 10,000 dollars a year or better; habitat: most any state in the Union) were headed for the hills of Tennessee. Most of them would have master's or doctor's degrees and every effort was to be made to insure that they be asked to make the minimum of environmental readjustments. The problem was, simply stated, to provide an environment which would offer no unavoidable conflict with their temperament, their routines and their habitual living standards. Our directive — as the army used to love to call its instructions — automatically removed our operations from any control by standard war construction practices. Comfortable homes of permanent construction, with gracious living rooms, fireplaces, electric kitchens and automatic built-in heating systems were authorized. Facilities normal to a permanent community were a necessity, complete from nursery through to high school. This was constantly stressed. Our clients — these individuals, largely scientists — would mostly be married with families and they were to be treated as highly volatile geniuses, given the best cotton-batting treatment.

Of course this was easy. All we had to do, apparently, was turn out a quaint little Cape Cod village with just the right amount of California mission style, then beat well for ten minutes and season to taste with a touch of the great Northwest. Those hills of Tennessee had something to look forward to! Girls' domestic science courses, boys' manual training shops, gymnasiums, basketball courts, music schools were trimmings we hadn't expected and they surprised us. There were spaces allocated for the living and the dead — like churches, temples and cemeteries for Jewish, Catholic and Protestant — each quite separate. We worried about the ultimate settling of the red-light district, where all faiths could mingle. Anything and everything needed to permit these people to continue their creative work uninterrupted in this isolated spot was to be provided.

There were some interesting sidelines on the actual physical site planning. Consider for a moment the responsibilities inherent in the proper street-naming and house-numbering system. Think of the hours and hours that would be wasted if the system was not clear and people got lost trying to find their friends' houses. And think of those critical hours between two and four in the morning when even the best system might fail. We encountered historical and political pitfalls in naming streets in a Tennessee town after Union generals, or vice versa. We never found out for sure just where Tennessee stood in the Civil War. Street naming was even more difficult because of our type of site development, which involved long, curved streets with no end. Our respect for the Pullman Company geniuses increased as six of our best brains worked for over seven months on the problem of naming the streets and lanes of Oak Ridge.

A man's present-day state of helplessness is profiled when one inventories the goods and services required to keep him happily tending his job. At the outset, as a worker, he is apparently an individual, but he ruthlessly mushrooms his requirements 250 per cent because he is *not* an individual; he is a family, a married man with a wife and one and a half children. To keep him and his family contented while he works eight to ten hours a day, an appalling number of things must happen. For instance, he will need .0012 per cent of a barber chair, with that part of a barber standing fractionally behind it. His wife will need .00658 parts of a beauty shop booth and she will spend an average of one hour there every two and a quarter weeks — and wish she could spend longer. In case we happen to be interested in feet, by multiplying the expected community population by .00107 we can arrive at the number of shoe repairmen we will need. Each of these craftsmen will keep twenty-three hundred people neatly shod by averaging three and a half rehabilitations per person per annum. For every three thousand people there will be a chiropodist on hand. Of course, if anyone should break a leg or come down with a cold, these formulas break down. Our science-minded man needs one-half a square foot of drugstore space set aside for his family — a little higher than the average man. Five point seven square feet of food store will keep the larder filled.

And so, settling the health, safety and happiness of thousands of people whom we would never meet, with slide rule in hand, we proceeded to determine the sizes and numbers of police stations, beer halls, churches and fire stations required for our sedentary population. Inadvertently we produced some defective formulas. In determining the size of our first hospital we used the national average in supplying obstetrical facilities. In Oak Ridge something went wrong. Perhaps it was the increase in the town's size or, as someone said, people had nothing to do nights. But whatever the reason, the obstetrical department reached a state of utter chaos within nine months of the opening of the town. The birthrate was running well over twice the national average.

Behind the retail facilities and the logistics for human consumption and care existing in an ordinary town lies a complicated system of assembly and distribution of goods, which is in reality the wholesale facilities of a community generally taken for granted, their size, scope and complexity never realized. For us the solution of this problem at Oak Ridge was one of the minor miracles of our success. From a physical point of view it involved the designing and building of miles of railroad sidings and switch tracks, the construction of thousands of square feet of wholesale and storage warehouses and trucking depots. Jan Porel, borrowed from the Glen L. Martin Aviation Company, solved this problem, a bottleneck which could have frustrated the building of our town.

Twentieth-century cities were growing obsolete; they were an expression of urban living in the pre-automobile era, and their abnormality was obvious. It was apparent that everyone who could possibly earn enough money to do so was moving to the suburbs. Admittedly concentration of industry for economic reasons required the concentration of people; but it didn't have to follow, since we were starting from scratch, that these people needed to live in the lee of belching smokestacks, chase rats out of vermin-infested alleys or spend two or three hours a day commuting in order to avoid it all.

At that time our cities, with the exception of just a few, were very young. Ninety years ago there were only 26 cities in the United States with populations of 25,000 or over. Forty-six years ago there were only 122, and of those, only 20 were 100,000 or better. So we felt it fair to say that our present concept of a big city had not proven itself and did not need to be accepted as a permanent fixture in our American economy. We were faced with the same problems at Oak Ridge that one faced in any growing small town. We did not know the ultimate population size so we determined on the nucleus — the neighborhood — as the basis for satellite growth. In this country we have, in effect, a nation of villages; therefore, why not start at Oak Ridge with a healthy, natural unit, the village? This we did.

Our scientist and his family and his baker and his butcher and his mortician and their families were to be our clients. It was their health and their welfare and their happiness that concerned us. We were single-minded about that. Their houses were to be oriented for sun and prevailing winds, ample land provided so that the grass and the trees and the flowers might grow. The alley in the gridiron city plan was banished. Here in one stroke we could eliminate many of the vices inherent in existing city plans. A single lane, a service lane, easily reached the kitchen and furnace rooms and garages of the houses, and naturally took the place of all this. On the opposite side of our houses were the living rooms and recreation areas, facing either a field or a park or an individual garden.

Man-made ordinances and zoning laws melt in the heat of man's greed. To protect the basic principles of health and safety and happiness in a community, our safety devices were built into the permanent plan.

Following the pattern of our firm (a number of satellite small offices within the aegis of a large organization) we planned a number of villages to be within the overall aegis of the master plan of Oak Ridge. To carry out this idea, each village unit must be largely self-contained, everything within walking distance, sized to support efficiently the proper combination of educational units (which turned out to be the junior and senior high schools), shopping centers — all facilities common to the neigh-

93

borhood. Each village of fifteen hundred families produced five thousand to six thousand adults and eighteen hundred to two thousand children. My own Indianapolis Park Avenue neighborhood was in the back of my mind.

We did not dare (being experts) admit to this nonscientific formula. Therefore we adopted the same general policy of secrecy for our specialty as that we met with in the Army Corps of Engineers in their dealings with their secret projects. We began to look and act mysterious. We clutched our briefcases and changed the subject whenever the army asked for any information. We hinted at satellite towns, talked of concentric systems of planning, ribbon-type cities as developed by foreign-named people like Hilberscheimer. We discussed mystically new concepts involving the theory of interdependent settlements. We would have submitted to torture rather than admit that all we wanted was a series of homely little American villages tied together with a road to take care of the long-distance traffic and permit the men to be on time to work.

The road serving the residential areas was designed in long, winding curves. This made commercial use improbable. Thus we avoided later invasions of blight: the future intrusion of scattered commercial facilities. Our first directive for approximately eighteen thousand people produced three villages; one project finally expanded into nine, each group of three having a town or community center with minor emphasis on the business section. The high school, with its track, football, baseball and basketball facilities, served the double duty of providing community facilities for gatherings, theatricals and dances.

As the demands for population increased, these self-contained villages could be added one by one, tapped into the major traffic artery — the highway forming the string, the villages the beads. Oak Ridge lay in a long, narrow valley bordered by rugged, wooded foothills and was ideally situated for this technique. The

94

final populated area stretched out over ten miles and was less than two miles wide at any point.

Louis Skidmore and I found ourselves the center of swarming talent gathered from every field of planning, engineering, architecture and building; strangers to each other, unused to working together, separated from their families, available only through an APO address, unable to explain why they were away or where they were. The miracle was that by creating an atmosphere of amused desperation suggestive of Alice and the Mad Hatter, for three years we were able to maintain a state of controlled hysteria.

Throughout that rugged, heavily wooded country I was often struck by the nostalgic charm of quaint little cemeteries among tottering cabins, tumble-down barns, patches of tobacco and sugar cane, which we viewed as we tramped along narrow, rutted roads in pastoral scenes. In theory this terrain offered the perfect opportunity: a kind of clean, uncluttered, uncommitted area with nothing to stand in the way of an ideal plan. But each of these cemeteries, nestling so peacefully in the rural scene was, with exasperating regularity, found to be nestling in the center of a high school gymnasium or between two main road junctions or in some ideally located six-room house. These cemeteries were untouchable. We were defeated. The maddening thing was that they were not big ones — just dozens of little ones scattered at random over the countryside. They were inviolate. The dead could do what the living could not.

When we settled on location in the hills of Tennessee, the city of Knoxville did not hold out her arms to us. We moved into town at the rate of fifty to sixty people a week by Pullman coach, private car, station wagon and bus. The ballroom of the Andrew Jackson Hotel — Knoxville's best — was soon superbly appointed with a sea of cots serving as temporary homesites for an ever-changing and heterogeneous mass of architectural, engineering, planning and surveying humanity. Among these were the Texans. Our survey parties were made up of Texans. We had a hundred or more: six feet tall, strapping, armed with bolos and axes in their belts, tough as nails. One was uneasily reminded of the gold-rush days or the cattle towns of the western front on payday when these men moved in to get their paychecks. We felt it expedient to do all of our necessary firing of personnel in this category by telephone.

The army was badly organized and in one thirty-day period our offices were moved twenty-six times. With this shuffle things got lost and people got confused as to our location. After one such move an army officer called the old office. Apparently the phone rang for twenty minutes or so and was finally answered by a Texan, our chief of survey, whose name was Clink Hammer. The officer gave him hell for not answering sooner. Clink Hammer asked him why in hell he didn't come over and answer it himself if he was in such a hurry.

To make sure that it conformed to the natural terrain, every mile of proposed road was walked, staked out and walked again. In this way John Merrill became acquainted with the country and discovered many lovely building sites tucked away in inaccessible areas. He became extremely judicious about disclosing these locations, since they turned out to be about the only trading point we had with the tough Corps of Engineers. When an army officer began to treat us kindly, we knew he was looking for an ideal homesite. The word went out: See John Merrill.

Once the roads were set and the rhythm established, a curious kind of urgency developed which, more than the Corps of Engineers, kept goading us on. Sixty-four-hour weeks were common enough. When a decision was made, the trap was sprung, the greyhounds unleashed. There was no time to change one's mind. Released in the morning, built in the afternoon. There was no time to correct errors or restudy anything. Once done, there was no alternative. Through heavy timber, rocks, thick underbrush, uphill and down, our boys would scramble along, staking out roads and sewers and water lines. The constructors followed closely behind, led by axmen, dynamiters and the great bulldozers. Occasionally a sharp deflection in the road system occurred, not always caused by cemeteries — which can only be explained by the uncontrollable zeal of the bulldozer operators who followed along so closely behind the staking parties that sometimes the boys ran out of line and took to the bushes in order to avoid being run down — with the bulldozers plowing right in after them. Or so the story goes.

With this kind of high-pressure effort, alcohol was a welcome stimulant, but the rules against bringing in liquor were stringent on the reservation. This being the case, any evidence could be used against us and it was difficult for us to dispose of empty bottles. Knoxville was dry anyway and had blue laws as well. Each newcomer in our personnel was told to fill his suitcase with liquor — he could buy clothes when he arrived. Cars were searched regularly going into the reservation, and if liquor was found it was confiscated and sold by the guards at exorbitant prices inside the grounds. Our men were outraged at this unfair treatment. We wondered why the military police didn't notice a tendency of our female help toward a bumpy plumpness going into the gate, and a sharp recovery coming out.

The red soil of Tennessee caused a great deal of difficulty. When dry it was a very fine, all-permeating dust, and when wet was thick, sticky gumbo. Once John Merrill turned up in the rain at a large meeting, barefooted. The mud had sucked off his boots. He was so absent-minded that this wouldn't have seemed strange even if it hadn't been raining. Merrill claimed he didn't know they were missing. Later, when identical trailers were brought in, Merrill is alleged to have gone home one night, eaten dinner, washed the dishes and sat down for a smoke when the two secretaries who lived there came in and screamed, and he realized he was in the wrong trailer.

The problems of internal financing required by this enormous project, plus two offices and two other key Manhattan District jobs, were mine and Gross Sampsell's. Since 1936 our local bank had expected to extend loans without security. For a while on this big one they didn't take alarm, but when our requirements reached half a million dollars they asked me the same unanswerable questions we had asked the original Corps of Engineers officer. What is the loan for? Where is the project located? How soon will we be paid back? Five hundred thousand dollars was just about four hundred and fifty-six thousand dollars more than we were worth — and still no contract with the government. Finally, as often seemed to happen at the zero hour, I got the contract, walked out of the colonel's office at Oak Ridge and fell flat on my face in the red gumbo mud in the pouring rain. The red shows on that contract to this day — not blood, but it might well have been.

8

A Man Can't Live
Where a Tree Won't Grow

AT WAR'S END, and after ten years of practice, I was once again at the crossroads. For those of us who were not in the service, the end result of our concerted effort during the war years so far seemed to have resulted in a lot of people being blown to bits at Hiroshima and Nagasaki. After the world's fairs the slate had simply been wiped clean. This time it was as if our labors had been dissolved in a nuclear blast.

There were uniforms everywhere. Too young for World War I, too old for World War II, left out, I was smoldering inside. We had prospered while our contemporaries had lost out in the service. And what had we become? Certainly not designers in the classic sense. We were entrepreneurs, promoters, expediters, financiers, diplomats; we were men of too many trades and masters of none. Depressed, at wit's end, I heard of the beginning of a new volcano starting at Paricutín in the state of Michoacán in old Mexico and immediately went down to see it.

At the beginning, Paricutín was only a whiff of smoke in a farmer's field, and the farmer put his sombrero over it to put it out. He then called in the church, through the services of the village priest, who offered incantations, but they seemed ineffectual. In fact, Paricutín was hourly growing larger. Finally huge, red-hot rocks the size of automobiles came spewing out and tumbling down the newly formed slopes of the modest cone. The sky for miles around was filled with pumice, cinders — dark, forbidding, like the beginning of the world, I thought; and as I watched this full-fledged volcano building higher and higher, spewing out lava, pumice, cinder, smoke and flame, I felt better. I had felt like that, too: violent, explosive, driven to get back to the participation in the business of planning some of the basic needs for the family of man on a permanent basis.

Perhaps for me Paricutín released the tensions that, unreleased in Skid, had caused his ulcers. But however we released those tensions, our offices continued to grow, strangely disparate in their relationships. With his combination of rare selectivity and shy sensitivity, Skid had carved a niche for himself and SOM in New York City with its seven million people, buttressed by Bun, Bill, Walter and Bob who, in their turn, had developed a hard core of associates: Gans, Posey, de Blois, Soverns, and a dozen more who could program, design, and produce anything that Skid could bring in. The New York office was perfecting high standards in "quality control" for architecture.

The New York office, mostly through Skid's efforts, sometimes helped by me, soon filled with neat, prestige jobs and seemed well launched on the road to fame. The early stretches of this road were well marked by four distinct milestones, and, through these trying times of great imbalance, the only thing that held the offices together was the unquestioning confidence Skid and I had in each other. It was as if our gut fibers were inextricably entwined.

First came the opportunity to design a huge veterans' hospital to be located on a windswept spit of land. Robert Moses had jurisdiction here and gave Skid his chance. Never having done a hospital before, he looked at the problem with the clear-eyed candor of an innocent child and asked embarrassing questions. The answers he received convinced him that even in the metropolitan centers in 1939 the art and science of medical clinics, hospital design and laboratory development consisted of one-third witchcraft, one-third ritual and one-third tradition, the results often spreading infection rather than functioning as a design to prevent it. He discovered that hospital planning was generally predetermined by existing lot size instead of the reverse, which would have been much more logical, and that the orientation of the patient's room was not a program requirement. Skid must have impressed the right people, because we were awarded the commission. The New York office followed the pattern we had planned to follow and established a research program, bringing in outside companies, such as conveyor experts and communication specialists as well. Architectural specialists in the hospital field were generally up in arms at our being awarded the contract. The reply, typically Skidmore, was, "We have never done a bad one."

At Fort Hamilton on New York Harbor, where the views were superb and the sun therapeutic, the New York office developed a great cliff of single-room floors with four-bed wards terminating each corridor, all floors facing the view. With the picture window protected by sunshades, tier on tier it rose, the solution suggestive of a resort hotel in the Caribbean — and what was wrong with that? Might not the experience of hospitalization be made as agreeable as possible? The experts didn't know, but one way or another the idea stuck. Orientation of rooms became a basic principle of hospital design and is standard today. My satisfaction equaled that of my colleagues in New York. I was proud of their great cliff of veterans' hospital standing solidly against the sea.

Then came the firm's opportunity to design our first in the ancient and honorable category of inn, or hostel, or hotel. Once again, never having done one, we were anxious to make this an exciting contribution. The education and character of our responsive client, Jack Emery, a third-generation builder with a

Harvard-Cambridge education, would ease our task considerably. This job was carried on entirely in and by the New York office, but it started on the twenty-fifth floor of the Tavern Club in Chicago, where Jack Emery and his associates were interviewing me. Was SOM qualified to carry out the design and working drawings, and supervision of construction of his proposed six-hundred-bed Terrace Plaza Hotel in Cincinnati, Ohio? While we were having a drink high above Chicago we somehow got off those technical questions and on to dreams of concept and decided to raise the Terrace Plaza's lobby and subsequent tower of rooms high above Cincinnati's busy business district. To a lesser man this would have seemed a risky thing to do since no one had ever done it before — but not to Jack Emery. This could easily be accomplished since the site, owned by Emery, was on the corner of busy business streets and would fit the requirements of a department store superbly. In fact anything seemed possible there — high above Chicago — on the twenty-fifth floor of the Tavern Club.

Jack Emery was a modern Medici with a drive to build something fresh and new to add to his already impressive empire, which included Cincinnati's largest and best hotel built by his father before him. We could offer him our large staff still intact from Oak Ridge, and add to it our bubbling enthusiasm. With Emery's approval, Louis Skidmore and Bill Brown proceeded to design a hotel room from the inside out, leasing a suite in the existing Plaza Hotel in which to experiment. They designed beds, tables, chairs; considered the facilities needed for daytime as well as night; revolutionized the guest's bathroom with a large counter around the washbasin. My contribution, entirely overlooked in hotel literature, was the introduction of holes in the bottoms of the soap dishes in the tubs and showers. Joan Miró journeyed to America to paint a charming mural in a circular bar high above the street; and Steinberg drew intriguing murals on the dining room walls while Skid and Jack installed one of Calder's first major mobiles in the lobby. The high level of theft of matchboxes, ashtrays and hotel silver was an indication that our efforts to improve the design had not been in vain.

The first bank building ever done by SOM was only four stories high and was dubbed a "glass lantern." Louis Skidmore was entirely responsible for bringing this major commission to us. Hap Flanigan, chairman of the board of the Manufacturers Trust, was an old friend, and he brought to us the site on the southwest corner of Forty-third Street and Fifth Avenue, nearly at the epicenter of prestige of upper Manhattan. Skid, sensing the opportunity for a masterpiece, conceived the idea of a competition among our young and eager designers. Here was an opportunity to shake up the conventional architects' approaches to banking. They were encouraged to come up with whatever popped into their heads, and the history and tradition of banking be damned. Charles Evans Hughes III, grandson of the jurist, won hands down. His four-story, glass-walled bank, an apartment and a garden on the roof, featured as the central drama of the scheme the great bank vault, traditional symbol of banking. With a circular many-layered door, fastened together with great glittering rivets and bolts, the gleaming polished-steel vault stood in full view of the public as the sculpture feature of the composition. It was the special creation of industrial designer Henry Dreyfuss. No other element of a bank is more complicated or complex, and, with its shining tooled steel, more beautiful. Other innovations followed, such as the brilliant idea introduced by Gordon Bunshaft, of abstract sculptor Harry Bertoia's monumental metal screen running the entire length of the second-floor banking level. Gordon Bunshaft devised one of the finest spaces conceived by man since Santa Sophia, particularly in the subtle spacing of columns, making them either disappear or gain prominence in the design. Mike Rapuano, my classmate at

103

Cornell in landscape architecture, designed a beautiful park on the penthouse roof. The final result was the creation of a noble space with a noble park on top.

Lewis Mumford called the glass bank a lantern, and surprised us all by relating the design to the Victorians and to the eighteenth-century dreams of all-glass cities. Mumford spun a glamorous and exciting aura around Skid's bank and suggested facets of creative genius of which neither Skid, Hughes or Bunshaft had ever dreamed.

Again, entirely conceived by Louis Skidmore, through his imaginative use of Marshall Plan funds for foreign building designs, like a meteor in the sky came an Arabian Nights' job: the Istanbul Hilton Hotel on a promontory overlooking the Dardanelles in the magic city of Istanbul. With the Santa Sophia and the Bosporus for inspiration, we had to do a great building. The result is a salubrious blend of strong Turkish architectural motifs and American plumbing and heating. Sedad Eldem, our associate, a resident of Istanbul, master of five languages, proved that the legendary toughness of the Turks extended to the character and fiber of their architects. Sedad Eldem is famous for having defeated Bunshaft on his own ground, maintaining the supremacy of rich, lush, romantic Turkish architecture over Bun's more classic international predilections. The resulting building is considered by both Sedad and Gordon as a satisfactory compromise between two worlds of culture.

But these four projects were only preludes to the climax of the fifth act, where the crisis was reached and the finale was a product of the efforts on all our parts, merged into an indivisible whole: the conception and creation of our best building, even now judged so over thirty years of practice. Lever House was built in 1952 but goes back to 1946 in Chicago, where, in a gesture of frustration, I expressed my last full measure of despair at the postively Stone Age attitude of all the office building managers of the world, individually and collectively. I felt that they were to the building industry what railroad unions (who require firemen on diesel engines) were to the railroads. I was tired of remodeling ancient though beautiful relics of a bygone but lucrative age. This tight little group who stood in the way of rebuilding the central city should be stung into some action — or reaction — and I arranged a debate with their acknowledged prophet, George Bailey, on "The Office Building of the Future"; or, as he put it, "The Building That Will Never Be Built." This was staged at the 1949 National Convention of Office Building Owners and Managers at Hot Springs, Virginia, said location guaranteeing a full audience on this, to me, important occasion. By way of a scarehead I sketched the bleak and grimy visage of Wall Street, La Salle Street and Montgomery Street, deserted and empty while the suburbs flourished. As an alternative to this I suggested action smack in the center of the downtown business districts anywhere in America. No less than half a city block would do. There, in the setting of a park with a garage under it to pay for the land — which was the equivalent of suggesting the transplanting of Walden Pond to La Salle Street — a slender shaft would rise on only a small part of the whole. The shaft would be sealed, free from dirt and sound.

George Bailey rose nobly to the bait.

Mr. Owings is *not* going to build this building with his botanical gardens, its flying window wipers and grass-covered parking lot. I could not resist this facetious allusion to Mr. Owings' conception. All of us recognize the value of environment and individuality, and speaking for myself, this conception is the first real departure from the ordinary that has been offered to us for serious consideration in connection with our downtown properties. It requires some temerity to suggest the acquisition of a half a block of valuable city property of which only one-eighth will be subject to major development. This we will at once concede: that such a development would have identity and advertising value, it would without question appeal to tenants, it would permit unusual conveniences, it would provide a maximum of light and air and it would permit the development of a main building of maximum efficiency, and also without question would constitute a unit of civic pride for any city in which it was erected. Any appreciable stabilization of our present economy might very well change our ratio of income to investment to such a degree that such a development will become entirely feasible. Who knows? In twenty years we may enjoy the presence of many such projects within our cities and live to see their third-level esplanades connected by bridges across the streets so that we may move from building to building with only the beauty of fountains, flowers and fir trees to distract us instead of the nerve-shattering scream of the irascible automobile and the stupid clank of the unlovely trolley car.

The idea fell flat and lay moribund until George Fry and I got drunk together on New Year's Eve two years later. A consultant to businessmen on how to run their affairs, he often explained that he was willing to put his own problems aside in order to solve theirs. We usually spent New Year's Eve together. This time we got involved in a crap game, and after a long run on the dice I seemed to have all George's money. At this point I felt so sorry for him that I gave it all back and he in turn was so moved that he asked me to help in a confidential matter of business. The business involved Lever Brothers in Boston, and within two weeks I had the contract for their new building, location yet to be determined.

I remember meeting the then president, Charles Luckman, who was a good client, and any unkind suggestions that he picked their particular site on Park Avenue for Lever House so he could watch the building being built from his apartment at the Waldorf are apocryphal.

But there was a time during the early part of the design period when some thought he went a little too far. The topmost floor of the building — the twenty-first floor, the size of a modest house site in the suburbs — had been laid out by Luckman for the personal requirements of the chief executive of the com-

106

pany, Mr. Luckman himself. It contained an exercise room, luxury apartment, dining room and board room and, almost as an afterthought, tucked away was an office. Along the south side of the building a long balcony projected where Luckman could survey the city at his leisure. One day while he was studying the model of the building in our office, he questioned the height of the railing on the balcony. "Three feet," we said. "Why, Charlie, are you afraid you'll fall?" "No, be pushed," he said.

Lever House turned out to be news. An empty lot wasn't news, but as soon as we cleared the taxpayers from the one on Park Avenue between Fifty-third and Fifty-fourth, planted it with trees, shrubs and flowers, and then put a building over it starting at the second floor in such a way that the park remained — that was news.

When we put the narrow tower, just wide enough for two sets of offices and a corridor between, with its narrow end toward the avenue — that was news. All other towers were broadside to the avenue up until then.

When we put parking underneath the park, and another park on top of the pavilion, too — that was news.

Lever House was completed in April of 1952 and was immediately hailed as "handsome, inventive, remarkable." Twenty-one-story Lever House on New York's Park Avenue filled the block between Fifty-third and Fifty-fourth streets and was designed to house 1250 employees. It was air-conditioned (new then) and fluorescent-lit, and every inch of the 290,000 square feet of office space within 25 feet of the windows. The building cost six million dollars (about eighteen million today), and we could "kick away" two hundred and fifty thousand dollars a year in ground-floor rentals in order to leave room for a patio to create the illusion of no ground floor. Critics called the structure "dazzling" and suggested that it had been conceived in part as an advertisement for the company, ranking along with the Empire State Building as a "monument to American industry"

— although the critics were quick to point out that the owners were Dutch and English.

We could answer queries from the press with: "We were fortunate in having clients who were aware of advertising and prestige. They didn't want just any building, they wanted Lever House. They let us get away from the tired shape of the ziggurat form of the standard New York office building."

Aline Saarinen called it a "handsome geometric mass of shimmering blue crystal, a lively light mass literally lifted into the air, unlocking the crowded New York skyline to give immense openness to the city scene." Lewis Mumford praised the building design in *The New Yorker* and Ada Louise Huxtable said of it in the *New York Times*, "It is the best example of modern architecture in New York."

Lever Brothers moved to New York because the price one pays for soap is 89 per cent advertising, and the value of the toothpaste inside the tube is even less; and the advertising agencies of America were there. Very few people realized Lever's quiet strangle hold on practically everything that bubbled, foamed or floated, from fats to detergents. In 1950 Leverhulme, the British company, controlled all soaps in the British Empire. At the same time the Dutch company, Unilever, controlled all soaps outside the empire; and the joint chairmen of the board quietly stated in their prospectus, "The Directors of both companies are the same." After a certain amount of preliminary skirmishing, Lever House was built under the supervision of two of those directors: Sir Geoffrey Heyworth, a tweedy Englishman, and Paul Rijkens, a bouncy Dutchman, with a passion for each other's company which could only be explained by their apparent lack of confidence in each other's judgment in the absence of the other.

I consider that I contributed two basic ideas to the design: first, the nonbuilding or park at street level; second, the placement of the tower perpendicular to the avenue instead of parallel. Beyond this, all the credit goes to Gordon Bunshaft, designer in charge.

People were impressed that we hadn't hung a big sign on the building saying "Lever House," and the building became better known than if we had. Lever became an important word. Even taxi drivers talked about it and told stories of how sailors sometimes bribed them to drive their cabs over the curb onto the plaza and wind their way in and out between the pillars; of one nice couple who had pulled in under cover on a rainy Sunday to fix a tire; and how children roller-skated on the paths in the little garden.

We thought we knew something about glass. We had researched everything from glass balls spun into fiber (we had helped invent a machine to do that) to huge panes of plate glass in colors to separate out certain rays and cut down heat. We decided to seal the clear, straight shaft with sheets of tinted glass. The wall around our shaft would rise from the street level to the twenty-first floor, a sheer unbroken exterior surface of three hundred and thirty-nine feet; and, except where floor spandrels occurred, just one quarter of an inch thick.

In 1950 Park Avenue was still lined with beautiful, nearly authentic Renaissance palaces. The luxurious Marquery Apartment House was typical. Designed by John Russell Pope, it faced on tree-lined courts, giving the avenue a quiet elegance which was further enriched by Saint Bartholomew's Church, designed by Bertram Grosvenor Goodhue; and McKim, Mead and White's masterpiece, the Racquet Club. Then there was that very special vacant lot: the block between Fifty-third and Fifty-fourth streets. In 1952 Lever House was built there and added its own slender beauty to the lovely old-world charm of that part of Park Avenue.

Then shortly sad things began to happen to the avenue, things we had not anticipated. It appeared that the wide publicity Lever House received gave other corporate giants the idea of seeking the advertising value of this beautiful design, Seagram's for one. Then followed a series of progressively aggressive structures, causing the demolition one by one of the richly clad residential landmarks until only the Racquet Club remained.

One might ask why Lever House caused such a stir, and is still looked upon as an important prototype of modern architecture in a city where skyscrapers are a dime a dozen and where Lever-size buildings are torn down to make room for skyscrapers. Lever House is only a yard taller than the 1903 Flatiron Building. It is smaller than the smallest of the Rockefeller Center buildings, on a lot less than one-twelfth the land on which the Center sits. Its highest main structure is only two stories high and only fifty feet of it touch the valuable Park Avenue frontage, while the Lever tower itself is perpendicular to it. Why does this combination create such a stir? Is it possible for us to fully comprehend the technical triumph of a building sheathed by a sheet of glass a quarter of an inch in thickness?

When one can predict with certainty which play on Broadway will be a hit, then this question of what constitutes great art in building can also be answered. There are so many separate factors, each with a distinct influence on the ensemble, none under any individual control, that such predictions become impossible. Unlike painting, sculpture or even musical composition, design is the product of the sum total of often unpredictable events. The creation of that product is not done by the architect alone but by all the other elements as well. If the outcome is successful, that is a miracle.

9

A Chicago Plan

CHICAGO, pulled by three powerful beasts — commerce, industry and government — had to be handled as an entity.

This phenomenon of Chicago is all explained according to the Book of Genesis. When God created the earth, He did so by separating the waters which were there in the first place. Lake Michigan was already there, with moods that would make a salt-water sailor blanch: dictator of temperatures and shifter of winds, producer of a climate overgenerously described as "winter and the first August." Man-made Chicago is a tattooed marking against the foaming edge of the lake, stitching down the flat nothingness of the land — nothing, that is, if God hadn't thought to include nearby extraordinary quantities of iron ore, tungsten, manganese, limestone, copper, and that fossilized plant life, coal. Truculent, always varying from surly to brilliant, Lake Michigan dominates that part of the globe. At the grinding edge, men and lake have turned wild onion swamp and Indian portage into the converting center of the world. Under a perpetual head of steam, land, materials and men have generated commerce and industry, American style.

The Near North Side of Chicago that Emily and I knew was still a kind of museum without walls, with introverted characters out of the Chicago Historical Society performing for the benefit of each other. Our street was tree-lined, shaded and perpetually dusted by a gentle, steady sifting of soot — black coal soot. We lived at 1240 North State in a charming four-story walk-up row house with a garden and carriage house, within walking distance of my office. We rented it from Kellogg Fairbank on a sliding scale designed to average out the luxury price of such a location over a five-year period. The day we took over full responsibility for maintenance, the entire first-floor ceiling fell down. Consisting of old-fashioned wood lath and rock plaster, it nearly killed us, both physically and financially.

Soon Emily produced twins, Natalie and Emily, which phenomenon caused her mother to remark that nice people didn't have twins. Then three years later Jennifer, and finally a boy named Nathaniel. Our family grew and prospered.

In between children I joined the venerable Wayfarers Club, founded in 1830. Like Boston's Saturday Club, it consisted of thirty members who met eight or nine times a year, always at the Chicago Club. The ritual began with oyster soup and ended with a dissertation by a member. The members — Higgenbotham, Monroe, Fairbank, Harper, Tenny, Ryerson, Winterbottom, Wentworth, Douglas, Stewart — were all distillations of Chicago's sometimes brilliant intellectual past, representing Chicago's schools of poetry, architecture and education. There were vintage professors from the several universities and ancient and honorable names from the archives of the architectural past: Shaw, Talmadge, Clark. The Wayfarers provided a mellowing forum where a wide variety of views were expressed in moods ranging from acerbic calm to salty ribaldry. When among such rare intellectuals, I glowed with a sort of reflected erudition.

In between those meetings there was the Lake Zurich Club, a kind of country Wayfarers, and allegedly the oldest golf club in America. I never quite believed this, although its appearances justified the claim. Here was fostered the wit and humor of the last century resplendent in its rumpled tweedy best, and its nine-hole golf course was equipped with a pitcher of punch at most tees, ready to strengthen the tired intellectual's drive. There was the table at night, loaded with the Zurich farm's own roasts and vegetables, and the talk was as good as the food. The wine steward questioned one carefully as to his preference in wines for the different courses of shellfish, roast or fromage, describing the nuances inherent in each of the great years available — and then all were served the same wine, an especially sour brew of basement bootleg red. The colloquy of languages — Greek, Latin, plain alley talk — was mixed with heavy clouds of cigar smoke; university greats were converted into a better kind of half-Bacchus. Below in barrels in the cellar, oysters grinding cornmeal between their shells lulled the members to sleep.

Then there was another kind of club, where the almighty dollar was honored by honoring those who had done well by it. Commerce and industry created, then rallied around, the Commercial Club and the Commonwealth Club, where rarely was seen any specimen of *Homo sapiens* other than the merchant prince. An architect in such an atmosphere was rare indeed. Somehow or other I made it into the inner sanctum and ranged their habitat, took on their protective coloring — for the moment, one of the Establishment at play. This contact with the captains of the corporate structure was sinfully productive.

The practice of architecture is essentially the getting and executing of jobs. These spring from opportunities. There must be clients to offer these opportunities. The first step must be the creation of the client in the right shape and for the proper predetermined purpose. Sometimes that client is a city, sometimes a detached individual — the extremes of a wide spectrum. I struggled to gain for architectural design an equal status in the evaluation processes. Architecture usually came after rather than before or during the consideration of the social, economic and political factors in the decision-making processes of these merchant princes. My goal was to seek out and prove to the Establishment that architectural input, properly applied, adds value.

Plenty of fresh ideas bubbled from every nook and corner of our attic office. Led by Ambrose Richardson, our crew stretched and widened their concepts of the cityscape, gained perspective on the relationship between the subject building, its neighbors, the street network around it and the neighborhood in which it rested.

When one project surfaced offering an opportunity to bring back the lowly fallen, formerly glittering, mansion-filled heyday of the Prairie Avenue area through the revival process offered by urban renewal, we came forward with an exciting solution called "Sidewalks in the Sky." The New York Life Insurance Company was anxious to experiment in social housing theory and saw opportunities in our proposal. Our sidewalks in the air consisted of two thousand-foot-long, eighteen-story, single-apartment-deep buildings, each in a sheer cliff, each reached by a series of outdoor sidewalks. They stood clean along the lake, and any other name would have lacked the drama this solution merited as a counterpoint in scope to the grandeur of the vista.

For what seemed a long time we worked away at this sort of thing in the SOM attic high above the lake, where we pampered our clients. The early ones didn't seem to mind the climb. Watching the lanky form of Rufus Dawes jacknife up the flight of stairs after the last elevator stop was a joy; I could almost hear his joints creak. And I could barely hide a smile when the ripe pear–shaped Dr. Pusey waddled up that last flight to check on his architectural partnership. We were paying him at what we considered downright usurious rates. He had his money back three times over in two years while we were still on five thousand dollars a year each. Slyly he teased us when we added Merrill as a partner, and upped our draw. Then, sadly for us for we loved him, the pact was terminated. He died in 1940 at the age of eighty-eight.

Just as the partners in the New York office had established certain milestones in their first four great buildings, we established certain basic principles in that South Michigan attic, arrived at through chance crossed with necessity. We learned the value of giving generously of professional services for a public purpose. One example was the Chicago Building Code.

At luncheon one day with Dr. Leverett Lyons (a rare bird among Association of Commerce executives in that he could think and was a trained economist), we were bewailing the building slump in Chicago when we hit upon a possible cause and a remedy: a standard building code to replace Chicago's present obsolete one. This was, and is, a technical subject too complex to attempt to explain. The obsolescence of building codes was the whipping boy for all the slack in housing construction — and of course the prefab myth was big and getting bigger. Lyons sadly agreed that such a code would do wonders, but would take a year and fifty thousand dollars. The Chamber didn't have it. Then — a solution for us all — I suddenly envisioned a masterwork. John Merrill would write the new code and SOM would contribute this service for a full year free of charge, asking only the assurance that his work have official status.

Commerce, industry and government at home and abroad accepted our generosity with paeans of praise. For Merrill, it was his kind of work. No one but Skid ever knew how luck followed our giving a needed gift. Because the building performance codes, documents prepared by Merrill, were seminal in the field, the work became a major milestone in reforming construction practices. It also marked the beginning of the acceptance of SOM as a major factor in matters of civic concern.

In 1948 the newly elected reform mayor, Martin Kennelly,

appointed me to the chairmanship of the Chicago Plan Commission, and at forty-five I became the first architect to hold this position since Daniel Burnham.

A planner can have great vision, dream dreams, project into the future and, unlike the architect, doesn't necessarily expect to get anything built to show for it. L'Enfant, held in reverence in Washington, D.C., and Daniel Hudson Burnham, held in awe in Chicago, were my two sources of inspiration. Planners were loners; architects came in clusters. Daniel Burnham had been a dropout in college, gaining his fame through the 1893 Chicago fair. Then city planning was called landscape architecture. Today no university or college is without a planning course. Cornell has three: political, regional and city.

Mayor Kennelly gave me a free hand. I had no precedents to bother about. But our commission was advisory only and had no power. Persuasion was the principal weapon. Chicago had grievous problems when I took over. The Burnham plan, begun in 1902, had been superimposed on an unplanned, seventy-seven-year-old Chicago, and the parts of that plan which had been executed were held sacred by all; the rest was in a state of rigor mortis. Chicago generally had the same grievous problems when I resigned three years later.

Even so, those three years saw the Plan Commission reorganized, using funds wheedled from the fifty-ward council. But there was a futility about it all. Crime and corruption prospered. The mayor, people said, was ineffectual, naive, a man playing the piano in a whorehouse without knowing what went on upstairs. Words, words, words — all to no avail. The 1902 Burnham plan was a bouquet of flowers presented to a sick patient (Chicago) : sweet smelling and a considerate thing to offer one in such serious condition, but to no avail as a cure for her illness.

Planning is un-American. The American people hate planning. They work on impulse. The planners themselves are at fault, having a way of talking double talk, like this: "The immigration of ethnic groups in terms of the competition of the periphery in our cities with a core as it relates to the physical and economic aspects of the situation . . ."

The expert is trying to say: "A man sat down with his wife in the kitchen in the city one night and said, 'Look, I'm making enough dough now so we can move out into the country where Johnny won't be likely to get run over by those automobiles every time he crosses the street, and where you can have a garden that won't be smothered by soot, smoke and filth.'"

Daniel H. Burnham's advice to "make no little plans" was heeded by the bad guys as well as the good guys and applied to the American Automobile Association and the Association of Commerce and Industry, who were often on the side of special privilege. Underneath the glossy surfaces were many special interests — some ugly — represented on the Planning Commission who were there to stop real progress. These men seldom showed their hands but operated effectively under cover. To achieve physical change through our commission — closing a street, for example — required strong countertactics causing political fireworks and often forcing the enemy into the open. At first incredulous, but convinced by harsh evidence, I discovered that the large-scale projects, large enough to have a real impact upon the environment and therefore requiring city action, were the ones that the commission was organized to stop. Because of the street closing we saw that our project involving the New York Life on Prairie Avenue would be one of those to be stopped. I made up my mind that this wouldn't happen.

I became frustrated with the role of chairman of the Plan Commission. It tied my hands. There was the matter of conflict of interest. I said to hell with it! I found that our massive housing program, introduced to clear slums and rid the city of festering sores, was opposed by owners of the high-return slum rental properties in the area; and the opposition was not based on moving blacks into a white area as alleged, for the blacks were already there. It was the profits created by those slum conditions that they didn't want to lose. The New York Life officials made it clear that they were depending on us for guidance and would withdraw their support if either I or SOM were forced out.

The Chicago *Tribune* at this point objected to my joint role with an editorial:

> Nathaniel A. Owings, chairman of the Plan Commission . . . has taken an open part in the controversy over the vacation of Cottage Grove Avenue for the New York Life Insurance Company housing project. The transcript of the Plan Commission's hearing on this question shows that he presided and was rather cavalier in his treatment of one opponent of the project. If the New York Life project goes through, Mr. Owings' firm will collect more than a million dollars in fees . . . Mr. Owings should get off the Plan Commission without delay. No man should be asked to render objective decisions on public matters in which he has such strong private interests as Mr. Owings had in these two . . .

I was all for ignoring them, but Huston McBain and Jim Palmer, heading the powerful department store Marshall Field and Company (the *Tribune*'s largest advertiser) didn't think so. They decided to stop this nonsense and, over my protests, we all drove out to Winnetka one Saturday afternoon to see Don Maxwell, managing editor of Colonel McCormick's "Greatest Paper on Earth" — certainly a graphic confrontation if there ever could be one between the power of the advertising dollar and the freedom of the editorial policy of the Fourth Estate. As our uniformed chauffeur guided that Cadillac sedan around the Maxwells' modest driveway, barely making the turns without backing, I thought I saw Maxwell peeking out from behind the curtains in the parlor window. Saturday afternoon had been chosen by my supporters because it was rumored that Maxwell drank beer, played hi-fi recordings and stayed mildly drunk all weekend.

Maxwell greeted us in open shirt and slippers and mentioned a visiting aunt from Rushville, Indiana. "I'm sort of from there myself," I said, and he replied, "My God! Of course we are probably cousins!" That settled everything, and in the first three minutes of play. From that date of nonconfrontation, the *Tribune* fell silent on the issue. Of the wide spectrum of crimes available and tolerated, open conflict of interest openly arrived at seemed most trivial and certainly something to tolerate in order to rehabilitate a big chunk of Chicago's worst available.

For three years I pleaded for a consolidated "single city" from Waukegan to Gary: a metropolitan area. I proposed this master plan (for Chicago was the epitome of "diversification," many-faceted) at a joint town meeting, laid the plans on the table, and quit the commission. In 1972 those proposals are still valid and have slowly taken form, but twenty-two years is quite a while to wait.

At an appropriate moment a publicity-wise realtor came to us with a four-hundred-million-dollar plan he had conceived: a project to tear down forty blocks of existing dreary honky-tonks in and around the Chicago River, and rebuild. The project, brilliantly named "The Fort Dearborn Plan," was bound to appeal to a sentimental Chicago, and the realtor wanted an architect to design (for free) plans, models and promotion material for this exciting mile-square development. My partners didn't think I should commit all that money but I went ahead, protesting that the exposure would be worth the gamble.

Ironically, the Fort Dearborn Plan never passed beyond the paper stage.

One night, out of a Chicago snowstorm, ex-football coach Curly Byrd came up our attic stairs. As a football coach he had always been a breezy, informal man, and as president of the University of Maryland he hadn't changed much. His contract agreement with us was breezy and informal and fascinated Gross Sampsell:

Dear Nat:
　Your emolument for the Glen Martin Engineering College and wind tunnel will be six per cent.

Cordially yours,
Curly Byrd, President
University of Maryland

Considering the sheets of closely written verbiage packed between the blue covers which usually preceded — and often ended — otherwise perfectly good professional relations between client and architect, was this short note adequate? Sampsell said yes, more than adequate. We have never reached such distilled purity in contractual relations since.

Curly Byrd's qualifications for president were apparently considered ideal since he had served as the football coach at the university through an unprecedented string of unbroken victories. His total unfamiliarity with the science of aerodynamics matched ours. He and SOM could start from scratch on the subject contract.

We proceeded to pursue the history of the art and science of aerodynamics, beginning with Icarus' wax-attached wings which had fallen off in the heat of the sun, and in a very short time we were ready to share with the Board of Regents our findings. Our technical recommendations for the design of the wind tunnel were accepted unanimously, but the envelope we had proposed to enclose this wind tunnel, to be built of indigenous red brick, was rejected forthwith by the same Board of Regents with equal unanimity. Only an exact reproduction of a Williamsburg Colonial exterior was acceptable. Senator Tydings said it didn't make any difference, since nobody ever looked at a building twice. I countered with a suggestion that we use Paul Cret's ivy.

They countered with a demand for Williamsburg. I countered with a resignation.

Twenty-four hours later, there we were, Curly Byrd and I in my attic in Chicago where he authorized me to proceed on our contemporary design. Confused by this complete reversal, we were enlightened some time later when, scarcely allowing the completion of the project, President Byrd produced a four-column prefabricated Colonial façade which he had wheeled to the site and installed over the central entrance of our contemporary structure. To this day there stands the evidence of the conflict between the shadow of the Colonial past and the future of the SST.

Creating clients, getting jobs; both took time and patience. Lee Block of Inland Steel had spoken to me in 1949 of a new building, but it was five years before he authorized the Inland Steel building which would be the first new office building to go up in Chicago in twenty-two years, squeezed in among the smoke-stained, weather-worn monuments to another era. This was one of Walter Netsch's endless ideas which forever tumbled in profusion, evidencing a spirit and a talent which almost consumed him. As a solution for just such a building, and in order to compete with the cheaper conditions in the suburbs, he would eliminate inside columns, thus providing a stack of rectangular loft spaces like hot cakes one on top of the other. To do this, all services — elevators, power, sewer, water, toilets — were consolidated in an attached outside vertical shaft, services freed of entanglement with the twenty or thirty or forty floors of the useful building space.

In between jobs the size and importance of Inland Steel, where a more natural place to look for suitable sustenance than Indianapolis and the circle, to seek out old friends?

When I was twelve, Harry Vanuys Wade's family lived ten blocks north of us in Indianapolis and was about that far ahead on the economic ladder. A fellow Sigma Chi at Cornell, he was known to most of us as Webfoot Wade. This was because he had fallen arches, wore large rubbers, carried an umbrella and owned a 1925 Dodge. His steady girl, Agnes, was a Phi Beta Kappa, reflecting intellect enough for two — which was a good thing.

We all kidded Wade a good bit about the sewage disposal plant for the island of Guam which he chose for his senior thesis. We said this was because he couldn't design a building above ground. He was, of course, just forty-five years ahead of his time — sewage disposal now being the "in" thing. When he received the senior award gold medal matching mine for my Rochester Library tower, we established a subject for debate for the ensuing half century.

Another link was Eloise. She, Agnes, Harry and I, Hoosier bonded, shared Cornell and the postcollege New York days; and when Harry and Agnes (he turned insurance company president) moved to Indianapolis, he did the thing that best friends should never do: he let me design his office building on Fall Creek Boulevard. With the ever-present dialogue of the sewage disposal plant we finally got the building done, and over the long years the warm nostalgia of our college days has never really passed. But at that moment, that job was not scorned by me. It was the link that helped Chicago span the gap.

Sadly, in the process of working on another job on the circle, with my sensitivity to the past still undeveloped I helped destroy the 1850 Victorian English Hotel and Theater. The structure which replaced this gem was a simple limestone façade fitted to the circle's curve with a scalloped portico projecting which cast an interesting shadow on the long, plain curve. On the Sunday following the dedication, the minister of the little Norman church next door bewailed this act of vandalism, labeled it a stone curtain and suggested that Russia's Iron Curtain was but a step behind. The doorman of the club across the street took issue on this subject and was supported by the taxi drivers lined up outside waiting for a fare. Facing the same problem today, I would support the minister in his passion.

Through a strange sequence of references, Arizona's Barry Goldwater made his way to our attic in 1945 with his brother Bob. They owned one of the really good department stores in the Southwest and now they were thinking of a new store for Phoenix. I said such a store, located in the colorful state of Arizona, must have an indigenous character and we would have to do some research. We would look for inspiration in the rock formations of the desert.

Barry knew every fold in that arid land and was enthusiastic about showing me the country. The prospect was exciting and I eagerly made my way to Phoenix and his store, carefully stepping around clumps of blanketed Navajos watching as the electric eye–operated entrance doors mysteriously opened and shut, untouched by human hands.

For nine days Barry and I toured the wonders of the West with sleeping bags, toothbrushes and a mattress in the back of the station wagon, breakfastless, with lunches from a paper bag. Globe, Show Low, Canyon de Chelly with Cozy McSparron's trading post ceiling full of arrows, each marking a departed New Year's Eve, all were extra glamorous under Barry's vivid leadership. I claim I saw a petrified pumpkin patch, complete with pumpkins — even broken ones with seeds — which nobody will believe even though all was recorded in photographs taken by Barry himself. More believable, there is one photograph also by Barry, nearly life-size, of the head of an ancient Hopi, each silver whisker glinting in the sun, his inscrutable face telling all and nothing. We saw the most famous ruin in Canyon de Chelly, the ancient cliff dwellers' White House, intact after nine hundred years, the pueblo tucked away in a great cave halfway up the sheer cliff wall gleaming in the sun above the canyon floor. We could hear the Navajos singing in the night as we lay in our sleeping bags on the rim of the canyon. We found there a great natural cantilever of sandstone thrust out into the blue space which became the inspiration for our final design, the main pavilion suspended above and facing the avenue, thrust out in a strong cantilever.

At the Grand Canyon the next day I called Emily from El Tovar and agreed to the move to the Southwest she had always wanted to make. I was suddenly aware of the power of the land.

The house of Goldwater was never built. Their taste in architecture — if not architects — was expensive and their present store adequate, and branches did what a new store would never have done: brought the merchandise to the ever-growing suburban areas around Phoenix. But the unbuilt store moved me and my family, serving the basic function of a rerooting from black dirt to another kind of soil, red adobe.

10

World Way Stations

EMILY AND I chose a high mountain valley in Spanish-Indian-Anglo country. Near Santa Fe, at Pojoaque, we found our perfect ruin: an ancient pueblo with three-hundred-year-old walls in the Tesuque wash, crumbling in an ancient valley watered by an ancient system of irrigation ditches established before the white man had dreamed of intrusion. Fed by the melting snows and summer rains drained from the watershed of the Sangre de Cristo Mountains to the east, our high valley lay under a great blue vault with white stuffed clouds tucked in folds and billows, held in place between the jagged teeth of two mountain ranges: the Sangre de Cristo and the Jemez. Here we remodeled our ruined adobe in the heart of three living cultures little — and much — changed from prehistoric times, making a partial transfer of residence, she and the children being in Pojoaque and I being nowhere.

All of a sudden all over the globe commissions for new towns blossomed: in Asia, Sumatra, Venezuela. Job followed job in tumbled confusion. Many were simply grist for SOM; some were unique form-givers of the twentieth century. But of whichever kind, there was a thread of continuity.

Back in the United States, Henry Ford II asked us to come to

Dearborn. The yellow room we were ushered into was intensified by fluorescent light and on a dais sat Henry the Second and Ernest Breech. We had placed on easels some projects selected at random to demonstrate the scope of SOM's professional work. With the problem at hand unknown, this procedure was awkward. Half-blinded by the intense light, I pushed through the preliminaries and extended an invitation to come and visit some of our appropriate works. But even better, why not describe their problem to us? With our techniques of programming and diagnosis, hopefully we could produce something creative and uniquely theirs. Then I laid down my pointer. Skid stood there, as he always did, looking embarrassed at his partner's indiscretion.

Heading for the lobby where our SOM staff were waiting to take us to the train, we were stopped by a Ford aide. "Don't go," he said. "I think Ford wants to see you." "You have the contract," Ford said when he finally saw us, adding proudly, "Fast decisions like this are something General Motors can't do with a board meeting."

We boarded the train tired and hungry, entered the diner and realized that we were both stony-broke. Henry Ford waved gaily as he passed us in the train's aisle, cordial in our new partnership. We, with a million-dollar contract in our pocket, had just the price of a pot of coffee between us.

We were hired to design an Olympian executive office building for Henry himself and his directors, the top floor to be filled with steam baths, handball courts, a state dining room and, of course, an apartment along Lincoln Continental style lines transcribed into architecture. The building was rushed into completion in time for a state banquet for directors and VIPs, and the garbage disposal lines in the kitchen were inadvertently connected to the air-conditioning ducts leading to the dining room. The garbage accumulated from a well-prepared meal was sprayed all over the dining room when some thoughtful person decided

126

to try out the air conditioning before the guests arrived. French doors served as ventilation that night, and evidence of the garbage was removed in time. Another version of this story, undoubtedly more accurate since it stems from Walter Severinghaus, goes like this: "The cleanout plug in the waste line had been removed after testing, to use as a temporary drain from a leak in the terrace above, and not replaced. The ground-up ham trimmings, celery and lettuce were sprayed over Arjay Miller's desk and easy chairs. He was then comptroller, and approved our bills."

Mistakes are bound to occur. The first really big one that happened to me was on a job for one of my best friends, Jack Kimberly. He had entrusted me with the Kimberly-Clark headquarters office building in Neenah, Wisconsin. When one end of the building started to sink he called me and raised the question as to whose fault it was: our engineers, the contractor, the architects or the outside engineers? Each pointed a finger at the other. It turned out that the building was resting on a peat bog at one end of the site and, unfortunately, not at the other, so the building didn't sink evenly. Actually, it shouldn't have sunk at all. I told Jack I was not interested in whose fault it was; our role was to protect the owner and I would fix it up. The cost to us to remedy the situation in this case was just over one hundred thousand dollars, but over the years it saved us much more. Our own staff, for example, were more watchful of possible errors since, uncaught, the cost might come out of their pockets.

In 1950 my old professor of civil engineering at Cornell suddenly contacted me and soon had his former student, Owings, doing all sorts of special assignments. I had lost track of Urquart, hearing vaguely that his departure from Cornell had been anything but academic. This information turned out to be quite accurate. For Urquart, the cloistered halls of an ivy league college left something to be desired and during my years of study with him he did little to stifle a compulsion to get drunk and break things up. But it was not until the late thirties that he tried to combine this harmless but disruptive pastime with his teaching. Rumor had it that one day the Hungarian-born Urquart strode into his classroom, holding in his giant arms the corridor Coke machine, which he smashed to bits before his students' unbelieving eyes; dismissed his class; resigned from college and joined the U.S. Corps of Engineers. This new assignment seemed to fit his temperament. Promptly granted a full colonel's commission, he rose to the top in the chief's office in Washington, D.C.

It was Urquart who thrust me smack into the center of a behind-the-scenes interservice war between the army and the air force, where the immediate issue was the handling of the Far East Command's construction program. MacArthur had asked the corps to send him an architect-engineer tough enough to handle both services. The assignment called for arbitration and on-site preparation of site plans and designs to fill the needs of both services — this work to be done in Tokyo and Okinawa under MacArthur's supreme command. Everything remotely connected with MacArthur was under his "supreme command."

As time passed we were to observe this general, who lived up to all previous billings. He stood out. He went far to replace the Emperor in the minds of the Japanese people. They worshiped him, and by the tens or the hundreds or the thousands, as the occasion warranted, would stand in awe and admiration while MacArthur performed the slightest function — like going home to lunch. With pomp and circumstance equal to a high school football game half-time parade, promptly at noon outside his office in Tokyo sixteen gold-helmeted military police in white spats, white armbands, white gloves, white belts and Sam Browne straps, with huge pistols in holsters strapped elaborately at their sides, would appear from nowhere on each side of the walk. A bugle would blow and out would march MacArthur, shirt open at the neck, gold braided cap pulled down over his hawklike nose. Striding resolutely out, eyes straight ahead, he never swerved from what was clearly his duty to do or die: get home for lunch. Aided into the big tan limousine with much slamming of doors, pistol-sharp commands and further flourish of bugles, MacArthur would disappear. By the time this bit of theater was completed, half a thousand or so Japanese had stopped or deliberately gathered to watch the spectacle. I suppose he came back from lunch the same way. I never waited to find out.

We learned slowly to adjust to things Japanese. I watched fish-allergic Walter Netsch turn green as he settled his six-foot-six frame into the approved Buddha squat, eyeing a very dead, unblinking fish on a plate before him at our first official Japanese dinner in Tokyo. I have often wondered what would have happened if that fish had blinked.

There was the publication of a special issue of the Japanese equivalent of our *A.I.A. Journal.* The text, unbroken by a word of English, left portraits of Skidmore, Owings and Merrill as the only clue that SOM and our Okinawa project were the subjects of the handsome volume with its brightly striking Japanese ideographs. With no idea as to whether the text was laudatory, damning or neutral, I conceived the idea of sending copies to a selected mailing of our friends, clients and prospects. With each I enclosed a personal note suggesting that while I knew they would be interested in this Japanese story on SOM, I begged forgiveness for the inadvertent error and resultant inaccuracy which occurred on page sixteen, column two, second paragraph, fourth line. I had, of course, picked this line at random, having no idea of what any of the article meant. The curiosity of several recipients was triggered. Japanese-English translators were enlisted — and the joke was on me. There *was* an error in that paragraph!

Hurricanes and typhoons and the war had leveled the Okinawa portion of the Ryukyu Islands several times over. The shores and beaches were a mass of mangled ships and landing craft, bombed out or torn apart by recurrent typhoons. The rugged northern tip of the island was where the Japanese had made their last stand. We were told that the plugged entrances to the caves along the Buckner Bay beach were filled with Japanese who had suffocated there because they didn't know the word "surrender." The inland areas were pitted with shell craters from the war or littered with United States barracks flattened by the typhoons.

Congress had appropriated huge sums to pay for the damages of Typhoon Emma and Typhoon Fanny and so on through the alphabet. Then there were more funds for permanent military bases to be strategically established to watch Japan — these to be for the use of the air force and the army. Lacking a harbor, the place was hated by the navy, who would have no part of it.

On the island of Okinawa the military barred the consumption by Americans, either military or civilian, of any "indigenous products," so nights and early mornings we would steal down to the villages and bootleg indigenous eggs from indigenous chickens whose indigenous masters were crowing happily from the peaks of their lovely clusters of huts — and thereby hangs a tale of the problem of indigenous materials.

We had inspected many of the lovely villages nestled in the rugged terrain, where the red tile roofs of these charming, untouched villages standing picturesquely intact were obviously of ancient vintage. A closer inspection of these indigenous products of the island indicated that these were no ordinary red tile roofs. They far surpassed those on elegant pseudo-Spanish haciendas of Hobe Sound, or the Bermudian grandeur of the gleaming estates of the rich in the Caribbean. These tiles were on the Grand Plan. Baked rich red, the handmade irregularities catching the light and bringing out their inherent plasticity, these tiles would cost a fortune in the United States. Suddenly in an opening between the hut clusters in one of these simple villages we saw squatting around a smoldering charcoal fire, naked skin gleaming in the reflected light, men in loincloths molding wet clay along their thighs and lower legs. When completed, the wet clay tiles were stacked neatly around the fire to dry. Here, at the very moment of creation, were the tiles we had admired so much.

Our mission on Okinawa was to design housing at Naha and Kadina for air and ground troop installations, housing that would withstand typhoons and hurricanes. It looked as if the natives had the answer, as well they might after a thousand years of trial and error. In painful bilingual discourse I found that: yes, the pigs, chickens, mats and even wives might be swept off in the fierce gales, but the roof tiles, weighing tons, never. The gales passed through or over them, leaving the basic structure of the house undisturbed. Here we had found an incredible break for an American occupation on foreign soil. We had found a solution produced by the natives on site, made from the clay under their feet, shaped by feet and hands and legs attached to their bodies. We could utilize skills passed down through generations. We could produce the impossible: an indigenous house produced from indigenous materials made by indigenous personnel at no cost to the taxpayer.

Enthusiastic, we shipped models and perspective drawings in color off to the general staff and the Congress in Washington, where they were rejected forthwith and resoundingly. War and beauty did not mix. The military must not produce or be associated with handsome or expensive-looking housing. There was the danger of scandal. Freighters bound from the United States continued to unload tons of Johns-Manville and Cellotex tar and gravel roofing. Roofs continued to be flat and typhoons continued to sweep our structures away. The military and Congress remained undisturbed by either their consciences or threats of charges of waste by the taxpayers.

Four years and a billion or so dollars later we had, with the aid of General MacArthur, the Far East Command, the Corps of Engineers and SOM partners, accomplished our mission — the total effect of which seemed to be the destruction of the scant flat land used for sweet potato farming by the Ryukyuans, converting it into useless airfields and troop quarters; and the training of another echelon of brilliant young associates for SOM.

From time to time Urquart had his own form of playing games with me and would call me back to the States. In the peremptory manner of final exams in a course on thin-shell concrete, I was once ordered to design and produce a prototype light concrete igloo for field ammunition storage. Formed, gunited, covered with earth, the igloo seemed to gather itself to resist the impact of the Sherman tank crawling painfully, inexorably forward. Having taught me all I knew about thin-shell concrete design, Urquart should have been concerned for my safety, but as the tank crunched slowly forward over the summit of the smooth dome he stood amiably by while I crouched inside the igloo, so certain was I that it would hold up.

Still in one piece and in the round after this experience, I boarded Pan Am's big four-motor propeller plane, Stratocruiser flight #100 in San Francisco, headed for Tokyo. These planes were underpowered; their swollen double-decked forward cabin with cocktail lounge below probably offered too much wind resistance. Hardly ever had we gotten all the way to Hanida Field with more than three motors working. With a stop at Honolulu, it was a long flight, a sleeper flight — but at twenty-five thousand feet above the cold Pacific with only a quarter of an inch of metal holding us together, I didn't sleep very well.

On this particular February 1945 flight, every seat was taken. My seatmate bustled in, refusing to let the stewardess take off his camel's-hair coat, every pocket bulging. "No," he said, "you couldn't lift it." Checked luggage was weighed and limited. Commodore Sullivan, U.S.N., confided that his pockets were loaded with cameras and such to sell to the still strapped Japanese.

Sullivan was a retired navy specialist in the demolition of sub-

merged craft with the rare title of commodore, and he confided
that his every plane trip had ended in near disaster. So, he explained with a wan grin, this should be an interesting one. As he
expanded on his subject, midnight advance sorties in slick suits,
the planting of charges in sunken craft in advance, we neared
Tokyo. The commodore became visibly gloomy; no disaster.
About an hour out of Hanida heavy snow swirled us into an
opaque white blanket. Two hours later — the commodore posi-
tively glowing with cheer — the pilot announced that we would
have to try for a northern emergency field. We were almost out
of gas. At that point I knew what it was like to make peace with
God.

We landed at an abandoned fighter airfield near Sendai in
northern Japan, seventy-five of us — a motley crew. The field
was staffed by one American sergeant, five privates, and about
a thousand Japanese. We could be massacred in our sleep, I
thought. The rolling, snow-covered rice fields were beautiful.
Someone had built an officers' club à la Frank Lloyd Wright
with a great stone fireplace. But more important to us were the
frozen steaks and whiskey in bulk. As the storm continued, more
stranded planes came in, one with a name band booked for the
Imperial Ballroom in Tokyo. Dancing began when nurses from
the Sendai base showed up as if by magic. There was a man with
something to do with living cancer cells which had to be delivered for testing at Hiroshima, who had to keep his precious
charge in ice cubes.

Inseparable by now, for three days and nights the commodore
and I made sunrise trips to the wild duck feeding grounds in the
snowy rice fields — officially to shoot ducks but actually to savor
the beauty of the place. Finally returned to Tokyo, I called
frantically to tell everyone I was alive and well, only to find that
no one cared. Snowbound Tokyo, with the wires down, had wor-
ries of its own.

War had devastated the indigenous Ryukyuans, their families,

133

their society and their civilization wiped out in a conflict between two alien nations: Japan and the United States. A few
GIs turned monks asked us to design a monastery for them. I
happened to be a devout Unitarian (if there is such a thing);
our commanding officer on Okinawa was a devout Catholic. He
brought me together with a small group of bearded Benedictines
who were attempting to teach some few of the thousands of
orphaned Okinawa children who had been left to wander over
the island.

We all chose a site — a magnificent site for any monastery —
on the ancient walls of the bombed-out palace. With the wind
whipping their beards and their black and purple robes snapping
around them, the monks stood high above the bay of Naha on
those ruins as we outlined our plans to them. They were ambitious. Our monastery reached a finger to the sky. We had not
forgotten Mont-Saint-Michel, and neither had they. Finally, as
we all waxed eloquent, inspired and euphoric over the yet unbuilt structure, the father asked what form of compensation they
could make. Suggesting that my problem was being a Unitarian,
I asked if he would intercede for me with heaven, either directly
or indirectly, in return for this small effort on our part. Roaring
with laughter that rose above the gale, our good father blessed
us and agreed — and I am certain that his intercession will not
be forgotten when the great day comes.

And then the ubiquitous Urquart surfaced once again, this
time in deep trouble (along with a private architect-engineer),
apparently tempted by what, from his limited view, were lush
government contracts. The bait: five huge Moroccan air bases
on a crash contract. On the theory of a romantic boondoggle, the
private architect-engineer drew his work force from the arts and
crafts towns of Carmel and Pebble Beach — people curious about
Casablanca, Bogart-Bacall style. One applicant's qualifications
were that he could count sheep. It was a complex project, complicated by the French Morocco protectorate. At a dead stall, we

were asked to reorganize, restaff. Apparently incapable of turning down a job, Walter Severinghaus took over and got the job rolling, and the fighter and bomber bases finished. The square miles of paved runways for use by supersecret airplanes were completed just in time to be turned over to Morocco — quite available to an enemy. Following a distinct pattern of wasting the taxpayers' money on abortive defense schemes, these bases were never used by the United States.

The dividend was an acquaintance with several very beautiful cities: Casablanca, Rabat, Fez, Marrakech. My memory calls up billowing clouds of dust, white-sheeted Arabs, slim, dark, mysterious people slipping by us as we sipped gluey coffee and negotiated for beautiful Moroccan rugs from the rug sellers' stacks; the graceful outlines of crenelated walls of the ancient cities, the inhaled smells and reflected sounds, the soft hordes of people, the monochrome palette, walls of beiges, tans and browns, the land and the cities of clay, the people: cream-colored, tan, beige, buff, brown, chocolate and black. Morocco is one of the beautiful places.

11

The Continental Divide

HREE THOUSAND MILES away from Skid's "round table in the Oak Room at the Plaza" could be found at almost any time of day or night the West Coast's best-known architect, seated at his own round table in the bar room of the Bohemian Club in San Francisco. His name was Timothy Pfleuger, and he had known Skid for a very long time.

When industrialist-philanthropist J. D. Zellerbach asked Tim Pfleuger to retain as a consultant an eastern hospital specialist, Pfleuger simply reached for his round table telephone and consulted his friend, Louis Skidmore, at his.

Although Skid's eyes could still blaze and mesmerize, he was withdrawing, retreating to the sand, scrub and holly of stark, bleached-shingled Fire Island to a house surrounded by nothing but wind, sun, sand and the deep green satin leaves and red berries of the holly trees. Exposure he avoided, so he stayed either safely hidden indoors, or upon some unavoidable errand. Wrapped up, sunglassed, in checkered woolen shirt and muffler and khaki pants, regardless of the season — he could be seen making his way across the sand dunes, sharing his solitude with his monumental ulcers.

I answered Pfleuger's summons to San Francisco to avoid further strain on Skid's physical condition. Ironically enough, Timothy Pfleuger dropped dead shortly after my arrival in San Francisco. To meet these added responsibilities I immediately established an office for SOM in San Francisco in a charming space high in the Renaissance Crocker Bank fronting on Montgomery and Post streets in the financial district.

I established John Barney Rodgers on location and jointly with Tim Pfleuger's brother Milton we set in operation the design and construction of an experimental patient's room. This was a new idea to the trustees and the staff; it won wide favor and generated some sizable contributions.

SOM's third office immediately opened up a wide spectrum of opportunities. In this coastal city there was a special quality of light and attitude toward work and exciting new jobs available for the asking. Caught up in the tempo of the city, the jobs and the people, I maintained a schedule like Phineas Fogg's; and the luxury of the transcontinental luxury trains made the time spent on them between San Francisco, Portland, Oregon, and Chicago part of the fun. I found that I could stand almost anything as long as it happened in a charming place and involved a dramatic situation. In and out of town, gourmet experiences and architectural challenges went arm in arm. The ethic of a great meal sometimes seemed to equal the aesthetic of a great design. There was an obligation to fully savor local specialties in San Francisco. I remember the sliced fresh figs, the huge ripe strawberries, the Rex sole, cold artichokes with mayonnaise, cracked crab and the Napa Valley wines.

When our fourth office opened in Portland, Oregon, it mattered to me that it would be located not far inland from Oregon's lovely, wind-swept coast among the rain forests, lakes and rugged terrain in "The Boston of the West." This area was bound to grow and needed advance protection in the environmental sectors. Perhaps this could be our training ground for what I already believed to be the future trend: a concern for the ecology of our nation.

Portland's leading architect, Pietro Belluschi, had moved East and asked me to take over. For a period of five years the new firm was to be known as Pietro Belluschi and Skidmore, Owings and Merrill. This firm name must have caused a good bit of confusion. Young Elliot Brown, partner-in-charge, was likely to answer the standard telephone call at the office along these lines: "Yes, this is Pietro Belluschi and Skidmore, Owings and Merrill, architects and engineers in Portland, Oregon. Can I help you? Mr. Belluschi? He's in Cambridge. No, Mr. Skidmore is not in town. Mr. Merrill? Which Mr. Merrill do you want? We have three. No, they're all away at the moment. Oh, yes, Mr. Owings. Unfortunately, he's in Rome. Can I help you? My name is Elliot Brown."

Portlanders seemed to possess a special breed of western energy crossed with Boston culture. The lush, moist climate put color in their cheeks and in their characters. There were skiing and mountain climbing, fishing and wildlife and breathtaking wilderness, all within an hour's drive to trailhead. With this kind of background the Portland office developed. Excellent SOM men were generated there. Today under Dave Pugh, the office has become an institutional part of the Northwest.

With the waves crashing against the Pacific Coast, decisions were easy and the chain of jobs formed link by link. Old acquaintances from the East helped, both in San Francisco and Portland. Stanford's venerable trustee Leland Cutler, cousin of Rufus Dawes, managed to get SOM hired to do a master plan for the huge estates owned by Stanford University; and there was a Corps of Engineers colonel, now a general retired, in Portland who helped us land the first big renewal project for that area. There was old Chicago friend John Boit Morse, who introduced me to his father, overlord and baron of Pebble Beach, California, S. F. B. Morse.

Better known as Sam Morse, the 1907 captain of the Yale football team still hadn't come down from the Yale fence even by 1970. Hale, hearty, vibrant, Sam Morse owned, operated, dominated, controlled, influenced, bullied and beguiled a large segment of the Monterey Peninsula population who resided within and without the thousand-acre compound known as Pebble Beach, which in reality was the Del Monte Properties and Sand and Gravel Company. Morse was a benign dictator and promoter extraordinary. His annual Crosby Gold Tournament actually put Christmas and Easter in second and third place on the calendar, though he could never have done it without Colonel Allen Griffin, owner and editor-in-chief of the distinguished, "small" (thirty thousand circulation) Monterey *Herald*. Under the colonel's personal direction the newspaper undertook crusades, risked losing advertising, and was generally "one hell of a good newspaper." He sensed the value of what Morse was trying to do and backed him up all the way.

By buying back land within the "forest" in the depression and reselling it under strict aesthetic conditions, Morse operated a near ideal real estate development long before the word "ecology" was heard by anybody outside Harvard. Untouched by the zoning laws of state or county, behind gates guarded by private police, on self-maintained road systems but with a sewage system dumping raw material into the bay, Sam Morse maintained the aura and near myth of his social, civic and commercial supremacy until his death. Then, as suddenly as a mask is dropped from the face of an actor, there was exposed at last the sand and gravel business dredging away the unique, irreplaceable white sands of the beaches of the peninsula. All of this had been a traumatic experience for the senior Morse son, John Boit Morse, who had early on washed his hands of the matter and dedicated his life to painting on a big scale; and a first-class painter he was and is.

Monterey's luxuriously beautiful old Hotel Del Monte, built in 1887, was bought by the United States Navy in 1943. With the money Morse made from this sale, he hired Gardner Dailey, justly famous for his "Bay Area houses," and me to expand the more profitable Del Monte Lodge. When this job was completed I offered SOM's services to the navy direct for the Post Graduate Technical School which they proposed to build and they handed us standard barracks plans which, if applied to that beautiful site, would have required the destruction of its dozens of ancient oaks. At this point young Walter Netsch, fresh from Oak Ridge, faced with his first important architectural opportunity in SOM, simply refused to proceed with the barracks plans; and, aware that he was committing an architectural form of mutiny punishable with termination of the contract by the client if the plan for change was unsuccessful, asked for and got permission to appeal this monstrous plan to the admirals in Washington, D.C. I agreed in principle, but from a practical point of view, how were we to crack this one? I turned to Skid's great friend, George Ferris, chairman of the board of the Raymond Concrete Pile Company, who had never failed in some thirty years to produce just the right man. The right man was Admiral Herman in the Bureau of Yards and Docks. Netsch made a model.

Admiral Herman, a man of ships and guns, was transfixed with amazement as Netsch cleared the model's terrain of oak and eucalyptus trees and covered the flattened surface with standard-plan barracks — and then, in swift sleight of hand, resurrected the trees from destruction, neatly fitted in between the gleaming pavilions, leaving the reincarnated countryside intact. At that time not just navy men but most educators were doing their academic planning by the seat of their pants. Not Netsch! He won over Admiral Herman and gained a thirty-day period of grace in which to put up or shut up.

Netsch moved his San Francisco crew to Annapolis, Maryland. At night the admiral would come over to their barracks workshop-bedrooms and share in this first taste — for him — of research and programming.

Fitted in among the great trees, the Navy Post Graduate Technical School has won its share of medals. But somehow Admiral Herman, who was principally responsible for its success, was passed over for advancement not once, but for a second time. We hope it was a coincidence but we do not know. Admiral Herman blew his brains out.

About that time, in 1953, I was fifty years of age, had been married for almost twenty-two years and was the father of four children: Emily (a poetess) and her twin Natalie (already forming her mother's social awareness) ; Jennie (thick, black, voluptuous hair to her waist and an artist to her fingertips) ; and the youngest, a boy, Nat, who eventually survived three sisters and grew thirty inches in thirty months to become a strapping six-footer. From a slow start Nat was to sharpen his intellect and launch into a career in fighting communicable diseases.

My wife, Emily, and the four children had, for ten years, been living more or less permanently at our home in New Mexico. I, in the meantime, was peripatetic and only incidentally took time from what I considered to be SOM's business. Everything and everybody received my attention except Emily and the four children, and they were learning to get along pretty well without me. In fact, Emily was about to divorce me and marry again immediately.

Emily's plans for divorce were still unknown to me when, early in 1953 — February 5, to be exact, on my birthday — I returned from touring some of those foreign places, Istanbul, Tokyo and Okinawa, armed with kimonos, obis and Noh masks. There was a cocktail party in progress, presumably to celebrate my birthday, in our casita at the Leaning Wall Ranch in Pojoaque, New Mexico. Emily had just introduced me to Margaret

Wentworth Millard and this extraordinary apparition startled me so that the glass I was offering her missed her proffered hand. Shattered between us, the glass lay in its own pool of ice, glinting a little on the red brick floor in the evening candlelight.

Margaret is a presence, an elegant presence. There is an aura about her: tall, dark hair piled high, her clothes at once spectacular and inconspicuous, indivisibly the hands of an artist and the penetrating eyes and mind of an intellectual. In Margaret's person came my first total experience superior to my own ego. My priorities collapsed at once. Indianapolis, Cousin Georgia, Dr. Wicks, Cornell, Dean Bosworth, Mother, Eloise and Skid, group practice, SOM, cathedrals — all telescoped into the background of one complete experience.

Margaret Wentworth Millard, recently divorced, mother of a young daughter the age of our twins, moved away to another part of the portal with the grace of a ballerina and talked to other people.

Through the slender thread of Margaret's daughter Wendy's and my Emily's sharing a tutor, I managed to weave a fabric to bridge and hold firm our never settled, tumultuous interactions. As she receded, I advanced in a wide arc of containment, foiling her every avenue of escape. Finally bringing her to bay with the Pacific Ocean at her back, I courted her. A nineteenth-century, wide-ranging, heavily buttressed stone manor house anchored on that rocky coast provided a fitting setting. A sheltered court among the feathery lemon, eucalyptus and Monterey pine was a good place to be married. Wendy and my three daughters, each with Victorian nosegays held firmly at their waists, sanctified a true miracle of convergence of the crossing of desire lines through some mysterious gravitational pull.

Margaret and I were married on the last day of the year 1953, "for tax reasons." Margaret Wentworth wasn't inclined to equate "tax reasons" with love, marriage or a way of life, but this kind of consideration was typical of the "corporate accountant" I had become. Her agreement to marry me was based on some fairly radical commitments. I agreed to move to San Francisco, to promptly seek out a site for a permanent home on the south coast in the area called Big Sur and to use the New Mexico ranch only as an alternate homesite.

Upon the occasions of International Date Line crossings things traditionally happen; ceremonies prevail. Our marriage was, for me, a passing of the symbolic International Date Line. The passing wasn't easy. My pre-Margaret self wouldn't stay dead. It persisted in popping up like an unruly and unholy ghost and had to be put down again, to my embarrassment.

Stripping me of my wrist watch was an early step in her process of de-escalating my internal time machine. When I had stopped automatically checking that watch, Margaret announced the first progress. But I sped past the mark, past the signposts set up by an ever-hopeful Margaret, past the objectives she held sacred. I sped past, turned around, returned and sped past again, until it was almost too late to readjust.

Having my office in San Francisco helped a lot, turning me from visitor to resident. My way was further smoothed by that same John David Zellerbach, our client on Mount Zion Hospital, whose own family's modest beginnings were appealingly expressed on a bronze plaque secured to the base of his Crown Zellerbach Building. It reads, "The Crown Zellerbach business was founded near this spot." It had to be that vague because collecting rags for the fine paper-making that had started the business had been done from his grandfather's pushcart as it moved through the streets near that area.

Rarely is an architect so fortunate as to have a client like J. D. Zellerbach. Because of his extraordinary grasp of the aesthetics, he provided a strong sponsorship of strivings for great design. J.D. and I spelled out a partnership in arts and architecture, climaxing in the creation of his company's headquarters building in San Francisco. J.D. and I knew that here lay an

143

opportunity to develop a significant building and simultaneously re-create a major blighted area in San Francisco. We looked around to see what we could see.

First we discovered something that was perfectly obvious to anyone who would trouble to look: Market Street's sleazy, shabby, junky appearance was only skin deep. Market Street was San Francisco's greatest potential. Straight and wide from the Ferry Building on the waterfront to the Twin Peaks foot-hills, now neglected, it could, with loving care, become one of the great boulevards of the world. In such cases, first starts were necessary. There was a superb island site near the waterfront among gin mills in the last stages of blight, with drunks and winos, which would cut away the rotten fabric of this central core of San Francisco and re-establish in it an environment worthy of that great city.

Our modest, twenty-two-story, single tower would require only one third of the entire island site. J.D. seemed reconciled to go ahead without buying out the total of that site. I knew this wouldn't do, so we lunched. Then I led him along Bush Street to the site and pointed out the developing vistas that his build-ing would provide when we built it. As we reached the corner of Bush and Battery he realized at once that the four-story existing Parrott estate building standing on the corner would cut off the view from his new building and thus lose in visual impact and money value several million dollars. That afternoon he ordered that the block be purchased, no matter what the cost, and the Crown Zellerbach Building thus gained the setting it deserved.

Modern planning can accommodate more people and keep more open space. For example, pre-Zellerbach there were five hundred workers on the site; post-Zellerbach, five thousand workers enjoyed a park covering two thirds of the area as well as a building in which it was a joy to work.

With a plaza that large I was nervous about what some future chairman of the board might decide to build there, so we designed a kind of toy bank in order to kill such an idea. It was a carousel — "banking in the round" — as a change from banking on the square. A kind of horizontal rose window served as the pavilion roof. At this charming little branch bank, which served the dual purpose of a "meet me under the clock" place and a depository for money, the bank's business zoomed to astronomical proportions in spite of predictions by the experts of dismal failure.

The problem of controlling signs with corporate executives had always bugged us. The Crown Zellerbach solution was a triumph in this regard. The sole identification consisted of a six-inch-high bronze nameplate. The building, in fact, needed no identification. Unique, it seemed to float in its own park, framed in a cobblestone plaza accented further with a bronze fountain and a grove of eighty-year-old olive trees. The trees were moved from an Orange County, California, olive grove just in time to avoid their destruction by an approaching eight-lane southern California freeway.

I had problems with the C-Z interiors. J.D. was safely in the American embassy in Rome on the day when I was called to the eighteenth floor of the Crown Zellerbach Building — the executive floor — for a confrontation with all the assembled vice presidents who had seen their offices for the first time. Some didn't like the furniture or the pictures. Since they had been carefully designed and selected by SOM, it was up to me to defend them. I didn't. I simply said, "Okay, you live here, gentlemen, and you spend about a third of your waking hours here. I don't care what you do with your offices but you have to do something, and you have to select the pictures and the furniture yourselves. You can't delegate it a second time." Outdoor men, at home in the woods among tall trees where they administered lumbering operations, they were lost indoors, especially in their own offices.

As the design for the building progressed, I moved to Rome as architect in residence at the American Academy. Since 1927 I had been hoping to finally fulfill my ambition of spending a year in residence at the academy. In the years since college I had been burning up native resources intellectually and spiritually and the time had come to recharge. It would be good to try putting down my roots into the rich culture of ancient Rome, even if it was for only a year.

I had never shaken my feeling of inferiority as a professional. I felt sincerely that only through full involvement in the American Academy in Rome could this block be removed. The president of the academy, my 1927 classmate Michael Rapuano, provided the invitation to come to the academy as a professor in residence and Margaret and I took Comfort, our Pekingese, and sailed for Rome, where we moved into the seventeenth-century Villa Aurelia. Laurence Roberts, the director, and Isabel, his wife, were the unofficial American ambassadors to Italy. They boasted the best chef in Rome and the Robertses' gourmet meals, with their native charm and conversation, made the academy the most popular center for Roman citizens as well as visiting dignitaries from America.

The buildings of the American Academy stand among a broad sweep of topiary-shaped ilex trees. A seventeenth-century palace is the nucleus. Enclosed by ancient walls marking the Appian Way, the Villa Aurelia is skirted by major aqueducts and inside all is elegance. In the soft Italian sunlight my native energy revived, and I felt strong enough to reintroduce collaborative problems at the academy for the first time after a lapse of forty years. The fellows in sculpture, painting and architecture agreed to try to combine their talents and enthusiastically went to work. One combined group undertook the design of a chapel supposedly for a rich American cardinal who had died in Rome; another group tackled a flea market — in reality a series of shops — which they designed like a ruin sprawled along the Tiber River.

Margaret's and my Roman adventure proved to be a confirma-

Chicago: "Big John" and the little Victorian water tower. *Hedrich-Blessing*

Indianapolis:
Soldiers and Sailors Monument.

Nat watches Rufus Dawes sign
contract for the Sky Ride, Chicago
1933 World's Fair.

N.A.O. — Eagle Scout on
Jamboree.

tion of classic values wherever my eye rested: in the Roman Forum, in the Campodoglio, at Assisi or the towers of San Gimignano. But Saint Peter's, of course, is the greatest of them all: the open arms of the embracing colonnade, the disciplined rhythm of the seemingly endless, subtly blending rows of giant columns suggesting eternal rhythm — awesome enough, yet comforting, too. We found there a sense of consolation, a haunting one, deep and abiding in the formal unity of the masses and the ambience of light and shade.

In 1958 a pope died and was buried there in Saint Peter's; and a new pope was elected from the College of Cardinals and elevated to the throne in ancient medieval splendor. We saw the long procession, the thousands of cardinals, bishops, monsignors and priests from the world over. In that long line there was not one woman — something which gave us pause for thought. From our seats high in the dome of Saint Peter's, thousands of tiny colored heads were only jeweled pins clustered in a lush cushion. All motion seemed frozen in that moment in time, all at rest under the huge enclosed vault, the noble volume crosshatched by rays of light dimly blurred.

Between funerals and coronations of popes, and collaboration problems at the academy, J.D. and I searched for large-scale sculpture, seeking a "noncontroversial" piece for the pavilion of his new Crown Zellerbach Building. It soon became clear that no existing sculpture would fit and the task of choosing a new one would be delicate, involving both the ambassador and his wife. Then we discovered Mascharini, a Triestino living in that ancient seaport on the Adriatic. He worked in bronze with lines inspired by the Charioteer of Delphi. His work was fresh, contemporary, safe, with roots in the ancient culture.

First Margaret and I visited Mascharini in Trieste. Then the sculptor appeared at the embassy in Rome early one morning with wax models of his proposed design and asked for a cold bath, which turned out to be not for himself but for the wax

147

models. A model was approved in principle and a few months later an unofficial, off-the-record visit to Trieste by the Zellerbachs was arranged so that they could see the final clay model before casting.

Trieste was a hotbed of intrigue and a diplomatic tinderbox, teetering in loyalties between Yugoslavia and Italy. It was no place for an American ambassador! But the proper sculptor was not easy to find and international incidents must be risked for the sake of art. The city of Udine was the nearest airport location considered safe for landing a military ambassadorial plane, and, as our plane leveled off to land, the Zellerbachs, Margaret and I saw below us a sight we couldn't believe: a military parade in full panoply, band playing, troops lined up in parade dress. As we stepped out of the plane on this very nonofficial trip a light wind whipped the ladies' dresses, and along that rigid line of young Italian soldiers there was no motion except that every eye in that line followed the swaying skirts and the shapely legs until the angle of human vision had been exceeded.

Thus through crowded streets we moved to the jammed front stoop of the Mascharini studio, television cameras all focusing on little J.D., whose bald head was framed by the generous clay bosoms of our proposed Lady of C-Z. Handsome Mrs. J.D. made frantic gestures to intercept the news cameras as they inexorably bored in and around that interesting conjointure of contrasting shapes.

The inevitable time of decision came. Would the ambassador approve the sculpture for casting? There was no answer possible short of a war between Yugoslavia and Italy, except yes.

Some hours later J.D.'s aide found Mascharini and me seated at a café table on the quay quaffing such liquids as might calm our jangled nerves. The very proper aide, standing straight in his pinstriped trousers and tail coat, his briefcase clutched tightly under one arm, announced that he was there to pass on the ambassador's final instructions to the sculptor. "These," he said as he cupped his hands (as much as he could without dropping his briefcase) over the spots where, on his wife, would be bosoms, "must be reduced to this — " glancing down to his flattened hands still in the same position. With a nod of understanding, Mascharini and I had another drink. To this day I don't think Mrs. Zellerbach likes that sculpture.

One day after his return to San Francisco J.D. complained of a headache. Within a week he was dead, and with him died a unique spirit. But the pavilion and the slender tower of his Crown Zellerbach headquarters building, standing in a park, will always remain — I hope and believe — as his living monument.

J.D. placed his new Crown Zellerbach headquarters building among the most cherished of his life's works, and I place my opportunity to have worked with him alongside.

12

From Air Force Academy to Circle Campus

B<small>Y THE TIME</small> Mrs. Harold Talbott told her husband (secretary of the air force under Eisenhower) that Eloise Skidmore was a darling and that Louis Skidmore had done a lot of free work for her New York Women's Hospital Board, it had become clear to friend and foe alike that SOM would be a formidable competitor for the commission to design the proposed United States Air Force Academy.

I did not know that Mrs. Talbott felt this way about Eloise and Skid. Even if I had I wouldn't have depended upon it. Government is too complex to depend upon any one facet. I had quite a few reasons for wanting that job myself. The academy would be permanent, and God knows I was tired of our all-out efforts on temporary-emergency projects; weary of pouring energy, talent and tax dollars into installations for war more often than not obsolete, or abandoned, or both, soon after we had completed our work. It would be great to have a hand in creating from scratch a contemporary academy as a counterpoint to Classic Annapolis and Gothic West Point.

Such a job would not only be exciting architecturally but would go far to break up the rigidity and separatism in our four offices. We needed a big job to shake up, heat up and reliquify our blood. It was only natural that partners did not want to move around from city to city. When working in Chicago, New York or San Francisco, for example, one should and does put down roots. But the Air Force Academy had enough sex appeal to actively stir everybody up and a certain amount of healthy homogenization occurred.

I didn't know about Mrs. Talbott but I did know about Chicagoan James Henderson Douglas: statesman, scholar, humanitarian, and a graduate of Corpus Christi College in Cambridge, England (a fact which stood us in good stead when the chapel came up for criticism), currently undersecretary of air and Talbott's special confidant. Douglas was an old friend. The trouble was that he was also an old friend of my most dangerous competitor, Chicago architect Alfred Phillip Shaw. I saw a way, through a decoy, to head off Shaw — also an old friend of mine. It so happened that the current air force job in hand was the selection of an architect for some highly visible, glamorous-sounding air bases to be built in Spain, similar in scope to ours in Morocco. We let it be known through the grapevine that entwines all professionals that we were hot after and would probably get these bases. With this information, our dangerous competition, in a fury of activity, went after those bases. We stepped nimbly aside. They, having won the Spanish bases, were safely out of our path, since no one firm could have both.

Our SOM presentation for the Air Force Academy was a national effort. The result was a hard-backed brochure exactly two inches larger in each direction than any known file drawer or wastebasket in existence. Our brochure would be kept on top of the desk — not in it or under it.

We went after the job hard, claiming full in-house competence, refusing association with other firms. As more of our competitors began urging us to join up with them it was clear that the word had gone out that we had the job — and even clearer when Secretary Talbott invited Skid to lunch at The

Brook. Skid returned from that lunch looking like the cat that swallowed the canary, but with nothing more important to report than that the company was charming, the food delicious, and the surroundings elegant.

Shortly thereafter a ten-member board of heavily starred generals, chaired by Jim Douglas, began interviewing at length some dozen of the three hundred–odd architect-engineer firms competing, whose brochures had apparently been large enough to remain on top of the table. The contestants' offerings varied from vague promises of what they would do if awarded the job to actual designs and models. Our own presentation consisted of a fifteen-foot-long, six-foot-high folding screen divided into three-foot panels, each devoted to one aspect of the total problem: research, programming, scheduling and design of the academy. A different partner explained each section of the screen. After I had completed a summary of our proposal, I was asked by a four-star general if I proposed to design the academy in sandstone, as recommended by Frank Lloyd Wright. "General," I asked, "would you build an airplane of sandstone?"

The story of the design and the construction of the Air Force Academy is a success story. When completed, the total ensemble looked and functioned the way we had hoped it would. The story in its many facets illuminates the role of the architect versus democracy, involving from start to finish conflict and controversy with the military establishment, the federal civilian bureaucracies, the country's elected representatives, congressmen and senators from all the states. We were, in fact, engaged in a great civil war, an undeclared war in which all contestants were determined that we were not to accomplish what we had been hired to do as professionals. At the end of the job we were out of pocket one million dollars in cash, exclusive of overhead, a loss few architectural firms could have sustained. But this was a minor consideration since our design ideals had survived. We had won out in this classic struggle for a worthy "Grand Design." We had by-passed mediocrity.

From the beginning we had been dealing with a confused air force. From my first wind-tossed flight over the proposed site at the foot of the Rampart Range, where my pilot advised me to stop trying to fly the tiny plane with my stomach, and the day I answered the kitchen phone standing in the hot New Mexico sun outside our ranch house and heard Skid's laconic "Well, we got the job. Harold just called me," we charted a rugged course through long, troubled years of conflict. We guided the air force into agreeing with our own plan for locating the academy on a high mesa, and the involved flow diagrams of the cadet functions were a key factor in gaining that approval. Flow, function and architecture were so closely allied that the approval of one automatically settled the design of the rest; and thus, with the approval of the academy's functions, the buildings that would serve them were in essence approved. Louis Sullivan's formula, "Form follows function," applied here perfectly and thus we reached our goal. Among the secretary's advisers in the military some were surprised, others amused and still others chagrined when our benign deceit was discovered — totally unaware that in approving the functional integrity of this design they had also approved a contemporary design for the academy buildings themselves.

Ictinus and Callicrates and Phidias probably had to fight to get the job of doing the Parthenon, and even they didn't have the free hand that architects dream about, since the site had been worked over for several millenniums. But the Parthenon had turned out pretty well; and the Acropolis had, in fact, held its own since 346 B.C. against all comers: Roman, Gothic, Renaissance and Modern.

Under that grim appellation, "military academy," lay in truth an institution for the education of twenty-five hundred young men at a time in a new environment, an environment which we might be permitted to create — or at least take a hand in molding.

Without tradition or alumni, and despite all the pulling and stretching and debating, an instant academy dedicated to the cadet was assembled into an extraordinarily unified architectural concept expressing the power of one idea. Ancillary facilities, like housing for professors and staff, were subordinated to the cadet. He was the key idea. He could eat, sleep, go to class. He would have swimming pools, tennis courts, football fields; he could reach all within a ten-minute walk. His father and mother and sweetheart — along with the population of the United States — could watch him if they cared to drive slowly and carefully around on a peripheral road which would encircle the academy. His professors and instructors would live at the foot of the mesa in a town for about ten thousand support personnel providing housing for faculty and academic staff, warehousing, laundries, bakeries, power plants, sewage. The alumni — when there were some — could come and see the boys play football in a stadium seven thousand feet above sea level — which, considering the thinness of the oxygen, is quite a feat.

We arranged to have a full-scale cadet room built and furnished on site. There were to be two cadets to a room and they were to have bunks, desks, closets, clothes and uniforms of the day (which consisted of several changes) , bookcases and closed-circuit TV. We decided on one bath adjoining two rooms. Final approval was withheld by a board of four-star generals, who, traditionally having hidden their own contraband food behind the dampers in the old West Point fireplaces, wanted to know (sheepishly enough) where the boys could hide theirs. Behind the TV sets, we said.

Each part of the grand design fell into place at last and one great structure after another was integrated into the varying levels of the mesa, the split-level quarters meshed midway between the two upper and the two lower floors, reducing stair climbing to two flights and making access easy. The dining hall, with sky-lighted pavilion roof, four hundred feet to a side (a conventional city block), rested on sixteen columns, four to a side. Twenty-five hundred boys could eat there at one time, to experience the "unity of the Corps." Cadets lined up four times a day before their quarters to march to the dining hall or class.

At this point our associate partner in charge of engineering, Ed Merrill, in typical engineering style, pointed out that the last cadet in the dress parade would walk twelve hundred feet a day, or a hundred miles in a semester, more than his more fortunate captain of cadets, who would be in first place in line. We could offer no logistical solution to this problem.

When the time came for final government approval the going was hard. Perhaps because he was a humanitarian first and an air force general second, the academy's first superintendent, General Harmon, supported our plan. But the balance of the elite officer corps was opposed to the location of the campus on the mesa and only capitulated under pressure — generally with bad grace. How could one oppose such a magnificent site? The Acropolis-like top of the great mesa jutted out from the twelve-thousand-foot backdrop. The buildings would fit the mesa, framed by the Rampart Range of the awe-inspiring Rocky Mountains.

Secretaries for air came and went: Harold Talbott, then Donald Quarles, an engineer who could read plans. Finally, our favorite secretary, Jim Douglas, who had been there all the time.

There was always that disturbing problem: just who was our client? By definition this at times could and did include every official with an opinion. On these terms our client's name was legion. There were the President of the United States, twelve to fourteen members of the cabinet, some ninety-six members of the Senate at that time, four hundred and thirty-five members of the House, the bureaucracy of the armed forces with special

155

emphasis on the secretary of the air force, the undersecretary and the generals. Somewhere at the heart of that complex there was always somebody who had to give the final opinions and decisions.

Our initial presentation effort to Congress was truly Olympian, our production great theater. To see it we arranged that from Washington, D.C., the congressmen, the senators and the newspapermen would be flown to Colorado Springs aboard great air force jets. This we thought would start them off in the right frame of mind. We emptied the handsome Colorado Springs fine arts museum of its normal contents and therein installed a vast panorama of the Rockies against the walls: giant murals. In order to prepare for this we rounded up fifty thousand Fuller brushes, since they make ideal trees. We forested specially prepared artificial plaster slopes with the brushes until they melted into the photomurals of the Rampart Range beyond. Within the museum the ramps and stairs were arranged so that our visitors could ramble around throughout the various sections of the model and view the parade grounds, the athletic fields, the quarters, the dining hall, the academic buildings. Like Paul Bunyans they strode across the miniature academy, inspecting the playing fields, pavilions and domiciles of the Lilliputians.

It wasn't long before our clients began to identify themselves. We were attacked with authority on all sides by senators and congressmen — mostly men from small towns with narrow but fixed ideas about design, often aesthetically influenced by their local pseudo-Colonial library or a western courthouse or city hall — backgrounds and judgments not ideally fitted to guarantee a high standard of design.

The press carried some interesting comments:

Architectural designs for the Air Force Academy were tabbed today by some of the score of Senators and Representatives who saw them as "heavenly," "radical," or "modern and futuristic."

156

They went on to say:

> Senator Herman Welker, Republican of Idaho, described the design as "heavenly." "I have nothing but thrills in my heart for the cadets who will enjoy this academy," he said. He added that he thought the designs should include "more Western architecture—more good, red Colorado stone."

"The academy looks like a modernistic cigarette factory," said Representative Porter Hardy, Jr., Democrat of Virginia. "I'm not saying that's my idea, but let's call it unique."

Senator A. Willis Robertson, Democrat from Virginia, said that our chapel looked like "an assembly of wigwams"; but the chairman of the committee that gave or took away our funds for the Air Force Academy went even further. He called the chapel "an insult to God." There must be fire behind all this smoke, or so Congress thought, and on July 13, 1955, the House Appropriations Committee met and abruptly stopped all construction on the hundred-and-twenty-five-million-dollar Air Force Academy project in Colorado Springs. The papers said "the Committee based its action solely on the proposed design for the chapel for the Academy, which has stirred criticism in Congress and elsewhere."

All this caused great inconvenience and long delay in accomplishing our objectives, but we drew support as well as criticism. On June 30, 1955, on behalf of the board of directors of the American Institute of Architects, Executive Director Edmund R. Purves said:

> The design for the proposed Air Force Academy for the United States, Colorado Springs, Colorado, is receiving a certain amount of adverse criticism and this criticism has been widely publicized. In view of the importance of this project historically and architecturally and in view of its significance to the American people, the board of the American Institute of Architects felt it should state the institute's position with respect to the engagement of and

157

confidence in American architects. In arriving at a selection of architects and architect consultants for the design of this important work, the secretary of the air force followed ethical and objective procedures that were in the public interest. The architects and architect consultants selected by the secretary of the air force are among the most distinguished of American practitioners. Any structure or work of art will find itself the target of criticism, sometimes voiced without a knowledge of the problems involved.

At the heart of our interest in the Air Force Academy project lay a kernel of old-fashioned, sentimental idealism framed in history. Louis Skidmore not only had begun to look something like Churchill but also shared some of his sense of history. This sense of history in its essence was epitomized in the problem posed in designing a chapel. Since no one felt very deeply about religion anymore, and since the Air Force Academy chapel must house *all* principal religions under one roof, what did one do? SOM would rise to the heights just this once and build to the Virgin instead of the Dynamo — even if she was a warlike Virgin — and we would raise a house to God with a passion and a meaning of its own. It turned out that our avenging angel in this case was Walter Netsch.

One day Jim Douglas, by then secretary of air in his own right, called me and said, "I've been on the Hill for five hours before the Senate Finance Committee. One hour and forty-five minutes were spent on next year's entire budget for the air force, about four and a half billion dollars, and the other three and a half hours on your damn chapel. I got it approved just as you fellows have it designed.

As is set forth in 1 Kings 8, in Solomon's prayer at the dedication of the temple:

> And Solomon stood before the altar of the Lord in the presence of all the congregation of Israel and spread forth his hands toward heaven, and he said, "Lord God of Israel, there is no God like

Thee in heaven above or on earth beneath . . . but will God indeed dwell on the earth?

"Behold, the heaven and the heaven of heavens cannot contain Thee, how much less this house that I have builded?"

Congress seemed to feel a good bit like Solomon about the air force chapel. This had called for a certain amount of double talk, as subsequent clippings from the *New York Times* reported. The stakes were high.

Regarding criticism of photographs of a chapel model for the academy, Owings said: "In the development and study of any great religious building, you go through a period of evolution. The published versions showed a model of a chapel in the location we propose to place it . . . this design, which was serious on our part, has found many adherents. However, it is a first step in a long period of evolution which we expect to take full advantage of in the time available—approximately three years."

In the final approved chapel roof system there are five miles of one-and-a-half-inch-thick stained glass strips between the tetrahedrons. I know this because the design was laid out entirely by hand on brown paper, rolled up foot by foot as Walter Netsch drew and colored it in on his living room floor. Showing it to anyone who would look, he carried a model of the chapel around with him everywhere in a little case, with Christmas tree lighting that could be hooked up to the nearest outlet, gaining from each of his partners approval to fight for that chapel's inclusion in the plan. With its seventeen tetrahedrons and five miles of glass besides, unchanged, the original design was finally finished two years after the rest of the academy was in operation. The framework was a lacy skeleton of tubular steel tetrahedrons stacked one on top of the other, reaching a hundred and fifty feet toward the sky — still the most striking example of this relatively new kind of structure in the United States.

It is a rare thing when a chapel can be built with any of the
religious sense about it. The air force chapel is the only building
in existence where three different religions occupy sacred soil
under one roof. We asked the Catholics to accept the crypt, or
lower level, because the Protestants above needed those extra
seventeen-and-a-half feet for a head start to heaven. There was a
Jewish chapel and a nondenominational one for some thirty-
seven other faiths as well.

We walked away from the Air Force Academy job with no
regret. The one million dollars' out-of-pocket loss would be re-
covered. All personnel, from Walter Netsch to the last superintendent on the leaking chapel, were swept away into new fields
on new ventures. An adequate demonstration of the Gothic
Master Builders theory which we had worked toward since Paddington Station, our joint effort under Walter Netsch, John
Merrill, Carroll Tyler, Bill Hartmann and Gordon Bunshaft
had proven that theory was not theory but fact. I remembered
Goodhue and his disillusionment on the state capitol at Lincoln,
Nebraska. Perhaps no work where a democracy is the client can
be great because the client must instill — as the Virgin did in her
cathedrals — a personal spirit. Is there a bright flame in a democracy?

The fruit of the SOM tree, by the laws of pure genetics, had to
have some resemblance to the tree, no matter how exotic that
fruit might be. Like steel filings drawn to a magnet, the result
would be in orderly rows: straight, stiff and rigid. The Air Force
Academy had to be an impersonal derivative of the conscious
and subconscious rule of our order. When we refer philosophi-
cally to humanity, to warmth, we think of soft, pliable surfaces,
of depths, of things that give, have texture. These were things
we couldn't do — yet. But in the evolution of people as well as
architecture, in the development of Walter Netsch or Chuck
Bassett, we can see later on the widening of the vision, the en-
riching of the palette.

When the University of Illinois decided to experiment with their Chicago campus, which had no dormitories and was centered in the heart of an enormous freeway interchange that would bring students to it from every segment of Chicago, Walter Netsch would draw on the rich compost resulting from his work on the Air Force Academy. The result — the university's Circle Campus — is the plastic and concrete yang of the academy's steel and glass yin; the one for twenty-five hundred cadets, the other for twenty-five thousand Chicago youths — richer for the work done at Colorado Springs.

The Air Force Academy was never submitted for an award or a citation for design. When an expansion program was launched, SOM was not invited to submit its qualifications as a possible architect-engineer to do the work; and I was too proud to ask.

The press carried a report of my reaction:

Both Nathaniel Owings and John Merrill (now retired and living in Colorado Springs) of Skidmore, Owings and Merrill were on hand. The academy is having another architect plan and oversee this expansion. Speaking to the press before the Purves Memorial lecture at the academy, Owings deplored not the loss of the contract to another firm but the deviation from the master plan that the academy has allowed. "The deviation from the site plan is disastrous," says Owings. "The government doesn't have the right to destroy the integrity of a national monument."

I am proud of the Air Force Academy design. Free from fad, the whole sits well. People like it. It is a useful institution of learning regardless of the changes to come in educational curricula.

13

The Rockefeller Story

IN ALL THE WORLD, past, present, dead or alive, there is no city to match the high concentration of humanity to be found on the tiny southern tip of Manhattan, where Woolworth and Singer and 40 Wall were raised to the honor of the American ideal, commercialism, to heights rivaling the width of the island on which they are built, mostly replaced now by even taller ones dedicated to the same ideal; where the desire lines of people and things are crossing in the most intense concentrations of any place in the world; where banking, insurance and exchange have centered since 1633; where the crooked, narrow street plan and the outline of the battery of Fort New Amsterdam have remained unchanged and Wall Street is still the address of the first chartered Manhattan bank, and 32 Wall Street is the Stock Exchange, and the Sub-Treasury Building (where Washington took the first oath of office) still stands more or less intact in spite of the 1930 bombing. In these dark, narrow canyons can still be seen the striped pants, the frock coats and the derby hats of the "runners" bearing dispatch boxes with securities from one depository to another.

In this urban Grand Canyon quaint structures like the Aquarium, the Front Street Fish Market and the clear view of the Statue of Liberty are exhibits in a Victorian museum. Narrow Spring Street with its variegated ancient and new granite, limestone and old brick structures still smells of spices and the sea, a bittersweet flavor of a nostalgic past. There are to be found the towering phallic symbols of the 1920s expressing another kind of ethic — right for that period — of stock markets rising and falling. Then, in a kind of prophetic climax today, we find the long vista terminated with the steeple of Trinity Church; and in a last gesture of respect, with the sun setting, shadows fall on the tombstones there at the foot of Broadway and Wall Street.

The idea of this ever-changing Wall Street and its financial district being moved to upper Manhattan seemed to me in the 1950s to be a threat as remote as London's Threadneedle Street moving to Piccadilly. Nothing could disturb this American phenomenon; Wall Street was immortal, a permanent fixture. But suddenly all this did *not* seem impossible. Was it in fact happening? Yes. In the 1950s it became clear that the unthinkable was happening, and was caused by a very simple thing: corporate heads were fleeing to upper Manhattan. The intrusion of Lever House into the serene enclave of the residential upper Fifties on Park Avenue seemed to have started the trend and the big banks were beginning to put their names on mushrooming blockbusters, huge and new.

Beginning in my junior days at York and Sawyer in the 1930s I savored the prospect of wandering whenever I could down through the echoing canyons of Wall Street on Sunday, aware of every footstep in the loneliness of the empty street. I never dreamed then that someday I might be involved in that street's ultimate destiny. In 1955, deep in the problems of building the Air Force Academy in Colorado Springs, where nothing could be further from my mind than Wall Street, Bunshaft reported that the then Chase National Bank had bought a sixty-four-thousand-square-foot parcel of land fronting on Liberty Street and had plans to build a new headquarters building on the site and asked

163

for help. According to Bunshaft, meeting David Rockefeller seemed to be the key, but how? Did I know him? Could I help? The New York partners didn't and couldn't. It just happened that perhaps I could.

Margaret knew David and Peggy Rockefeller, a friendship not to be polluted by trade. Bearing this in mind, I requested a meeting with him at the bank, but this resulted in David's invitation to spend the weekend at their home in Tarrytown, and I determined to win a few Brownie points from Margaret by ignoring vulgar business, no matter what. But every time I steered the conversation to David's beetle collection or Peggy's new wildflower books, David would bring up site considerations or wax enthusiastic about the prospects of such a project. By the time we got to chopping wood and later sampling David's rare vintage wines, the message had come through loud and clear. David wanted us involved; he thought we could help.

He was young — forty-four years old — and his board, of which he was not a member then, was extremely conservative. Chairman Jack McCloy liked only the classic architecture of the past, either Greek or Gothic or Italian Renaissance. David liked our modern architecture and hoped I could win over Jack McCloy from his personal devotion to the classic. McCloy, David said, would insist upon preserving the unity of the architecture of Wall Street.

David was an excellent tutor and by Monday morning an idea began to form. By Tuesday morning, somehow or other, our office had put together an aerial photographic montage, including a clear view of the southern tip of Manhattan. With this mounted on a board five feet by eight feet, we were ready for a meeting at the Chase.

I got off the subway at the Liberty Street station and reached the surface, crossed cluttered sixteen-foot-wide Cedar Street — entirely blocked at the moment for ingress or egress by a trash truck. On axis at the end of the street was a dim view of the

164

spire of the Trinity Church and on my left the handsome Sub-Treasury. All else was latent rubble — excepting, of course, the Chase Bank.

Thinking of the five o'clock rush when the new Chase building, towering forty or fifty or sixty stories above, would debouch twenty thousand scurrying people homeward bound into that narrow network of streets already jammed with existing traffic, I decided to ignore my partners' urgent pleas to hold my fire. To avoid any upsetting or unsettling criticism of the Chase directors' choice of site until we had the job would be, I felt, a form of dishonesty. The board should know that their long, narrow lot would not serve their purpose unless they took heroic steps to change the environment in lower Manhattan, using their building as the catalytic agent. It was no wonder there had been a flight of the downtown banks and insurance companies to the upper Fifties. Park Avenue and Madison Avenue were streets a hundred and sixty feet wide and the sun and air could at least penetrate into the canyons which their proposed skyscraper would create.

I was interested in the job from another point of view. If this project went ahead, a major commitment of this scope, then perhaps by this act, if decisive, the flight from Wall Street to the Fifties could be stopped.

It was clear to me that in addition to planning for a single site, Chase must consider a plan for a superblock; but on an even larger scale, Chase must lay the groundwork for the development of a healthy renaissance of the entire lower Manhattan area. Such was my state of mind before the meeting.

Walter Severinghaus, William S. Brown and I met with the board and, true to David's forecast, John J. McCloy, late United States high commissioner to Germany, expressed his desire for a building design that would conform to the existing character of the Wall Street area. If he would pick one out from the aerial photomural on the wall, I assured him we would be glad to oblige. The tone was lightened by discussions of the futility of the architects' efforts who had labored to produce these terminal architectural masterpieces, the aesthetic quality of which could generally be shared only by the pigeons. Finally a gentle chuckle filtered across the room and there was an unspoken nod of "touché." The architectural style seemed on the way to settlement. Nerves quieted and a more basic question came. What did we think of the site they had purchased? Severinghaus blanched as I took the plunge and said that the site, treated as for a single building, was impossible.

Several directors smiled. Obviously they thought so too. If their present site was the only downtown one available, then it would be far better to move uptown — which, in my opinion, would also be a disaster. It could well be the end of Wall Street if they made such a move. That too, of course, was unthinkable. But there was an opportunity here to take a bold step. Here, clearly, was the making of a city within a city and an answer for Chairman McCloy. We would break with architectural tradition. We had been asked to describe our ideas for a building design and we offered our client a design for a new town within a city. Chairman McCloy wanted his building to conform to the architecture of Wall Street. We recommended a way to change hodgepodge to conform to his wishes, with all the makings for a return (we naively thought) to the New Amsterdam village of yore: Battery Park, the "sea around us," shipping wharves — the old and the quaint. We dreamed of replacing the dreary parts of the area with row housing. We thought that with the Chase Plaza as a nucleus we could provide a balance between man's need to work and his need to live with open space and recreation at hand.

It was a simple plan: establish the overall environment for the entire lower Manhattan area and establish Chase Manhattan headquarters as the central focus. Of course this would involve a change of thinking and require research and planning in a manner to which the Chase board was hitherto unaccustomed. They would require of us: (1) detailed maps and charts prepared showing street patterns, traffic flow and transportation facilities; (2) height, age and obsolescence of adjacent buildings; (3) ownership and value of surrounding real estate.

But why not consider developing a superblock by consolidating the many Chase locations in downtown Manhattan? This could easily be done by closing Cedar Street to vehicular traffic, since the Chase Bank already owned more than half of the adjacent block. Moses could close the street with the flick of a pen. By applying the New York City zoning formula which made Lever House possible, with a tower which could then rise unbroken to infinity as long as not more than one quarter of the block was used, they could have a magnificent sixty-story shaft with three quarters of an acre of space on each floor, freeing a plaza of an area over three times the space occupied by the building. Around this twenty-first-century edition of the Boston Common in downtown Manhattan, Chase could be the visual and acknowledged leader, stabilizing the financial district in perpetuity. On the outside we could put the great structural columns which would support that tower rising eight hundred feet in the air, suggesting, in its visual form and shadows cast, the Gothic image so much desired by McCloy. In the five-year construction period necessary for such a great project, lead time would be provided in which many other structures would be demolished and Chase's example would encourage contemporary architecture to become predominant in the area. Other companies would be bound to follow. The great tower of Chase Manhattan on the Chase Plaza, guarded by the slender Trinity steeple and the classic Sub-Treasury, all together would establish the character of the area for the future.

Then, from the least expected quarter, came the miracle that I had learned to expect. It came from a wiry, vigorous little man named Frederick H. Ecker, chairman of the board of the world's largest life insurance company: the Metropolitan Life Insurance Company. He was then ninety-four years of age and it was rumored that his son would succeed him when he retired. At sixty-five, Frederic W. Ecker was still waiting.

This little man, who knew every detail of the operation of his vast company, spoke up. "Jack," he said, "this design is okay. This is the way *we* build these days."

On our way back in the cab Walter Severinghaus could only shake his head. That afternoon David and Peggy Rockefeller held a celebration. In the years that followed, the Downtown Manhattan Association plans burgeoned and our planned walk-to-work row house program had changed to the World Trade Center with one-hundred-story twin towers. The dream of the intimately scaled downtown village was lost but an armature remained upon which the dynamics of change could grow with health and strength. The environment of Wall Street, at least, was no longer in danger, which is more than can be said of the Stock Exchange as an institution.

My part in the Chase Plaza design was to supply an idea based on land use principles. The combination of a tower and a plaza, and the creation of a central square as a focal point to anchor a natural subdivision of Manhattan was a basic design idea, worth more to me than the chance to design the exterior or interior on any project from the Parthenon to Big John. From that conference with the board of directors of the Chase Manhattan Bank, five long years of work were required under Walter Severinghaus' direction, where difficulties arose daily: increased costs, labor shortages and strikes. The difficulties were met and the problems solved — a job he performed so well that twenty years later, in 1972, he is still the principal SOM architect for Chase.

Between that original meeting and the finished building and plaza there was no measurable change in concept. What had been conceived in forty-eight hours will stand perhaps for as many generations.

The Rockefeller Story — Part 2

When Laurance Rockefeller introduced me to Winthrop he explained to his brother that I collected Rockefellers. This wasn't so. Out of five Rockefellers only four were really clients and only David and Laurance were really active as such.

Laurance was a collector of exotic Shangri-las to be found in rare and beautiful locations where virgin powdered beaches and sparkling oceans met. Sun-drenched beneath emerald skies, Laurance's many-faceted acquisitions were generally fitted out as exquisite resort hotels blending with the environment in such a way as to add to the charm, detracting not at all from the commercial feasibility of the resorts. From ski resorts in New Hampshire to Caneel Bay in the Caribbean, he had many beautiful solutions of which to be proud and might have continued to add to them — without the benefit of SOM — but for chance: a cruise through the Caribbean with David and Peggy, Laurance and Mary, on the ninety-five-foot ketch *Wayfarer*. For two totally dreamlike weeks, all four Rockefellers turned working sailors gave this trip the sense of adventure one rarely finds. We were really at sea, stripped of a good bit of the plastic coatings of convention, artifice and false values one grows; down to jerseys and bare skins, salt water and wind. There was the sea and the hot sun. Every roll of the hull of that windswept sloop undid a few more snarls of the mind and left one free.

People will talk, especially sitting cross-legged in brief shorts at the very cutting edge of the bow. Thus I heard about Laurance's plans for a resort hotel for the big island on the Kona coast of Hawaii, where he had bought into the ownership of the largest ranch in the world; and where, on an absolutely empty coast, he planned to build a complete resort of one hundred to one hundred and fifty rooms. The bare suggestion of another

169

stack of "clifflike rooms overlooking the sea" was noxious to me. Whatever was done, we couldn't do a standard Hilton International Hotel type of thing. Something else had to be done.

It happened that not more than a month before, when I was totally unaware of even the remotest possibility of a trip on the *Wayfarer* or of the subject at hand, we had been sailing the wine-dark sea with Kenneth Van Strum among remote Greek islands where the villages clustered against each central mountain. I found the Greek village and the Indian pueblo of the southwest United States had much in common in concept. I found that the Greek islands' plastic, whitewashed, exciting, voluminous shapes were good — in fact, had been good enough to inspire Le Corbusier for some of his great works such as the Ronchamp chapel.

These universal Greek domed villages were a real discovery and I came back full of ideas. Here at the bow of the *Wayfarer* I poured out my Grecian odyssey and transferred my burgeoning ideas to the big island of Hawaii, where the rain seldom came and they never (they said) had more than four inches of rainfall in a year.

While Laurance was absorbing the full implication of this radical idea I checked it out with partner Chuck Bassett, and Marc Goldstein of our San Francisco office, and, as their minds and hands raced ahead, fabulous eye-catching visions of an entirely new community such as the world had never seen began to take shape. Working with the weather information at hand, Chuck, Marc and I developed the idea of arranging domed suites in bas-relief over the rugged black lava shoreline of Kona, with satellite-attached domes for luxury bathrooms and kitchens and various other facilities; all based on the principle of the Roman Pantheon with an orifice, unglazed, at the top of each dome sending slanting light down upon the sure-to-be-charmed occupants.

On seeing the models, various authorities on resort hotels,

unanimous to a man, damned our design, especially the decentralization of services. They said it wouldn't work. In fact they said everything was wrong; it was outlandish and crazy. Every one of these criticisms strengthened Laurance's determination to go ahead. He was convinced my idea would work, and so was I. Finally, the construction of an actual domed unit was begun on site, where it would fit into the master plan if the project proved out. Our concrete domed structure rose impressively against the sea and was made ready for final test. Furniture and fittings, glasses, china and silver were in place and it was planned that Laurance and I would spend the first night there.

The stage was set. The soft, voluptuous curves of the luminous dome shone softly in the light of the rising moon and the orifice cut the blue sky of the Hawaiian sunset in a graceful oval. Our beds had been turned back, the tray of drinks was ready, when suddenly, out of nowhere, came a black thunderhead, and it began to rain. It rained in a solid mass of tidal proportions. It rained in that orifice in such volume as to suggest Niagara Falls bent inward. Never in the records available to us had that much rain fallen, not even in a five-year period let alone in one evening. Never since the islands were formed by the hot lava rising above the angry seas had such rains come. That night we were drenched. I took to the solace of a series of bottles of Scotch, which didn't help any. To my everlasting gratitude, Laurance didn't fire me on the spot; and, fortunately, Mary had missed the deluge.

So Laurance sent me back to the drawing boards, a thing only a very tolerant and warmly understanding human being would do. From the ashes sprang a truly magnificent Phoenix. In six weeks the same Charles Edward Bassett and Marc Goldstein produced a totally new idea for the Mauna Kea Hotel on the Kona coast on the big island of Hawaii. It was as if some ancient Hawaiian god had found an Olympian fragment of marble the size of a city, had split it from end to end and laid it open, and from this had sprung there on the glistening shore of the South Pacific a fabled series of hanging gardens where human beings, transformed into gods and goddesses, could live. The new design could accommodate a hundred or more couples and there were no corridors to bore them — only terraces and balconies and lanais, courts filled with giant palms a hundred and ten feet tall and plant and bird life; courts leading from one series of quarters to another.

SOM's associate partner, Davis Allen, traveled around the world selecting treasures for the public spaces. He came back with charming, mysterious, glamorous things.

Constructing a luxury palace on such a forbidding and remote spot had its difficulties, but the golf course offered the most obstacles. On that coast there was no level space, no soil, nothing related remotely to a golf course. From this problem Laurance and Robert Trent Jones produced out of air, water and coral an eighteen-hole golf course. The fairways and the greens were first hand-carved out of the lava and spread with ground coral which, energized by chemical fertilizer, plus air and water, miraculously produced a living green felt about the consistency of that found on billiard tables. This emerald green felt-smooth surface, spread out in pools and irregular shapes interspersed with rugged, challenging lava-filled crevices, has made this golf course so beguiling as to make me *almost* want to play golf — but not quite.

How to fill the resort? That problem still existed, one that would give anyone of lesser stature than Laurance pause. Such a resort, regardless of its merit, excellence or beauty, was useless if it were destined to sit there idle and alone. We had to find a clientele. Just getting them there from almost anywhere else involved traveling halfway around the world. But meeting an Olympian problem in an Olympian setting was something Laurance could take in his stride. He would bring the people to the mountain by chartered giant jet.

Margaret and I joined two hundred and forty others at the formal opening, and all two hundred and forty of the richest, most worldly and presumably influential people applauded in relief when our jet plane touched down safely on that tiny air strip, the first to have ever done so. It was one of those "never happened before" things.

A nonstructure, our design refused to be defined, identified. It refused to become a building. One approached each facet of it intrigued and titillated, and jaded senses were unable to catch hold of it. It stimulated the imagination. Time has added to its attraction. The Mauna Kea has succeeded. Reservations are difficult to obtain, a condition dear to the heart of all innkeepers.

Springing from historical proof that in the plaza, town square or commons lies the necessary nucleus of central core cities, the Chase tower standing on the Chase Plaza anchors the downtown business district and financial centers about Wall Street. Nothing else could accomplish this. It also does a lot more. It offers an open sun-swept central area for people to use and to enjoy. To accomplish this is the ultimate purpose of planning.

In my own collection of bright happenings — urban and natural — the Mauna Kea and the Chase Plaza are special. Time and aging improve them. Through an inner quality of renewal, their richness deepens. But equally important are the great friendships formed and tested in this heat of creating shelter in the twentieth-century contemporary idiom.

14

Under the Banyan Tree

Sprawled around a deal table edging on an orange grove under a spreading banyan tree were thirteen disparate men varying widely in shape, posture and age. A score of years had passed since the Paddington pact. Those twenty years had earned for Skid his highly prized financial security, evidenced in this exquisitely appointed estate, and the partners were there in honor of this special occasion of Skid's retirement. The year was 1956.

SOM might be likened to a banyan tree. From spreading branches SOM had put out aerial roots, put down new trunks and strengthened old ones. The thirteen had journeyed to Skid's house in Winter Haven, Florida, on Lake Eloise from their separate fiefdoms across the land. From New York came Brown, Bunshaft, Severinghaus and Cutler — all too fixed in position, too involved with their own activities to have time or energy for real concern with the nationwide firm. Chicago was represented by Hartmann, Merrill, Netsch, Hammond and Kraft; San Francisco by Rodgers and myself; and Portland by Elliot Brown. Like feudal barons, we maintained operations that were essentially autonomous. Held together by that invisible bond of the

Paddington pact, what didn't show was the vital thing: creating a jointly marshaled band of strong associates, some destined to become barons in their own right. Luck and timing, as much as merit, too often seemed to determine the names appearing on the partnership roster — not that this implied error in the selection of those who did make it, but it might be argued that as SOM grew larger and older the firm became more rigid, losing the flexibility needed to handle discussion concerning controversial candidates. As a result, SOM had middle-ground candidates and compromisers together with its peaks of brilliance. But whatever happened, SOM somehow could run itself. The associate partners, participating associates and multidisciplined experts carried the enormous technical load, all held together by that band of partners.

Here at Skid and Eloise's home to hammer out a Magna Charta, those partners began the debate.

Was a Gothic Master Builder society still our prototype?

Were we a secular order or a brotherhood?

Could we still provide renewal through the infusion of young, new blood?

Was our objective still to prove that the only true economic value is beauty?

Were we succeeding in our efforts to merchandise individual creative design and to reach an ever-larger proportion of the still largely untapped markets concerned with habitat?

Were we providing a sufficiently complete architectural in-house, all-discipline service to the client?

Did we make effective use of nonconventional disciplines generally foreign to an architect's practice?

Were we actually furnishing the "complete package," with full management and interior design?

On the table before us lay a *Fortune* magazine containing an article called "The Architects from Skid's Row." The *Fortune* article had spoken of "these remarkable architects who produced the biggest and most advanced buildings in the United States, blurring their identities under the firm name of SOM . . ."

SOM wouldn't say, but the editors made an educated guess as to profits and backlog. Both, they said, were incredible. And all of those echelons, those strata and substrata, those hundreds of men and women were pursuing not only the mysteries of the scientific world but those of the humanities as well. Was it true? Exaggerated?

My personal uneasiness came from a look around. We thirteen didn't look all that good. Were we holding back better men? Did our system crush the sensitive, discourage the brilliant nonconformist, produce gray residues? Clearly the shadows of the years had fallen on each of us — and what of the shadows cast by our buildings upon the land? Were these reflections sloppy sentiment? As Bunshaft was prone to say, hoping for an argument, "We are only interested in design and *money*." Perhaps, but even so we wondered if the world was a little better off because of our efforts. We knew that our contributions had strengthened the aesthetic, the land ethic; and of course our interpretation of the "grand design" met Nietzsche's formula: "In the architectural structure, man's pride, man's triumph over gravitation, man's will to power, assume a visible form."

Just because we, as a group, were somewhat inarticulate didn't mean we didn't feel things deeply. If variety, dissimilarity as evidenced in thirteen totally different sets of genes meant anything then my uneasiness was unwarranted. Whatever our faults, it was not from having been frozen in a mold.

I thought of my own efforts to tease, bully or lead talented young men into the SOM system who could meet the Nietzsche specification. I thought of my first three duly elected partnership candidates and of the filtering process they had endured. One had already died of alcohol, Elliot Brown would die of cancer, and one, waiting until armed with his state architect's license, would move out like a bird leaving the shelter of a nest.

Other candidates went far to ease the anguish of attrition. Taciturn John Barney Rodgers had become the John O. Merrill of the San Francisco office. Lantern-jawed, he tended to drape his cadaverous frame over things in disquietingly unstable positions. Jack had come to me as an appendage of Mies van der Rohe's migration to the United States in which Jack played a part, having studied with him at the Bauhaus in Berlin.

There was soft-spoken landscape architect Fred Kraft, usually found at the piano at three in the morning, a recalcitrant client putty in his hands. In a totally different way from Jack Rodgers, he played backup man. Permanently dependable, meticulous, he created settings that became part of the fabric of Walter Netsch's designs.

And there was William Hartmann, sitting slightly apart under the banyan tree. With the inner glow of polished white jade, marked only by the soft glint of pale blue eyes set like turquoise in a Hopi fetish, his white skin was stretched over a fine skull. Although ten years their junior, he was held by all as one of the original partners.

Bill was tough, compact and valuable. I have never found anyone who would even hazard a guess as to what went on inside of him. When he won the Rotch Traveling Fellowship he chose to travel in Tibet. On an environmental basis, this spot was rejected by his wife-to-be as inappropriate for a honeymoon; and it shook up the parochial Boston Rotch trustees, unaccustomed as they were to approving travel in such alien lands. But Bill bought a yak or two and set off, a lonely stoic on a long journey.

Bill provided the initiative for action and held the reins as well; and SOM, Chicago, continued to support the quality of the city. When her Civic Center Plaza needed a supreme focus, Bill envisioned a monumental sculpture created by Picasso. The chill, white Hartmann fascinated the short, explosive Spanish painter-sculptor, who finally received Bill with open arms.

Picasso's metal sculpture in scale model, safely crated, passed a confused U.S. Customs. Was it scrap iron or fine art? Was it a lady or a horse? Master politician, Mayor Richard Daley, leaning on Bill for all matters aesthetic, was persuaded to approve this strange, distorted cartoon in the new U.S. Steel product, self-rusting Cor-Ten.

Bill guided each step: raised funds, retained the support of the mayor — more at home in the City Hall than with an elegant assemblage of the cultural elite — engaged the Chicago Symphony Orchestra at his own expense while, unguided by Bill, the moiling hippies with peace signs thronged like a scene from Goya's painting of the Spanish Revolution. Was it a celebration, a revolution, or was it peace?

As a light breeze stirred the leaves of the banyan tree I thought of Ambrose Richardson, Walter Netsch, Tallie Maule and a good many other young men who had come our way — gold nuggets of pure design talent discovered at Oak Ridge. Returnees from military service, these youngsters thrilled to the instant results possible there and helped develop unique techniques of research, programming and design. Freed of worrisome client headaches, budgetary squeezes and hemming and hawing, each new project they designed went up fast. Under these conditions their designs proved not only the boys' worth to us, but the system's benefit to them. They were potential partners, yet some had left us. Some didn't like our ideas. Some simply wanted to squeeze SOM dry. Some thought that anonymity was for the birds. Some couldn't stand the hard-driving tactics.

Clearly our style of practice involved the dispensing of a purely American nostrum compounded of idealism, pragmatism, the Master Builder, the Virgin and the Dynamo. Idealism, of course, applies to creative people rather than to things and it was our job to extend the idealism through young designers who could do things that had to be done. No design has only one solution; provided one adheres to the natural laws of balance, scale, proportion and the essential element of time, there are infinite variables. With our fluid system of satellite offices within the SOM complex, we did develop opposing systems of design, any one of which might prove to be better or worse than the other.

Strange — for an architectural group practice assemblage, where were the designers? In New York, who else but Bunshaft? In Chicago, who else but Walter Netsch? In San Francisco? Portland? For the general operation there were Skid, John Merrill, Walter Severinghaus, Bob Cutler, Bill Brown, Bill Hammond, Fred Kraft and, yes, myself — all coordinators of the overall product. And somehow, some way, unexplainable even now, design got done — and well.

Group practice? The Gothic Builders? The individual stars? The Bunshafts and the Netschs, and later the Bassetts and the Grahams? There was a lot more to it than that. There was a steady flow of creativity going on among the collective us, indefinable, sometimes unexplainable, but working extremely well. In fact, the success of this aggregation of creative people, professionals all, was living proof of the workability of miracles.

John O. Merrill, Sr., with his health in jeopardy, would soon retire in Colorado Springs, where his heart was. Louis Skidmore, we all felt, was near the end. But Skid's knack for thinking things out a long time in advance had insured that his planned retirement was phased to mesh. He and Eloise had systematically checked out a series of potential spots like Bermuda and California, and finally filtered out all but a ninety-acre citrus grove on Lake Eloise in Winter Haven, Florida — their choice of climate re-establishing the old principle of each of us doing his own thing. With the humidity such as to give the sensation of walking under water, Eloise and Skid settled into a beautifully designed, pavilion-like house which, of course, was fully air-conditioned, standing on a tree-lined lawn sloping gently toward the lake. The external sheathing of the house, unpainted swamp cedar which in time would turn softly white, caused the impatient local gentry to comment: "The Skidmores are too poor to paint but too proud to whitewash."

That we were there at all under the banyan tree I considered a miracle. The twenty-five-thousand-odd architects in the United States in 1957 were no more inclined to get along than their brothers in general practice had been back in 1936. This basic fact of human perverseness made my pride in the workability of this loosely joined brotherhood justifiable.

Soon to be alone as Senior Partner, I saw SOM as a tree — a tree adding yearly rings, producing fruit widespread among the boughs, the seeds of the ripened fruit scattered by the winds, the resulting fruit somehow identifiable with the name of the parent tree: SOM. How often have I been told of a bright structure in some distant town that gave people pleasure, only to find it the creation of SOM. Renewable, the partnership was proved organic; a wide-spreading organism responding to control from another source: "The thee in me that works behind a veil."

On the night of May 16, 1957, in Washington's Constitution Hall a large assemblage of architects had gathered for the American Institute of Architects' centennial celebration, where Louis Skidmore was to be awarded the institute's gold medal, the highest honor within its power to bestow. Margaret and I were seated at a table near the stage waiting for Skid to make his acceptance speech. He was bowing out in style and we were fearful that he couldn't get through his lines, carefully written out. The institute's citation accompanying the medal made us all feel good: "This high honor is being bestowed on you in recognition of your leadership in the formation and conduct of an outstanding firm which has made a major contribution to the architecture of this nation . . . SOM, whose organizational procedures permit the concentration of architectural talent simultaneously on a number of projects in many parts of the nation and abroad, has added a new dimension to architectural practice."

Too soon after that we were in France when the little postmaster, arms flailing excitedly, waved a pink slip covered with scrambled French and English. The words "la mort," "sorrow" and "Skidmore" gave me a clue. The first word of Skid's death was from architect Bill Wurster and reached me in the tiny village of Tréon just twenty miles outside Chartres. Year: 1962.

When a memorial service was held for Skid, we summed up our thoughts.

Skid was a mystic. "Man is a stream whose source is hidden." Skid could have been, had he chosen, a successful etcher or lithographer. He reveled in the richness of the twelfth century, in the light and shadow, in the mystery. In education he was a Norman and a Gothicist, dedicated to Mont-Saint-Michel and Chartres.

Yet somehow, out of the social, political and economic changes of the early 1930s, Skid emerged as if dedicated by a decision assigned to him at the beginning. He was proudest of the men he had drawn together and called that force "his life's work." Each member of SOM was a thoroughfare through which the stones of the cathedral were passed. So sure was he of what we might call "Man's furthest dream" that he convinced his host of friends — civic leaders, educators and men of business — in the validity of this dream and its achievement.

Louis Skidmore's service to humanity was to show the way toward this idea: a faith in great realities outside our present vision.

For a little while after Skid's death, Eloise and Mother were together again. Mother's last years were good. She was near her daughter. Her mind was dim enough to blur all the weight and worry that had been part and parcel of her life, and she died in her sleep.

The last half dozen years of Skid's life had been spent mostly right there at Lake Eloise, and, when he died, Eloise didn't change anything very much. She had become a consultant to the church on matters artistic and a trustee of the local hospital, and had begun to specialize in bonsai and Japanese flower arrangements. She had become a leader in the garden club and a captive hostess to the myriads of genuine and alleged old friends of Skid's and hers who wanted to "just drop in and hope it isn't too much of an inconvenience."

My sister neither married again nor moved away to a more sophisticated scene nor retired to the life of a recluse. She simply and quietly did her own thing, which I learned after all these years to accept as her right of choice.

BOOK II

Four Miracles

"... and a mouse is miracle enough ..."
WALT WHITMAN

1

Big Sur

GROWING OUT OF ROCK and sea wind like Big Sur itself was our house. Neither a weekend house nor a second home, it was not for shelter or children or community. It wasn't a house at all. Two independent spirits met, crashed into a kind of numbing calm, then saved each other and the marriage by building a kind of shrine to a shared ideal — an ideal on which we have both been working since we moved into Wild Bird in 1957.

No more than our house is a house, is Big Sur a place. It, too, is a frame of mind; or, more precisely, it is a changer of one's point of view about a number of things. Big Sur is the heart of a seventy-two-mile stretch of tilted limestone and granite: cracked, crinkled, fashioned by the lime-colored grasses in permanent pastures, the sage, the yucca, the turpentine plant and manzanita, paintbrush and brodeia, wild strawberries, and cucumber spreading out great swaths of searching vine, growing at an almost visible rate and producing spiny fruit. There is the redolent oil of the bay tree, the Victorian velvet of the redwood, the tanbark and coast maple, white rushing streams, and arid, brittle gorse side by side, tumbled together.

Big Sur scared this black-dirt, prairie Indiana boy, who found the tilted massif pressed against the sea disturbing. Between the mountains and the sea was the third basic element: the weather. There was always the weather, never the same. Each element of the weather on the south coast is visible, with a personality of its own. Mixing sometimes, apart other times, the swirling mist, the cotton fog, the jammed winds roar in, swell to bursting and then explode or quietly dissipate.

Big Sur is a thin edge of crinkled geological detritus backed up by sixty thousand remote acres of wilderness rough enough to provide a last resort for the mountain lion, bobcat and coyote. Until 1900 grizzly bear were not uncommon. Red fox and red-tailed hawk, ringtail cat and blue pigeon, canyon wren and sickle thrashers — and at least once a condor soaring against the Santa Lucia Mountains to the east — all worth learning to live with and worth fighting to save.

South of Big Sur we found Grimes Point, named for English-born Edward Grimes, common seaman, who skipped ship in 1852, settled in Big Sur and married Ellen Post on Christmas Day in 1879. All year round Grimes Creek rushes to the sea through steep redwood and bay tree–lined canyon walls, emerging at the foot of a rocky finger of land six hundred feet long, six hundred feet high and never more than thirty feet wide, arching out and down to the sea. To the south, directly below our point, lies the sheer cliff blocking approach from land to a rock-strewn, sandy beach, thresholding a cloistered bay where rich kelp beds rooted to the ocean floor give shelter to a wide variety of sea life: sea lions, sea otters, cormorants, gulls, sea urchins, periwinkles and abalones. Margaret knew about this place and brought me there. Perched on a great boulder, we picnicked on fresh peaches and warm champagne and immediately commenced to plan, wondering how such a perfect site could be unpre-empted. Perhaps the small, disheveled figure visible across the canyon observing our trespass knew the answer? She did.

Old Mrs. Whiteside dearly loved her canyon and precipitous

acreage, and planned to build her own house there in a hundred years. Sharing a wine jug of stored spring water outside her shanty across the way, we listened to her account of the monumental biblical history of the world which she was writing and which was going well. She had read a thousand books in preparation. The royalties from the finished work and the Hollywood movie rights would do the trick. "People live longer in Big Sur," she explained, "so I have plenty of time." Her obvious optimism toward longevity suggested an alternative. "In this century of literary gestation," I asked, "could we perhaps have a short-term lease — maybe fifty years?"

Mrs. Whiteside's eyes flashed the answer. "You think I'm crazy, don't you?"

"No, just durable."

A few weeks later, in Rome on our wedding trip, we received her acceptance to the offer we had made that day. We thought we had bought a dozen acres at the most, with no more flat space than would be required by a good-sized tent. It proved to be an astonishing forty-six acres of sheer beauty.

Even as recently as 1930 there was no road south of the Post cabin at Big Sur, but the road, when it finally came, brought in services: electricity and telephone. Water had poured from our own spring-fed stream from the beginning of time.

In the Big Sur there were mythical figures. The brothers Walter and Frank Trotter were Paul Bunyans who could lift things the size of small houses with their muscular bare hands, and could build things with huge rocks or redwood flitches; great, strong men who would stop midway in a hammer blow to watch a rosy finch place a straw in the nest on the eave above them. Pragmatic Walter Trotter grabbed the end of a six-hundred-foot piece of one-inch pipe and with a machete walked down the canyon wall while our engineers at SOM were still working out the detailed plans of how to build a road down the steep slopes so that they could install a water system in that supposedly impenetrable canyon. And Frank, Walter's brother, simply lifted the one-and-a-half-horsepower pump in one hand and a bag of cement in the other, and together they installed the pump and pipeline, already running when the plans arrived with directions as to how they should be installed.

There was Henry Miller, whose fame rested over the land like a shrouded mist long after his departure from Big Sur. One Partington Ridge resident — after having to rebuff the inquiry of a bearded face peering in at her in her shower — put up a sign before her house announcing (somewhat tartly, we thought), "Henry Miller? Follow that arrow." This was Louisa Jenkins, who had joined Clare Booth Luce, another Catholic convert turned skin diver, in creating and installing what was probably the first, if not the only, underwater shrine to the Virgin of Guadalupe in the world.

People in Partington Ridge, a thousand feet above us, looked down upon us — as well they might, since their intellectual attainments were as impressive as the nearly impassable, tortuous road leading to their stronghold. Suddenly struck one day with a yearning for an in-depth briefing on Easter Island, I let my desire be known at the mailboxes and a dozen rare and mostly out-of-print volumes covering the subject, not to be found outside of Leipzig or Paris, appeared at our door.

The bus of Ed the mailman was filled with much more than mail. With his special quality of weather prophet, grocery dispenser and carrier of messages if they were downstream, Ed tied the Sur together. Covering the sixty miles from Monterey to Gorda six days each week, in season playing second violin in the symphony, he was the friend of innumerable families whose mailboxes were the only part of their family life he ever saw. When his trip was interrupted by great storms and ensuing landslides, we residents helped carry milk up over the ridges to remote babies while reading the postcards and feeling the envelopes, in place of the mailman. While the slides were cleared away by bulldozers and big shovels we stood around with morbid curiosity, wondering whether cars or people would appear underneath. Once we met Kenneth Rexroth, the poet, slide halted on his way to Esalen for a reading. It soon appeared that the backlog of people clotted up at the slide were his total class, so he gave his performance, providing a theater in the raw which he used comfortably as a setting for his poetry.

The annual Big Sur theatrical required three months of four-nights-a-week rehearsals and only obstetrical cases, seizures or outright death could interfere. Mrs. Chenery, wife of the retired editor in chief of the defunct *Colliers* magazine, played the upright piano; and roles were always worked out for Walter and Frank Trotter, usually dressed as butterflies, requiring limited elocutionary talents. This mixture of Trotter and drama produced an entity unique to the Big Sur.

There was a row of Partington neighbors worth a grant for anthropology research. Giles Healy had, after graduating from Yale, discovered some temple murals in Yucatán, which he lectured on for twenty years. He also owned one of the last remaining (there were four) custom-built, 1903 Hispano Suizas, which he claimed to have purchased from the butler of the Duke of Alba. Elegant and Victorian, with the body of a teak boat hull, great brass headlights, mudguards shaped like the wings of a huge black butterfly and the back seat cut off from the front by thick plate glass, this wonder might be seen by any hippie who happened to be wandering through, standing under Healy's "porte-cochère" — a tarpaper shed. I remember arranging for Laurance Rockefeller's aide, Aldy Boyer, an avid car collector, to meet Healy. As the two negotiated in vain I watched while two of Healy's goats placidly consumed the stuffing from the fading splendor of the upholstered seats.

Harvard graduate Sandy Justice, bearded mountain man extraordinary, ran a kind of halfway house hideout for a miscellaneous group on his d'Angoula place. Living just below him was another Harvard man, Nicholas Roosevelt, one of the vintage *New York Times* editorial writers, author and ex-minister to Hungary. "Nobody here is average," he wrote of Big Sur. "We have a lumberjack who quotes Shakespeare. We have a garbage man who creates out of trash. We don't think it's so much a matter of who can afford to live here, but of who is capable of it."

Nowadays we like to think about the people who worked on the house, too, and almost everybody in Big Sur did. The grandson of the railroad tycoon, Sam Hopkins, rolled a wheelbarrow; Buzz Brown, whose twenty-foot metal sculpture of Christ, categorized as a billboard by the Big Sur master plan advisory board, was the center of controversy; Don McQueen, who built a trimiran outside the post office where his mother served as postmistress, worked on our wiring problems, often short-circuited by heavy discussions. Don was the unelected mayor of Big Sur.

Every step of the way in building our house was special, from the scale model of the site with every rock in place, through architect Mark Mills' sensitive handling of the working drawings, to the choice of the redwood timbers from the old Torre Canyon bridge. Boulders garnered from the road after each storm, some a soft celedon shade, were fashioned into sculpture turned fireplaces and chimneys by Gordon Newell, a talented worker with stone, sculptor turned mason. Construction chief George Whitcomb, like the captain of an old-fashioned four-masted windjammer, and his crew were busy there; and when the heavy fogs swirled over that motley aggregation — bare to the waist, tattooed arms and chests — and the men moved across the trestled scaffolding, pirates and a boarding came to mind.

After the house was finished, that trestled scaffolding was converted into Margaret's off-limits painting and drawing studio steeply perched against the cliff below our bay-shaded terrace, with a panoramic view to the sea. This isolated kind of log cabin fitted her inclinations and her background. She could work here, uninterrupted, on painting, drawing, collage.

Margaret's forebears, of the independent stock of Ponds and Wentworths, had been Massachusetts ministers, carriage makers and even governors, through successive generations for several hundred years. At eighty-nine, her mother still judged female friends on a graduated scale where her alma mater, Smith College, was rated number one. And in the male line, the heirloom monadnock-headed cane from Dartmouth and a mug of pewter and crystal symbolized her father. He was closely connected with Mills College, Margaret's guide to Echo Lake, Yosemite and the High Sierras, and cofounder of the California Save-the-Redwoods League, which had been a mere forerunner to the wider horizons in conservation still to come. But her father had provided the stones with which to build this structure.

In Margaret, born in Berkeley, California, a graduate of Mills College and Radcliffe, I found many diverse interests to meet my own and to hold the two of us together. Soon after we moved into Wild Bird I objected to her absence in the isolation of her log studio when she painted and she promptly redirected her energies to stitchery collage, which she could do in the big room while I read Proust aloud. The size of the O in her monogrammed "MOW" varied depending on the intensity of her feelings toward me at the moment.

From a distance our house in Big Sur is almost invisible, reflecting the natural forms of the bay trees around it. From the inside there is a sense of space with changing light and shadow, rather than recognizable house forms. In our living space I felt the need for a harpsichord. I could see Margaret's white shoulders in the flickering candlelight, long slender fingers (after a few easy lessons) hovering over the keys. So I attempted to order a harpsichord, only to find that harpsichords were then rare and elusive instruments fashioned by a few old-world craftsmen, mostly deceased. After chasing ghosts over western Europe for a while I let my frustration be known to the ever-present mail gatherers waiting for Ed at the Partington post boxes, and the treasure of the century in harpsichords, just on the market, appeared two miles down the road. Signed by Hugh Gough in London in 1953, it was just for us, we knew. When the strings snapped, as they often did on the fragile instrument, renowned harpsichordists like Margaret Fabrizio simply rearranged their repertoire to match the ones still operating. Or Ansel Adams would pour another glass of wine and improvise around the missing chords.

The wide, cool balm of the Big Sur coast and Margaret's spectrum of stitchery and wildlife offered open space and calm beauty. On a quiet walk toward the sea along the coastlands one fall afternoon she spotted a coiled rattler close up. Only a few minutes later on the same walk a butterfly touched me lightly on the cheek and I jumped, Margaret said, a foot. Like the moonwalker's first step on the moon, that foot was a long one. Today, at my insistence, a coiled rattler on our path is safe from harm; gently captured, removed and set free in the canyon below.

A new and unexpected force polarized our joint concerns and directed them to the rock-covered, sandy beach below. From our porch we could look down on the large herd of sea lions which basked in the sun and raised their young on the adjoining rocks of that inaccessible beach. On the large boulder closest to our point of view, towering above all the others, was an enormous white male who apparently had ruled the harem there for many years. In this, our first spring, five females with their young nursing at their sides surrounded this old bull. It was an absorbing unit of life to observe and we watched it, not daily, but hourly. Then suddenly, tragedy struck.

As Margaret wrote later in a letter to the Monterey *Herald* editor:

On Saturday, June 5, at five P.M. a car stopped on the coast highway and three shots shook the air, followed by a sudden silence among the sea lions. We watched with horror as the great white sea lion plunged off the rock and rolled into the waters where a cloud of red blood encircled the body. His end was violent as he dove and turned in the waves, but his life poured out. His handsome white coat became vermilion as he battled against a force he had no power to check. In a few minutes his strength was gone and he sank under the red stain on the water. We had watched a king die. The car, the man and his gun moved on. I was strongly moved by this incidental, needless murder, without reason, by a man who had extinguished a life quite obviously more noble than his own.

Following the extinguishing of that life — the firing of those shots — we soon discovered that all the three hundred sea lions below our house, their bark and laugh continuously making their presence known, were in jeopardy. As a species they had managed to incur the wrath of the salmon-fishing industry in the far northern part of the state. Their dire straits were disclosed by sheer chance: a two-inch notice of the passage of a bill before the state Senate designed to kill 75 per cent of the total sea lion population along the California coast. To quiet Margaret's tears at this exposure to outside attack, I counseled a good night's sleep and action in the morning.

In the morning Margaret hired a professional legislative lobbyist to stop the bill in the Assembly. He launched research to see if the sea lions really did eat the salmon as the fishermen claimed. Not so — the culprits were mostly trash fish, including the dreaded lamprey eel, the real curse to these fishermen. The actions that followed effectively stopped this initial thrust by outside forces against the security of the sea lion.

But man and his gun still stalked our shores, and one smirking hunter, posing triumphantly with gun in hand, his foot on the prostrate form of a beautiful mountain lion near our house, really roused Margaret. For this act of bravery — shooting a lion treed by a dog — the reward was sixty dollars' bounty from the state for a female lion and fifty dollars more from Monterey County. A year later an astounded California legislature discovered that somehow or other a bill had been steered through cattlemen, sheepmen, sportsmen lobbies and their own august bodies as well, which removed the bounty from the mountain lion for a four-year period. A time limit is always a face-saving device for beleaguered legislators. The Audubon Society, in a joint ceremony also honoring Rachel Carson, gave national recognition to what had been, to date, Margaret's local efforts: "Artistic, articulate citizen of the Golden State, a conservationist to whom the word means action . . ."

When the four years were up there was a second time around; and then began a quiet, moving bit of intense theater: the soft noiseless tread of the mountain lion and his reprieve from certain extinction, where most of the action was off-stage — an open battle between the powerful forces of the target gun disguised behind the benign-sounding name of the National Wildlife Federation and supported by the California Department of Fish and Game. Margaret, depending on scientifically researched data, with the aid of qualified witnesses and a broad-based vocal citizens' pressure group to drive the issues home, proceeded to enlist, rehearse and use techniques to move the legislation toward the goal of protecting the cougar, resulting in another four-year moratorium on hunting the lion. But the signing of this bill into law was only one of the diverse steps involved in living in Big Sur.

We have a "raggedy man" who does odd jobs around our place. Big, raw-boned, a gold ring in one ear and his hair in a bun at the back of his head, he appears and does a little work and disappears again into the hills. One night quite late he came, holding in his awkward hands a tiny, furry, muddy ball: an owl, all head, beak, claws and eyes. With those eyes, those golden disks, Genesis began to have some real meaning for me:

194

And the earth was without form, and void, and darkness was upon the face of the deep, and God said, "Let there be light," and there was light. And God saw the light, that it was good, and God divided the light from the darkness.

Fallen from a nest we never found, that tiny owl opened up for us an education in optics, stored memory, and in the occult and the obscure, generalized under the term "cybernetics." That owl confirmed my sure knowledge that science will never take the place of witchcraft. Watching the automatic expansion and contraction of the pupil as flat disks of yellow responded in range and scope to the light or lack of it, grew immense from pinpoints of fire as the light waned, I began to sense a technical competence in optics and the rest that was marvelous to behold. It is little wonder that a measure of daguerreotype from early photography would be half or a quarter of an owl's eye. To know that the little owl's light meter was installed in that furry ball a million or more years ago was a relief to me. It rather reduced the concern I had over man's ignorance and crude bungling in such things. The owl's equipment was an endowment, shared by us if we could but have the humility to accept it. In those yellow disks, as in the owl's thick ankles seemingly encased in heavy socks, fashioned with powerful, hand-like claws directed by the built-in computer, I read an awesome print-out from the same dim past — instructions which included details of the original techniques of search-and-destroy needed for survival.

This tiny fledgling owl had everything that IBM and GE could build in the way of computer control equipment, plus what they could never have: the power of renewal, of growth, and reproduction in its own image. But even while I stood in awe and wonder at the glory of the owl, I cast a tragic shadow of extinction. Man, by his own gloved hand, could snuff out this life without reason, justification or excuse.

What a difference between us, my owl and me. But the owl had the final determining advantage. I believed in owls, and he was the incarnation of them all down through the ages for me; therefore, I worshiped him. It would soon be my duty to release this wild thing because captivity would destroy its greatest heritage. But until released, the owl stared unflinchingly, unimpressed with double talk, his sole concern a raw, bony chicken neck one-quarter his size, inhaled in one swish. And how he eyed that mouse as it scurried by, contemplating an act of predation which would have to wait till either he was free or my wife was away.

The owl reaffirms my belief that "there exists in nature in myriad activity a psychic element, the essential nature of which is still hidden from us"; that the greatest mysteries are in the nonscientific, the worshiper of the earth goddess; that everything we have and use, and even are, comes from a few sticks and stones mixed with a little water and warmed by a little sun.

The Big Sur coast is famous for its wide expanse of sky, an invitation for UFOs. One often had an unsettled feeling, as if something unexpected was likely to happen, especially on stormy nights. On such a night one late November, rain was coming *up* in torrents as the wind howled off our point. Not a creature was stirring; only the big plate-glass windowpanes bowed. We were having our lamb "pink" because the electricity was off. The candles guttered as we animatedly talked of the "Form Givers" show at the New York Museum of Modern Art and Buckminster Fuller when a knocking loud enough to be heard above the storm interrupted us. There, standing neatly in a pool of water, was Bucky Fuller, come as if on a magic doormat straight out of the inky blackness into the rosy glow of our oak fire. I marveled at his gnomelike presence, his slight five-foot frame, his black alpaca suit chosen from the wardrobe of "the least conspicuous person alive: a third assistant bank teller." His polished,

196

hairless, bullet head, his myopic gaze through double-thick rim-less glasses, made it seem likely that he had just stepped from a flying saucer parked, no doubt, outside. It developed that Margaret had recently sent word to him of sighting an exceptional flying saucer and he had come for details.

Before long the house sheltered a wedding. Quite independent of my long friendship with Adlai Stevenson, my daughter Natalie met John Fell Stevenson, the youngest son, during the 1956 Democratic Convention in Chicago, when Adlai was nominated for the second time as the Democratic candidate for President. The ensuing pursuit cut short my daughter's formal education, but ended as such pursuits sometimes do with a wedding ceremony, this one under the arch of bay trees beside the tiny pool of water at Wild Bird, presided over by the gulls patrolling above and the sea lions calling below. It seemed as much an occasion for a festival in honor of the father of the groom as a celebration of the young people taking their wedding vows. Adlai's natural charm and warmth, along with the state and the nation's affection for a good loser, plus his seemingly unlimited number of personal friends, turned the pre- and post-nuptial logistics into a veritable nightmare. Actually, the space limitations of Wild Bird proved fortunate, justifying the tiny, prewedding luncheon that Margaret was able to give — which was not, however, without facets of interest, considering the inclusion of Emily and the ex-Mrs. Stevenson. The pressures for a large reception were satisfied by commandeering the nearby Nepenthe restaurant; and as Natalie and John Fell cut, and toppled, the four-tiered wedding cake and Adlai shook hundreds of hands, Emily, Margaret and I watched and savored the deep power of attraction of this man.

In the late 1920s Adlai had occasionally escorted Emily Otis to her debutante parties. One was a costume affair in which she especially remembered Adlai, dressed as an infant, sliding down a shoot-the-shoots with a large ruffled bonnet tied under the chin of his long, domed head.

With this kind of background inherited from Emily, my relations with Adlai from the start were informal. In the war years, having missed the first and determined to get into the second, I sought out Adlai, then special adviser to Secretary of the Navy Knox, and asked him how I could get into a uniform. "You're stuck with Oak Ridge," he told me a month later. "The army says they haven't got a uniform for that job."

In 1950, embarking for Japan to start the Okinawa job, I was armed with two letters signed by Governor Adlai Stevenson of Illinois: one "To Whom It May Concern" and the other one to General MacArthur. During Adlai's years as governor of Illinois we worked together to weed out the graft prevalent in the state's construction industry.

Adlai sometimes stayed with us overnight at Wild Bird. Once, upon his return from the Los Angeles Democratic Convention and the nomination of Kennedy and Johnson, he and Sissy Patterson stopped by. We picnicked on the ridge high above our house and I still have that pleasant memory of Adlai lying on his stomach playing with Natalie and John Fell's baby son, chewing on the end of a grass stem and simultaneously giving us the latest word on whether or not Red China should be admitted to the United Nations.

By 1964 Adlai was tired, disappointed and defeated. He had been almost certain — but not quite — that he could never have been the one. But that was his time, I think. He could have outdrawn Kennedy. Or, if President Kennedy had made Adlai secretary of state, there would have been a world basis for settlement, and Vietnam might never have gotten out of hand. It is hard not to consider what might have been. He was trampled upon, used, lied to; but with his invincible spirit he unflinchingly upheld both the honor of the United States and the United Nations until, in London, he died on duty with his boots on.

While Margaret and I could in our own way, collectively or separately, explore the deep, mysterious and ever-demanding areas of life we had only touched on before, one thing was very wrong for me. I had turned into an alcoholic and our bit of Eden was too often for both of us a glimpse of hell. There had been problems of winding down, all right. I was busy paving my own particular brand of hell with the finest available solid granite intentions. An especially unworkable intention involved sporadic dips into the philosophy of Alcoholics Anonymous. I remained in motion, galloping my pony express, exhilarated by an illusory sense of accomplishment, supported by my alcoholic crutch.

In November 1963, that alcoholic crutch collapsed and crashed to the ground, and I went with it. After that it was a new and strange sensation to find myself dependent, being done for instead of doing to. Loved ones all silently banded together helping — an ineffable sensation. Beside my hospital bed Margaret's doctor explained to me what the percentages were in favor of the various known means of the cure of alcoholism: about 5 per cent medical, 10 per cent Alcoholics Anonymous and less by the clergy. The brightest hope was Raleigh Hills Hospital in Portland, Oregon, where better than 65 per cent were cured. There, by association, I learned to revolt against the taste, sight and smell of all forms of alcoholic drink. A tissue release from alcohol followed. There was a sense of exaltation in arriving home on my birthday, February 5, 1964. Having taken the first big step, I then knew that, barring the accidental swallowing of alcohol, there should be no concern on that score ever again.

The Raleigh Hills treatment was not just a matter of relieving tissue demand. It helped me to free my mind for other things and I left behind the climate of total commitment to SOM, to which I had subordinated family and children. Now, a bit late, I could make a new try at family and children, walk into a new life with a new home, new energy and new interest in making a personal contribution in response to a new awareness of the social planning issues. And find *time* — and a lot of it — *time* to discover *nature*.

2

The Coast Road

As a boy I had been told of "the midnight ride of Paul Revere" and how, when the British were coming, he was to watch for the lantern's light:

> One if by land, and two if by sea;
> And I on the opposite shore will be,
> Ready to ride . . .

Our problem on the Big Sur coast was more complicated. The seventy-two-mile ribbon of land was matched by an equal seventy-two miles of sea and would require all lanterns up at once.

As an architect I naturally thought of people and land use. As a conservationist, Margaret naturally thought of the wild mammals of the land and sea other than man. Diversity was the order of the day and attack came from both land and sea.

I had been raised on stories of pioneer families crouched behind the log walls of their cabins while the arrows of hostile Indians whistled through the cracks, narrowly missing the sleeping infant in the cradle rocked by the foot of the fearless mother as she loaded the flintlocks. Or else the plot would hinge on the

lonely widow and the brutal cattle baron unconscionably pushing her around for not only her virtue but for the water hole
available only on her land. Pioneers, squatters, intrepid migrants
facing west always had implacable enemies and always came out
on top.

Things were not so different now. The great coastal sweep of
the Big Sur country, where mountains meet the sea in breathtaking grandeur, had built-in enemies threatening to invade and
ravage. This time they were highwaymen, and just as bad as
those who held up the old stagecoaches a hundred years ago. Our
highwaymen chose Dolan Creek as the site of their first en-
gagement. Dolan Creek bridge, delicate, almost fragile in aspect,
spanned with a large braced timber arch a deep, lush ravine and
was a beautiful piece of timber-craft.

The Highway Department suddenly announced that they
were going to tear down that bridge and fill that canyon with
rock and dirt. Margaret and I knew we were in for trouble. Our
Big Sur neighbor and seasoned ex-editor, Nicholas Roosevelt,
advised that we should fight. Nick fired the first shot. Headlined
on page one in the local press, in purple prose he thundered:

A gigantic fill, eight hundred feet wide, five hundred feet long and
a hundred and twenty-five feet high will replace one of the most
beautiful bridges on the coast highway over Dolan Creek south of
Big Sur. If the present plan of the Division of Highways is carried
out, three quarters of a million cubic yards of dirt will be gouged
out of a nearby mountain and the spectacular coast highway will
be defaced by a new and hideous scar. The planning for this bit of
bureaucratic vandalism was carried out in secret.

And Margaret wasn't just rocking the cradle and loading the
flintlock for others. Her letter to the Monterey *Peninsula
Herald* when the Division of Highways proposed widening our
coast road to freeway standards ran thus:

Last week my husband and I returned from touring Italy along its legendary coast where every curve of the road is a slowly turning page of a volume of world-famous views. Built when the swing of the pendulum was leisurely, the cars today drive slowly and we savor and memorize this glorious meeting of the mountains with the sea. We derived a prideful pleasure, knowing that our own Big Sur coast was its close equal. Upon returning home we were shocked to hear the proposed state freeway system included our coast road as a future freeway. A freeway is a method of carrying as much traffic as possible in the shortest time to its destination, while a scenic road is a pleasure to drive where the tempo is careful and slow, the curves — be they canyons or rocky headlands — still an experience; and a coast, I might add, is a delicate meeting of land and sea. I hope our coast road can respect this quality and remain a scenic road rather than a freeway.

The nation's press followed us closely, but the "home-owned" Monterey *Peninsula Herald* was indispensable, reliable and fearless. Colonel Allen Griffin, as owner-editor-publisher, made all the difference. He launched special Saturday supplements to cover special phases of the plan. His editorial column was always open to us. Ruddy-faced, aristocratic Colonel Griffin, a broadgauged man, was an unlikely combination of an activist liberal and a reactionary. While thundering for enlightened planning for land use on the one hand, he lived in the well-planned compound of Pebble Beach, a community detached from relevancy. Without his journalistic backing the South Coast Plan would never have succeeded.

Ecology, environment, the biota — all were beginning to carry some weight and draw something besides blank stares from the citizen-Californian. In 1961, still at the beginning of things, a sense of timing brought enlightened Democratic state Senator Fred Farr into the conservation field for a bigger share of the action. It was he who pressured Margaret's appointment by Governor Brown to the California State Park Commission.

Gently Fred Farr, Margaret and I began the education of the nervous California state and county political incumbents who were still uncertain as to how important the issues of conservation might become. As a part of this process, armed with my usual five-foot square of aerial photography — this time a helicopter shot of Dolan Creek gorge with overlays showing the devastation if filled and the beauty of the bridge without — I showed the governor the pictures and asked him about his state planning office. In response to my inquiry he found that no such thing existed within the state. This shocked him. How could California, with a hundred million acres, provide planning guidance without one? How could a seven-hundred-man, four-billion-dollar-a-year, *single purpose* State Highway Division be controlled when there was no overall master plan to guide them? He didn't know and asked for suggestions. We made them. At this point — certainly not by coincidence — the California State Division ruled that not only Dolan Creek bridge but all other bridges would be retained in all of the canyons, and fill was banned forever. Highway One was to remain two-lane. The legal climate was changing. County legal counsel, necessarily limited in their national point of view, absorbed new concepts of conservation with rare avidity from SOM attorneys, who maintained an admirable anonymity.

We reconvened the town meeting. The Harlan County (Kentucky) Harlans, land-poor, third-generation American Gothic pioneers, provided chocolate and angel food cake and steaming coffee, and demanded the right to be left alone. Scorning controls at any level of government, the Harlans left one such meeting, collided their truck with another, demolishing both. Hospitalized, without insurance, they began to wonder about the individual freedom they cherished.

The very rich landowners did the same thing, demanding the right without bringing the cake. Everyone claimed the right to do with their land as they damn pleased — a God-given American heritage, they said. Fortunately, the middle-income people were in the majority and many of them understood that such freedom, unilaterally exercised, ended by definition in chaos.

Planning imposes uneven restraints, requiring disciplines and sacrifices from some, granting unearned benefits to others, and therefore involves battles of sorts. These conflicts between land and people, rich and poor, commercial and residential, recreationists and urbanists, service interests of those who ran the motels and filling stations and restaurants and those who used them, the involved citizens who had moved down to Big Sur for peace and quiet, were resolved on only one point: they wanted to be left alone, free to do each as they saw fit.

That a rumored national parkway would be superimposed upon their coast was the people's greatest fear, and this fear unified the people scattered over the area through a coalition born of the threat. Such a heterogeneous group needed a corpus for action, money and leadership. Widely varying in income, uniformly proud, Big Sur people would not accept subsidies. How to provide the money and design talent needed? We must have a master plan. Margaret and I, through SOM, arranged that half of the expense would be donated and the county would find the balance. Thus the first classic step in any community planning — seed money — was provided.

For the research-minded there are some twelve feet of files on hand, but in brief this is the Coast Plan we reached for:

To preserve the natural landscape of the south coast for future generations; to control future growth so it will harmonize with the scenic setting; to accomplish these controls without turning over the land to a government agency; to retain Highway One as a two-lane scenic road; to establish density requirements of one house per ten acres of land along the shore and highway, and one house in twenty acres a certain distance east of the highway; to encourage landowners to deed to the public or give scenic easement to land along the shore and highway; to encourage the building of houses and commercial developments in clusters with retention of open spaces between clusters; to expand Big Sur Park to concentrate recreation facilities in the park rather than fragmenting recreational areas up and down the coast to keep the overall density of the area as low as possible, and to accept established communities as they stand.

With water in short supply, no industry for jobs and a narrow road for access to the area, the place could be kept relatively undisturbed not only for the residents but also for posterity. We enjoyed the doubtful stimulus of controversy. For two years final showdowns seemed to come about once a month.

Monterey *Peninsula Herald* headline: COAST PLAN WITHSTANDS BOMBING

The Owings plan was bombed by opposition for the greater part of five hours in the supervisor's chambers in Salinas and, despite the buffeting, at the end of the day Owings stood like Foch at the Marne and said the situation was excellent. In a packed chamber, Owings was called a "buzzard." The plan was branded as unconstitutional. One real estate woman said she felt "dashed that we are exposed to a super-race of people who alone are endowed with the qualifications to build on the coast." When the hearing was finally gaveled to a close, Owings was asked how he felt. "I am encouraged," he said. "We're on our way. I expected this turnout. Opponents always come in greater numbers than those who are in favor of something." Mary Koester, dramatic in the classic manner, denied that she was a "hired gun." She proved the darling of the opposition, along with short, spunky Barbara Brazil, member of the early Big Sur family, who wore dungarees and a sweater. She lacked articulation but really turned the squirrel gun on Owings. Miss Brazil wanted Big Sur country left as it was but her impromptu brass was returned by bearded Howard Welch, the garbage collector. "Shut up so I can hear!" Don Bloom called the entire procedure a "brainwashing." Owings called the meeting very beneficial. "We heard many expressions which we hadn't heard before."

206

It took three years to get our proposal for land use approved and enacted into Monterey County law when the Board of Supervisors approved the plan six for, to one against — great step, giving me renewed confidence in the planning process and in what might be expected at a modest county level of political sophistication without state or federal intervention. We had held good cards: a worthy objective, a strong plan, and solid, seasoned, middle-class people to support it.

While the land use ethic for people on the south coast was going pretty well, the distress signals began to run up along the coast for an interest in what Wallace Stegner called "all the little wild things," and a bloody drama began between two segments of that chain of life: the southern sea otter and the abalone, with sea urchin and kelp, interrelated and balanced but brought into conflict through overharvesting by the commercial abalone industry.

Along the California coast some one million sea otters had been reduced to near extinction by the turn of the century. However, in 1938 they were once again sighted along the Monterey coast. When they were declared an "endangered species," a one-hundred-mile refuge was established to guard them, and by 1970 the population count had reached one thousand and forty.

At this point a dying commercial abalone industry claimed the sea otter as the culprit. To placate the industry a legislative bill was introduced providing that "sea otters could be taken outside the California Sea Otter Refuge" if there had been a public hearing before the Fish and Game Commission. Since the word "taken" could imply "kill," and one third of the total southern sea otter population was outside the refuge as the bill was introduced, action was needed to defend the sea otter by defeating the bill.

To say that Margaret became involved would be an understatement. She created what can only be termed an institution: the "Friends of the Sea Otter," with an advisory board including Dr. James Madison, surgeon, but more importantly scuba diver and underwater photographer, William Bryan, Salinas lawyer, but again specializing in otter photography; a full-time research person in Judson Vandevere; and added to this, a number of distinguished professional marine scientists. They built up the facts, exposed the fallacies and settled the issues which became in essence a judgment of values. The membership grew out of a single mailing of some two hundred and fifty personal letters into an organization of over twenty-five hundred. Even people living in landlocked Kansas cared very much about sea otters. This was one of the most successful direct mail campaigns ever launched and the organization was born full-blown.

The bill in the state Senate was heard and withdrawn. With this victory one more step had been taken to defend the diverse web of life inherent in the land use and marine resources along the Big Sur coast. A kind of rural advocate planning system evolved through the participation of ordinary people in mass rallies, mass sit-ins, mass letter writings and mass demonstrations. People are instinctively wise, we learned, given an honest definition of the problem and an opportunity to vote. Advocate planning involves conflict and differences of opinion, and such procedures do not make friends. We found most people distrustful and suspicious in the beginning; and then slowly, through the process of town meetings and counseling of individual families, their criticism and suspicion melted and turned into respect, confidence and even love. Today the people of the Big Sur will defend their plan on both land and sea with their lives.

In 1968 Mrs. Lyndon B. Johnson decided to honor our scenic coast concept and give it national recognition through a formal dedication. Ceremonies were planned, and Stewart Udall, Fred Farr and Governor Brown would assist. Lady Bird would dedicate on this occasion a specially prepared bronze plaque mounted on a giant boulder and engraved with Robinson Jeffers' words.

> I, gazing at the boundaries of granite and spray, the established sea marks, felt behind me mountains and plain, the immense breadth of the continent, before me the mass and double stretch of water.

We did wonder, though, if this introduction of national politicking into our hitherto peaceful existence was worth it. We knew that the sudden recognition of the beauty of this two-lane, forty-year-old unimproved road was motivated less from a desire to dispense aesthetic justice than from the desperate political situation the governor and our state senator found themselves in before the coming election. They were in trouble.

Still, national recognition would help local and state politicians who revered publicity. As vice chairman of the Scenic Roads Commission of the State of California, I had worked to steer through a reluctant Highway Commission a five-thousand-mile potential system of incredibly beautiful, fragile, easily saved and easily ruined back country California roads. But the event was nerve-shattering. We were inundated by people who were "advancing" Mrs. Lyndon B. Johnson's party for the dedication of Highway One. Advancing involved a dry run — the rehearsing of the planned trip by a stand-in. Distances were judged, timing calibrated, photographic stances anticipated and time allotted for preplanned "spur-of-the-moment candid camera shots." Nooks and crannies were searched and possible sniper perches blocked off. Change upon change in plans was made.

It was clear that the gods were not pleased when, as Margaret was personally directing the placement of the giant ten-ton granite boulder she had selected from our own Grimes Canyon, the crane boom buckled, cables snapped and the boulder crashed with ground-shattering impact close to her feet.

Not only the gods, but a good bit of young America — well represented in Big Sur — were displeased with LBJ and the Vietnam war; and even Lady Bird, we feared, might have to bear the brunt. We expected trouble and, for safety's sake, had reserved the final placing of the plaque on the boulder until the morning of the dedication. At sunrise our fears were confirmed. Summoned to the scene, we found the rock smeared in its entirety with purple paint. But Gordon Newel and a sandblasting machine cleaned the boulder, and deep-set bolts secured the bronze plaque in place.

Big Sur's garbage collector, Howard Welch, whose engraved calling card carries "Your Trash Is My Treasure" as its motto, was the security guard on our gate during the long hours of the vigil before and after Lady Bird's visit to Wild Bird. Tall, handsome, neatly bearded, he knew everyone on the coast and his presence would put off anyone he didn't.

Howard had ethics and applied them rigidly to his profession. His routine included, before disposing of a collection of trash, the sorting out of objects of value that he thought might interest others. These objects, which one day happened to include a pair of beautiful pink ostrich plumes, were laid out on the canyon wall for anyone to view, and claim if desired. Upon seeing these plumes, a theater director — somewhat in awe — asked Howard where he found such treasures. Howard drew himself up and pronounced this code: "I never disclose the names of my clients." With credentials such as these, there was no question that we had on hand the combined equivalent of the F.B.I. and the Secret Service.

Following the dedication and Lady Bird's stop with her entourage at our house, Howard was so moved by his experience that he wrote it up:

Nat handed me a ring of keys and I sorted out the small, intricately shaped one to the magic gate, turned it lightly. It was as touchy as the space bar on an electric typewriter and the big gates began to swing closed before I realized that they were open. Admiring the perfectly lovely day and the sweeping scenery, I moseyed up to the mailbox, took off my coat, rolled up my shirt-sleeves. Ed, the mailman, drove up. I asked Ed if he had had any trouble getting through Bixby. "Hell, no," Ed answered with great dignity. "There's a mob of people there but I sailed right on. After all, I'm federal too, you know. Lady Bird isn't going to hold up the mail."

Suddenly an earsplitting shot rang out from a high promontory of bushy land. It was the piercing snap of a long-range rifle. I glanced up the mountain from where the shot sounded and spotted two men in blue shirts carrying rifles. I thought, "Holy Mother of Christ, what a time for deer hunters!" Or were they deer hunters?

I didn't want to throw a panic in the proceedings to the north so I personally decided to intervene. I called up to the men, "What the hell are you guys doing there?" "We're just hunting deer," they shouted in reply. "You know the President's wife is due along here any minute?" "Yeah. We decided not to hunt much till she went by."

Suddenly three trim, athletic-looking young men in dark business suits drove up — clean shaven and crew cut. Their eyes had a steely gray look. The leader said, "We're Secret Service." As one of them went up the hill to check the hunters, the rest started down the hill. "No you don't!" I said. "I want to see your credentials." I'd been planning this since I was a small boy — asking the F.B.I. and Secret Service to show their credentials. My eyes bulged as they drew out an expensive-looking black leather folder. "All right," I said, and they eased their car down the Owings' drive.

Radios crackled and chattered. The county deputies strutted in their handsome uniforms with white ten-gallon broad-brimmed Stetsons. "Has Lady Bird congratulated you on your hats?" I asked the sheriff. "No, she ain't said nuthin' yet. If she knows her history she'll know we were wearing these hats before Texas had anything but buffalo and Indians."

Finally three long black Lincolns appeared and I immediately looked for Lady Bird Johnson. I couldn't help but grin at her, this tiny little woman, a Texas housewife, a mother, a terrific symbol of a hell of a nation — she was beautiful with extremely black, piercing eyes. As the car went by Mrs. Johnson grinned back at me with a look of incredible surprise on her face. She actually swiveled and continued to smile through the back window as an S.S. man leapt lightly on the back bumper. It dawned on me why she'd looked. She'd finally seen an S.S. man with a beard.

Then came the big buses and a flood of photographers and news reporters. Starting en masse for the big open gates, my moment of reckoning was at hand. Three photographers, men draped with at least five cameras each, loped ahead of the herd. I flicked my magic key and the forbidding gates sailed shut. I stepped to the center of the charging crowd. The air crackled with "Oohs" and "Ahhs" and feminine gasps of dismay and disappointment. "But we must go down!" a chorus of resentment went up. Then an S.S. man moved over and said, "I think it will be all right." Some of the frail and more fleshy women reporters couldn't make it so I gave them little human interest stories about the Big Sur.

The S.S. man had given me a tiny tricolored metal medallion. I was mighty proud of it. Nat said, "Yes, they gave me one like that too but Margaret made me take it off." There was a wan smile on Nat's face.

3

Katchinism – Christianism

WHETHER UNDER the burning sun of August or a soft blanket of snow with piñon smoke curling up from the low adobe houses, there is always *mañana* pervading our part of the great Southwest, lending a quality of *festina lente* to our New Mexican casa, which we therefore called "Festina Lente." In that high mountain valley Margaret and I seriously follow the ritual of "making haste slowly."

Even though I had promised Margaret that Big Sur would be our principal home, the Southwest, Santa Fe, Pojoaque in particular, was a magnet for us both. Like the Hopi, who build afresh with any change in social or family aspect of their pueblo life, Margaret and I gradually abandoned the older sections of my ranch to tenants and built our own set of compounds adjacent to the barrancas on the site of an ancient pueblo of Jacona. Our ever-growing efforts took shape: essentially an adobe-walled, enclosed hacienda or farmyard which I envisioned filled with chickens, ducks, pigs, sheep and goats. Margaret saw to it, however, that this particular form of modified modern animism never occurred, and our succession of enclosed courtyards and plazas remained uncluttered, framed by handsome arcaded structures: guest house and studio, marked down the middle of the inner courtyard by a chamiso-lined straight brick path leading to a long, narrow "great room," the impressive volume of which is spanned by ancient bridge timbers found beside a stream near the little Spanish village of Las Trampas. Every piece of old wood molding, or door or table or chair, each piece of silver and glass, metal or fabric, is a gathered object of Margaret's loving care. With wide, thick, high adobe walls and wide, bone white worn plank floors, bultos and santos from the past, Margaret's stitcheries, and in one special section many, many Katchina dolls — limited, however, in their selection to reproductions of full-grown Katchinas I had actually seen dancing in the plaza of a Hopi village — here we have preserved and maintained the presence of another age to which I find I have an amazing affinity.

According to Colton, there are some three hundred and seventy-five distinctive types of Katchina which have been recorded since the days of 1883, when Jesse Fewkes began a study of the Hopi villages. I started collecting Katchina dolls in 1942 after I had witnessed my first Shaleco (Home Dance) of the Katchina at Hotevila, Arizona. To find even the sketchiest meaning of that word "Katchina" involves a career in research of Hopi Indian lore. The Hopi Indian is not about to submit to being a research subject. Having lived in the Southwest since at least the time of the birth of Christ, and probably a lot longer than that, these people have striven to be left alone to live their own lives. In the process they have been persecuted, harried and threatened by the white man, whether he be missionary, soldier, bureaucrat or just plain nosy do-gooder. Hopi have rejected the Catholic religion and have refused to give in to missionaries or basically change their own way of life, a way that I have found exciting, colorful and imaginative.

I try to follow the Hopi calendar and quietly make pilgrimages to the various villages at appropriate times of festival and dance. All are, to some degree, a religious ceremony. I have never asked the Hopi for permission to do so, nor have they recognized my presence in the thirty years I have been a spectator, except once when, all unthinking, I casually reached down and picked up a few grains of cornmeal from the dust of the plaza after one of the dances and was immediately pounced upon, warned never to repeat that act.

The visual impact is great when one comes upon their dances after making the trip from the outside world; the circuitous route is pure Alice in Wonderland. After landing in a big jet at the Phoenix airport, taking a smaller plane to Flagstaff, Arizona, then following the roaring traffic of Highway 66 through the horrors of that grotesquely signed and billboarded town to an obscure road just recently paved, I would then travel another almost invisible unpaved road leading to an even more invisible mud ruin that is no ruin at all but a thousand-year-old adobe village perched on a high mesa.

Inside that walled plaza I would find a scene that has to be observed to be believed. There would be anywhere from thirty to forty, or even as many as eighty dancers, functioning as a unit in the dance. Their extraordinarily luxurious adornments on bare skins — kilts, shells, feathers, casques, all tied together by the ever-rhythmic pulsing of a drum and the measured, guttural voices of the dancers — all spell out an unbelievable sense of discipline. Obviously here exists a set of natural cultural laws functioning perfectly. Except for the few visitors — the white people who have made their way there — there are no detractions, no commercial aspects, no stores, no admission charge, no police, no ropes to hold one back. There is a unity in the total concentration. All there are obviously of good heart.

I subscribe wholeheartedly to their philosophy, as far as I can figure it out. After the Hopi Rain Dance I find the Christian services drab. Both are given for the same reason: appeal to a god or two; and what is more pantheistic than the hierarchy of the Catholic Church? I find the dances more beautiful than any opera. They are a subtle combination of symphony, ballet and great theater. With their placement in the classic plaza and their totality of community effort, they are utterly removed from reality. Underneath this apparently monolithic effort I know that there are schisms, jealousies, hatreds, loves: but they are well clothed in a fabric that holds the Hopi together through thick and thin. Everyone of every age participates in the dances, from the infant in arms to the trembling, tottering ancient. All is great theater. All is a dance. All are a part of it. All are in the act.

The sum total of this experience has reflected toward my own work. I feel that what the Hopi has is what we Anglos haven't: a firm faith in something; a faith that combines in its diversity all the aspects of human nature. The Hopi religion is for every day, every season, and involves geography, geology, meteorology, astronomy and, more basically, rhythm and the dance — their spirit barely enclosed in living form.

Yes, I like the Hopi dances because nobody tries to take me in or convert me. I cannot assay the Hopi Katchina values or what they mean to me. I only need to say that I *feel*. To feel is a rare and endangered privilege in this country, one which I intend to retain.

Sometimes that feeling is induced with the force of a sharp ax severing one's hand from the wrist.

It is an hour before sunset. I am standing at the edge of a thousand-foot cliff, my feet on the dusty, bare plaza there. The big rattler is hanging sheer, dangling from the Hopi dancer's cheek by its fangs while the feather in the hand of the teaser vainly tries to dislodge its heavy, swaying form. This is not the eleventh century, nor am I in New Guinea. This is 1968 and I am a spectator at this sacred rite. I am Anglo-Saxon, Caucasian, skilled at the destruction of the world's resources: fossil, fiber, chemical. I am coldly pushing off into oblivion the wild things of the ecosystem: bird, fish, mammal, crustacean and insect. And, with all my Christian humility parroting "There is but one God," I know deep in my heart that there is a god living in every brook, every tree, flower, animal and bird. I know I am in the minority in this feeling. As we tool-using *Homo sapiens* expand in numbers, lemming-like, I know that every fiber of our collective bodies, minds and instincts is directed toward a speedier destruction of the biota, the environment, the total ecological complex.

But in spite of this, here we are, Margaret and I, at Walpi, one of five Hopi villages, each perched precariously on the edge of one of three mesas, each a thousand-foot sheer cliff. This is the final act of the eight-day ceremony of the Snake Dance — its climax. It is August. It is hot. This ceremony is bringing rain clouds and the Hopi know that the dozens of snakes being passed out by a hidden chief from the little kisi beside us will bring the needed moisture to the corn, melon and bean crops without fail. That snake hanging by its fangs from the dancer's cheek was so close that I could have pulled it off, had I dared. And so could the three horrified nuns standing there beside us, their cowled faces paler even than a nun's face usually is. We were all standing within arm's reach of the kisi, a small, cone-shaped shelter formed of cottonwood boughs, enclosing the sixty or more snakes which, one by one, were being danced around the plaza. The actors were a dozen Snake Clan chiefs, teasers and carrier dancers, their moccasined feet beating a heavy rhythm beneath their swaying bodies and blackened faces, every nerve centered on that writhing snake firmly held just below its neck by each dancer's clenched teeth.

After the kilted dancer had danced each snake around the plaza three times, he draped it over the arm of the dozen or so waiting members of the Antelope Clan lined up in front of the kiva for this purpose. At the finish all the snakes were thrown together, quite casually it would seem, into a cornmeal-marked circle in the center of the plaza. The circle was divided into the six sacred directions: North, South, East, West, Up and Down. Then, after being blessed by Hopi maidens costumed in black homespun togas, whose downcast eyes hid their concern for the dancers, each snake runner straightaway flew to one of the four winds, clutching a handful of snakes to be released on the plains below. It is said that these snakes send back rain to the Hopi fields.

To the white man's age-old question — how do the Hopi avoid dying from snake bite during their nine-day ritual? — the answer is no one knows. So far as anyone can tell, the Hopi don't tamper with the snakes, since they are worshiped as gods. They simply release the proud predator in the canyon below at the end of the dance.

The Hopi are animists, worshiping animals and birds; but they are also good meteorologists. Their Rain Dances produce rain too regularly to be a matter of pure chance. This success is, I am sure, based on the priest's predance knowledge of the highly favorable probabilities of rain. The Navajo laughs at the Hopi Rain Dance, but always brings a raincoat.

Most religions are based on catastrophe: Judaism and Christianity, Noah and the Ark, the flood. Even the American Hopi Indian bases his ethics and religion on survival and a great flood, always stressing survival. The Hopi is an optimist. He has had three disasters past, and one to come; floods through which the Hopi people make their way each time to another island of refuge successfully, but at great peril over great wastes of water.

An important segment of the Hopi religion, unique to the Hopi and providing a basic outlet for Hopi spiritualism, involves the Katchinum, an individual of the Katchina Clan. Although not listed among the world's great religions, for me it is a fundamental one. A Katchinum is a Hopi Indian transformed through the power of his thinking into a god. The Katchina may still be seen, though very rarely, at Walpi or Oraibi or one of

218

the other eight villages on the three mesas scattered in the high, arid country between the gorges of the Little Colorado and the Rio Grande. At fixed intervals through the annual calendar they do come onto the plaza, alone or in groups, and engage in magnificent ritualistic displays of deep religious significance.

The Hopi Easter occurs at the spring equinox and is called the Pauma, Anglicized to the Bean Dance. Just prior to this Easter celebration the Katchina return from the nearby sacred mountains called the San Francisco Peaks, where the Hopi say they have spent the winter. Hopi, transformed into gods by masks and ritual costumes taking the shape of anthropomorphic demons, animals and birds, become in fact — each individual man — a fox or a bear or a demon; and surely as the transformation occurs for the Katchinum, his human problems dissolve.

To try to explain to a non-Indian this complex belief of a religion of unknown age, never reduced to writing, is hopeless. One of the very reasons for Hopi survival is their secrecy about their indestructible faith, passed on from father to son in the darkness of the kiva, or under the stars on some mountain top; and their beliefs bring to mind a house built of dawn.

How could a Hopi have ulcers? All inhibitions disappear with the transferal of the man into that other world. As an eagle he can fly high and wide, or as a powerful buffalo dominate with the strength of ten. I have watched the Hopi dancing all day long in the hot sun or driving snow, bare to the waist, in casque, kilt and moccasins. All participate in the worship, to live with nature in peace and harmony, taking only what can be renewed and only what is absolutely necessary.

The white man has always said that the Hopi religion is dying out but the Indian GI, coming back from whatever war, has evidenced the need to enforce the old and sought to hold it. He has proven the strongest prophet, rivaling the old men in carrying out in faithful and meticulous detail the great ceremonies.

This is a worship nontransferable to the white man, who stands benumbed in awe as a spectator, following the Hopi annual calendar through the seasons of the year.

When the Spanish tried to press Catholicism on the Hopi in the seventeenth century, the Hopi rejected it, killing the Franciscan monks and destroying the churches they had been forced to build. The Hopi retained their original "primitive belief." They believed in magic and used impersonal forces conjured up by the shaman. The underlying principles of the Hopi religion are impersonal and their forces act automatically and obey whoever applies the right formula. The continuity is gained throughout the ages by making the succession hereditary, thus avoiding the pitfalls of democratic selection of personalities qualified to handle such important cosmic powers. The Hopi priest knows that his role is to interpret the often capricious will of supernatural beings, which he does through rigid procedures handed on by word of mouth, including incantations, sacrifices and prayers.

The Hopi has rejected the advent of so-called religion. He sticks to true animism, refusing to widen the gulf between man and nature. I see here an opportunity for us to learn from the Hopi how to get man back into balance with nature because, as far as I can tell, the Hopi believes as I do that every animal and plant has a soul. Over the years I have studied many petroglyphs etched into the walls of the cliff dwellers that go back to at least the birth of Christ. From these drawings it is incontrovertible that the Hopi and his predecessor believed — and his burial ceremonies show that he recognized — that with the end of life the soul did not die but departed and entered into another life, transported and transformed into a form of life that the Hopi considered more attractive and more powerful than his own: bird, animal, demon. He knew that the fox, the bear, the beaver and the snake had souls — probably those of his predecessors. The Hopi explains the facts of life by the assumption of a soul in the life-giving spring from which he draws his water. The branch of the spruce tree has a special power and each animal and bird has a tongue and a story to tell.

The Hopi has survived in this country for over a thousand years, and to do so has developed a bond with nature involving what of necessity has become "an ecological conscience." He has found it expedient to develop his formula for life into an integral part of the ritual of nature. The Hopi retains this flame of truth and he has survived through this spark of eternal life almost extinguished elsewhere. Obviously this has been retained by him, not as a new fad or a modern theory — not as a theory at all but as an ingrained part of his fabric. His beliefs are a part of him and have remained unchanged by all we whites have done over the last two hundred years to destroy them. In the Hopi's living culture as practiced today I find two key elements which apply directly to our modern problems. One is their form of pueblo as a central core unit applicable, I believe, to city planning. The second — and probably the more important — is their belief in animism as the basis for the development of a modern ecological conscience.

John Collier in his *Fullness of Life Through Leisure* wrote: "This is a problem and an opportunity of eternal human nature. No group and no individual can permanently solve the problem or realize the opportunity and then rest upon the achievement. Life . . . is a dance over fire and water. Whole societies which have veritably existed have danced that dance of life, though they have not called it leisure life, or recreation."

As parallels to my interest in the Hopi run the strands of the Spanish conquest of the Southwest in the seventeenth century. To Festina Lente it seemed appropriate to bring some of the strands of the Big Sur Coast Road experience. These were woven into a support strong enough to save, perhaps, a small but important segment of that ancient Spanish culture. The particular

221

area involved was known as the village of Las Trampas, a remote settlement established in 1704 on the narrow, winding stage-coach road between Santa Fe and Taos.

Such fragile areas were under attack on every side in the name of progress, of course. This particular one came to our attention through a clipping dated October 2, 1966, which read: "Village of Trampas — New Mexico Heritage Faces Destruc-tion." Rights-of-way had been acquired for the widening of NM 76, which would destroy the churchyard and pass within six feet of the Las Trampas Church itself. The Church of San José de Gracia, dominating the plaza of the village of Las Trampas, had been the object of scores of pleasant visits dating back to 1931, when a visit was considered hazardous and involved at least a day's trip, sometimes subject to unannounced flash floods when one might be marooned on the edge of an arroyo — or even in it — for a day or two.

In recent years my wife, Margaret, and I have had many a luncheon alfresco, resting by the sparkling spring, perched high above the church, its straw gold, crusted, blunt-edged adobe walls glowing in the sun, our luncheon basket balanced on the flume of hollowed-out logs that carries the stream across the gully dividing our hillside from the plaza.

The blunt twin towers of the church might have been a proto-type for Bertram Grosvenor Goodhue's Nebraska State Capitol and his 1931 Los Angeles Public Library. Since Goodhue had never heard of the Church of Las Trampas the parallel involve-ment of pure art forms was of especial interest; and thus I would try to help preserve this "American aesthetic." In continuous operation since 1704, the church had been neglected except for some remodeling in 1931. Now, thirty-five years later, here was a crisis.

As usual in a crisis, there is no time left to do anything. Those in the Highway Department involved in planning the road which would destroy part of the church had done their work well. They had kept their plans secret and had released the announcement at the latest possible moment, leaving no time for us to develop a counterattack. We were challenged to save not only an irreplaceable adobe mission church, but its walled cemetery and a beautiful plaza as well — if we could. I sought to make use of a new federal law passed that same year which provided the means to preserve historically significant structures if they were threatened by another federal agency. Las Trampas would prove the ideal test case. Here we had a fragile mud structure and a simple two-lane country road about to destroy each other. Surely here in the wide open spaces of New Mexico the two did not have to collide. There must be room for both.

The State Historic Structure Society Committee was aware of the crisis. Governor Jack Campbell called Las Trampas one of the most precious jewels in the string of early Spanish villages — Chimayo, Cundiyo, Cordova, Truchas, Picuris and Taos on "the high road to Taos" — and was willing to postpone action on the proposed road providing I could get a letter from Stewart Udall, the secretary of the interior, at once. On October 21, just three weeks after we had started our efforts, the letter came: "I would very much appreciate it if you would find it consistent with your personal views and official responsibilities to defer a decision on the routing of the proposed highway . . ." On November 1, Governor Campbell agreed to postpone action.

But the villagers' attitude was a different story. They did not seem to wish to preserve the church and the churchyard where their fathers and mothers and grandparents had been buried. They felt that the new road was not an instrument of destruction but a sign of progress. We were do-gooders, outsiders. The press took sport in poking fun at us "preservationists" and supported the road, "progress." One of the villagers summed it up: "If the church is in the way of progress as indicated by the building of the road, then blow up the church!" But Las Trampas had a fine priest, Father Rocha, who countered, "Under the church floor lie many bodies of your revered ancestors. You should not expose those souls to the freezing weather of the Trampas-Truchas climate by destroying your church."

I felt that the villagers had been misled about "progress." They seemed to think the road would bring them something they had been deprived of. Lacking their support, we created our own, the Las Trampas Foundation; and two villagers took their lives in their hands and risked banishment by joining.

Acting for the village, the foundation applied to the secretary of the interior for a National Park registered historic landmark designation for the church, which usually takes months — sometimes years. But the Santa Fe staffers of the Southwest region of the National Park Service produced a beautifully documented report overnight and the National Advisory Board's subcommittee, chairmaned by Dr. Melvin Grosvenor of the National Geographic Society, and famous archeologists and anthropologists Ned Danson and J. O. Brew, supported the work and approved it.

My dream was to project a way of life in the village based on the economy of the 1800s when the villagers raised sheep, sheared the wool, spun it into yarn, wove the yarn into homespuns and rugs and used or sold the products. This is still only a dream.

The landmark status was granted in one of the most expeditious actions ever taken by the advisory board. It has been referred to as the only case on record of instant historic landmark designation.

The secretary of transportation, Alan Boyd, a good friend, was also involved and he assigned another good friend, ex-Senator Fred Farr, to take care of the matter. The Department of Transportation had the final say-so, since they largely financed the roadway, and so representatives of the two cabinet offices, the governor of New Mexico and the two United States senators met and signed "The Treaty of Santa Fe" — all to save a rural church from the intrusion of a two-lane country road.

The bulldozers were stopped less than two miles from the environs of Las Trampas. The old road width was retained and paved in asphalt colored to match the adjacent adobe fields. A new wooden bridge was widened to two lanes and an opening left for cattle to reach the stream just as it always had been. The culverts were rock-faced and the fencing was wooden posts and rails. Standing near the bridge was a hundred-year-old cottonwood casting great shadows and providing a beautiful profile against the village. I insisted that this be saved, although an old man commented, "Why bother? There will be another one there soon, maybe in a hundred years."

The Treaty of Santa Fe had saved the church and the road was properly built, but the village itself was still hostile. To win them over we offered to repair the church, which was sadly in need of a new coat of adobe. Its roof was full of leaks and its baptistry was about to collapse. The handsome main gate hung on one hinge. We approached the village father who held the keys to the church to see if the Las Trampas Foundation could finance the construction, which was to be undertaken by the villagers. The famous Rancho de Taos Church had just been plastered in cement and we wanted to avoid this at all costs. There would be a new roof, new windows in the nave and transept, and a remodeled baptistry.

The villagers held many long, involved meetings in the schoolhouse about this. They finally agreed, but there was a hitch. Almost everyone in the village was on relief. If they accepted pay for their adobe work, this infraction would be reported and the work would have to be abandoned. This being a short-term job, nobody in the village wished to prejudice their status on relief and run afoul of bureaucracy and the law. After judicious counseling an agreement was worked out with the welfare agencies. They looked the other way and the work commenced.

The men and women turned out in force and it was a beautiful sight. Those fine, assured, competent women each settled to their special tasks — one to sift the selected adobe earth, one to sort and shred and mix the strands of straw, another to add the proper amount of water. One dug in elbow deep to mix the plastic substance to the right consistency. These women were supplied with mud and straw and water by the men who played a minor role in this interesting and ancient craft of the Spanish-American. The women were heroic in the classic sense — mistresses of a fine craft and very proud of it.

The application of adobe is an art. The amount of moisture given the surface before application was critical and everything was done truly in the ancient tradition. The surface was almost as hard as glass with a texture like homemade bread crust, and the entirety so beautiful, so aesthetically satisfying, that the question of a cement surface was too ugly to consider. In the use of adobe the need for renewal was created, a rhythmic renewal, and the festival of community effort could recur every several years. An ancient and splendid custom was thus preserved, and, like life itself, the ritual of renewal could continue.

One day an old lady came shyly forward and from under her mantilla she produced an old, faded photograph, undated but of Civil War Mathew Brady style. It showed her family standing before the church and above them were two capping wooden towers. We must restore those towers, I thought, but this was dangerous business. To alter a historic landmark, intact without towers for almost seventy-five years, was not to be done lightly.

John Gaw Meem, the Southwest's authority on historic adobes, designed the bell towers and thus forestalled any possible criticism as to their authenticity. Margaret and I provided the old

226

wood and the foundation paid the bill. Albert Livermore, a superb craftsman from Santa Cruz, built the towers and placed them where they can now be seen as one approaches the village. Then we hung a large bell, which for years had been on a chain below the balcony, to toll out the news that the church was ready. Father Rocha held his twenty-fifth ceremonial anniversary Mass at Las Trampas Church, choosing it over the four other churches in the area of which he was also priest.

The great day came. It was an impressive sight to see the entire village turn out — men, women, children, babies in arms — the women and the men in eternal black, as they filed into the church to kneel, sing, pray and listen to Father Rocha's admonition. The villagers had no reason to fear the Las Trampas Foundation, he said; nothing would be done to damage their village or their church because there was no helicopter he knew of large enough to carry the church away.

After the services all thirty-five members of the village joined us at the schoolhouse for cake and coffee — the cake baked in the exact form and detail of the church with everything edible except the ladder to the roof.

Before the rains and the snows came, the church completed and the road and bridge completed, the old bell tolled out the notice of the services from the new towers; and the interior of the baptistry, neat and clean, served for the christening of each new entry into the world of Las Trampas. Those who wished to visit the church could get the keys from one of the old men who were elected each year (as they always had been), and the visitors would have to look hard to see that anything was unusual or different about the road or the plaza. So far as I could see whenever we visited Las Trampas with a picnic basket, everything seemed especially fresh and as charmingly beautiful as I thought a New Mexican village should look. The seamed and weather-beaten faces of the inhabitants remained inscrutable, stoically accepting life as they always had. For them life was not a matter of approval or disapproval but a simple matter of endurance until death.

*   *   *

"The temples are not objects for admiration nor are they sumptuous, for they are very small with walls of mud and adobe, built without skill and at no expense . . ."

Governor Medezabel, 1663

4

"They Have Sown the Wind and They Shall Reap the Whirlwind"

THREE THOUSAND MILES away from that remote village of Las Trampas another people had landed on the eastern shore of the same continent and founded a nation "dedicated to the proposition that all men are created equal . . ." Their capital city was laid out around a pattern consisting of a gridiron of streets overlaid with a series of diagonals called avenues. The designer of this city plan for Washington, D.C., had also inspired — if not actually designed — the radiating avenues laid over the rectangular grid of the city of my earliest memories: Indianapolis, Indiana.

Within that Washington plan by L'Enfant lay a key avenue just the same length as the Las Trampas road, one and two-tenths miles long, this one connecting the President's house and the Houses of Congress, called Pennsylvania Avenue.

In 1862 the admonition to visitors was, "When you venture on the Avenue, watch your purse," and the chief disgrace of Washington was the area between the central market, Market Square and Fifteenth Street, bounded on the south by Pennsylvania Avenue: cheap gambling houses, slums, penny arcades and rooms that could be rented at odd hours day and night. The region between Twelfth and Fifteenth streets was an appalling slum

which became known during the Civil War as "Murder Bay."
In 1862 Hooker's Division camped there. When they left, so
many prostitutes remained that they retained the name
"Hookers" and the neighborhood was still called "Hooker's
Division." In 1962 the hookers were still there, but things had
changed. On the other side of the street was the Department of
Commerce Building, to which I had made certain artistic contributions and which dominated Pennsylvania Avenue by the sheer
majesty of its sterile, federal architecture.

On June 1, 1962, the President of the United States, John F.
Kennedy, appointed me to the chairmanship of the council for
the redesign of Pennsylvania Avenue. He did so through the
secretary of labor, Arthur Goldberg of Chicago, who was an old
friend. Goldberg did so on behalf of the President through his
assistant secretary of labor, Daniel Patrick Moynihan, whom I
had never heard of until the day he called. I disregarded the
advice of those who had every right to offer it: my wife, who objected to the potential alienation from Big Sur which the long
distances involved would cause; and my partners, who believed
nothing could be accomplished by committee.

A Presidential ad hoc committee established federal policy:
"The finest architectural thought for the nation's 'Grand Axis':
Pennsylvania Avenue." The desolation on the north side of the
Avenue was "to be changed." The nation's ceremonial way, inseparable from its adjoining area, should have a special character. It should do honor to its lofty destinations (the White
House and the Capitol Building) and should be harmonious in
itself, linking the city around it in both its architecture and its
planning, pleasant to traverse either on foot or by vehicle. The
Avenue must be reclaimed and developed as a unified whole,
with emphasis on private enterprise.

From the start our directives have changed surprisingly little;
only the means of accomplishing them have varied.

Facing a battery of microphones, television cameras and the

general press on the lawn outside the White House after meeting with the President in the Fish Room, I realized that my new assignment on Pennsylvania Avenue in the national capital would have considerable national impact. I was surprised at the reception my words received: "We will get somewhere with this because President Kennedy is the first president since Jefferson who cares about architectural design in Washington." President Kennedy did his best to see us through; in fact, he set a date — the Friday after his return from Dallas — to hold a "coffee" and introduce the plan to the leaders in Congress. The word of his assassination on November 22, 1963, came to me while I was in the canyon below Wild Bird. When Margaret shouted, I thought it would be word from the President to come to Washington to present the plan.

The assassination of President Kennedy practically ended my assignment and Congress repeatedly threatened to shoot down my efforts to gain recognition. Yes, I had plenty of opportunity to throw in the towel, but my Welsh blood rebelled. An empathy for this central one and two-tenths miles between those two extraordinary structures, the White House and the Houses of Congress, developed and is still going on.

LBJ could not be faulted for seeming to ignore the Pennsylvania Avenue plan. There were, admittedly, other things higher on the list of priorities immediately following John F. Kennedy's assassination. Fortunately, strong Avenue supporters had continued on: Charles Horsky, Presidential adviser for civil affairs; Stewart Udall, secretary of the interior; and there was Lady Bird, with her amanuensis, the unique Liz Carpenter, who had forged through the medium of the most fragile of weapons — tulips and pansies — a powerful environmental beautification campaign, a concept which would shake the nation and confirm the great sincerity of a great First Lady.

In this hiatus between Presidents it seemed best to sit still and wait for something to happen. I was doing just that when the telephone rang in my room at the Hay Adams in Washington, D.C., and a voice ringing with authority inquired if I could come over to see Mrs. Lyndon Johnson at eleven o'clock that morning (it was then eight-thirty) and would I bring along a Pennsylvania Avenue Report. I certainly could and would.

From the balcony of my room at the Hay Adams overlooking Lafayette Square I used to pretend that I was a guest of Henry Adams when he and Hay lived there together. I had a wide view of the White House — and pigeons — through the French doors. Sometimes I would find two eggs carefully arranged in the bottom of my wastebasket, covered by a large, bottle green pigeon. I have never been able to stay long enough to determine just what the full incubation period is.

It was a short walk across the park to the White House gate and at five minutes to eleven promptly I passed through the hurricane fence and the gold-badged, police-studded outer identification point. Then across the broad green lawn, past a ramrod-stiff, blue-red-and-gold-uniformed Marine to the front entrance, presided over by an ancient black man who must have served many Presidents as butler over the long years. With courtly grace he escorted me to a tiny elevator and we silently arrived at the third floor, where a depressed, woebegone-looking man sat all hump-shouldered in the corner, holding LBJ's equally hump-shouldered, sad-eyed hound dogs. Then down a wide, sunlit, flower-filled hallway to be greeted by Lady Bird Johnson, whom I met that morning for the first time in her golden yellow sitting room.

Apparently concerned that the First Lady would rush into a commitment with me, watchdog and entrepreneur Liz Carpenter, Mrs. Johnson's Cardinal Richelieu, rasped her way in and suggested that everything was tentative; that this meeting was unofficial. But Lady Bird's charm and serenity were supreme and we sat there looking over the plans, the pictures and the reports, discussing the history of Pennsylvania Avenue. Mrs.

Johnson noticed Jefferson's poplars, which had lined the Avenue in 1802, and we discussed the comments of Abigail Adams, who was less than pleased with the functional arrangements in the White House. There was the gentle urgency of Lady Bird's sense of participation in the Abigail story, to which she was writing another chapter now. We discussed open spaces and flower beds, and that tied in with the Pennsylvania Avenue plan. In the presence of that charming lady I would gladly have promised to take down every building and fill every space with pansies, tulips and azaleas. Coffee was served, and the historic china cups and saucers, and even the coffee, gave off the all-pervading sense, the rich aroma of American history savored in the making at the source.

There were many visits like that, each for an official mission. One I especially remember was spent in Lincoln's bedroom where in those sacrosanct quarters I had been asked to set up a slide machine, balanced crazily on the edge of Lincoln's giant bed. Lady Bird wanted to see our pictures of Las Trampas Church, and while waiting for her it was difficult to believe that the Gettysburg address I was reading — simply framed under glass on the open desk — was one of the originals actually written by Abraham Lincoln.

This White House visit had been scheduled to last one hour. There was a meeting to follow with half the top brass of the General Services Administration to discuss the Federal Bureau of Investigation Building design, which was closely related to Pennsylvania Avenue. Lady Bird chatted on and the clock hands kept moving inexorably forward, the quiet pace of our reminiscences of the Southwest uninterrupted by any thought of that small part of Washington officialdom waiting while the little Las Trampas Church had its day.

Still another time, following Stewart Udall's lead, the three of us were sitting on the floor of Lady Bird's sitting room studying a great long drawing unrolled across the carpet, Stewart squatting at one end, I at the other, and Lady Bird in the middle. We were telling her all about some new features on the Avenue that needed her attention when suddenly in swarmed LBJ, all six feet of him, infused with the outdoors and dogs and things. As his eyes swept the room, our little tableau caught his attention. "What in hell, Udall, are you doing down there on the floor with my wife?"

Another time we were rehearsing for our big presentation with huge photographs and drawings in the State Dining Room when suddenly LBJ stormed in again, this time with forty or fifty governors in tow. Spotting the dramatic display on easels around the room, he launched into a presentation of the Pennsylvania Avenue plan which, to my surprise, was accurate and exhaustive in spite of his dozen refusals to take the time to be briefed on the plan. Perhaps at one point he had been hiding behind the curtains!

Lady Bird would routinely gather a band of dedicated beautifiers in the State Dining Room to hear me describe the plans for transforming Pennsylvania Avenue and the Mall. Using a beautifully constructed large-scale model showing every item of the plan in detail, I would stress the Avenue's broad sweep from the National Square to the verdant Mall as a haven for pedestrians. On the third time around I asked Liz Carpenter what could be done to improve this speech and make it a more potent weapon for implementing the plan. She said, "Make it shorter."

Sometimes Mrs. Johnson invited us to White House dinners. A formal White House dinner can be great theater. Live bodies are seen attached to famous names. The women guests' make-up, hairdos, jewels and costumes are all-out concoctions, worn defensively, without self-assurance. The hawk eyes of society reporters look toward business; Margaret's hundred-rupee bazaar necklace drew their comment. A kind of uneasiness held everybody at attention waiting for the colors to come down the stairs, the band to play, and the President and the First Lady to appear. Handsome young marine, army and navy lieutenants dressed in their parade best were islands of refuge for the uncertain; and the table seating was always a lottery. Margaret drew Secretary of Defense Clark Clifford, who, in answer to her questions, gave a briefing on foreign affairs and defensive attitudes so exhaustive that other members at the table, like the general manager of the *New York Times,* could hardly stop to take a bite. At my side at my table, the ranking Princess of Iran gushed that she needed desperately a new summer palace for which she had always yearned. She knew just what she wanted and assured me she wanted me to be her architect. It was to be an exact reproduction of George Washington's Mount Vernon.

From the west White House balcony can now be seen twin fountains with shafts of white foam rising from the shallow basins of twin granite monoliths. Mrs. Johnson had wanted those fountains very much and asked me to be the architect for them, but as usual there was a catch. Under the bureaucracy of Washington the generous sum given for the fountains hardly covered the overhead. I reverted to Chicago World's Fair tactics; we would beg and borrow the necessary ingredients. The design was "the simplest art form in the simplest setting." Two unadorned blocks of granite twenty feet on a side and two thirds of a yard deep, each resting on a low pedestal, with a slender shaft of water rising from each center, would meet my criteria.

I sent John Galston to ask John R. Alexander, the owner of the greatest granite quarry in the world, for two samples of a certain special vein of granite. "Why certainly," said the unwary quarry head. "How large would you like them to be?" "Well, Mr. Owings thinks two pieces about twenty feet square and two feet thick would be just fine."

Pieces of granite that size hadn't been handled in one piece since the Pharaohs. Mr. Alexander was intrigued. He granted Galston's request and found rail cars strong enough to carry the monoliths — which, he explained, might wreck any tunnels encountered along the way, although he quickly reassured us the tunnels wouldn't do the granite any harm.

The two-foot thick, twenty-foot square, rough-hewn slabs, tops prepolished, shallow basins routed out, were gently freed from their billion-year-old resting place by the slow, horizontal cutting of sand and water. All honor to Alexander's name, he did not suggest — as a lesser man might have — that we cut the granite into pieces.

Those slabs finally arrived in Washington, D.C., after a two-week journey stretching from Minnesota to Florida on seven different railroads. Trucked at night over D.C. bridges, the two great blocks of granite were put in place. Standing up well under the student demonstrations in Washington as hordes of young people happily bathed in the tall spray, dancing and rejoicing in the two shallow basins, the great blocks seemed to belong there.

Most architects' approach to design is to scrap everything and start over. Contrariwise, I took steps to retain and strengthen L'Enfant's grand design; to create there an island of refuge. Since 1801 there had been cries of anguish about Pennsylvania Avenue, when Jefferson rode through its mud to his first inaugural.

Early we found that Burnham and others had erred in their treatment of Pennsylvania Avenue as a street when it should have been treated as the simple spine of a wide area of influence. Our planned ceremonial way was to be surrounded by a garden city with Pennsylvania Avenue as its heart. We could do this easily — in a vacuum. But the probability of diverse forces canceling each idea out was serious. Our design provided car parking under all structures — three open squares, comprising a beginning and a center and an end to the Avenue. We had vistas, grand space and intimate places, too. We planned residential row houses framing the historic central market square — trees, fountains, variety of form, color, shape — yet all to be tied together by the quiet harmony of materials and rhythm of light and shade. In the L'Enfant plan, Pennsylvania Avenue was but the hypotenuse of a triangle of powerful proportions which embraced Washington's major monuments, termed in its totality the Mall: the Houses of Congress, the Washington Monument and the Lincoln Memorial. We treated the area as a total composition, and our job, as I saw it, was to get all or part built in our lifetime; or, failing that, to give a guarantee that the pieces could fit together in later years as the plan progressed.

One day, with a freezing wind whipping our coattails, Udall and I were posing for pictures on a grandstand high above the Avenue. While waiting for the puttering cameraman, Udall said, "Who do you think would be a good architect for the Mall plan to go along with the Pennsylvania Avenue plan?" "Well, Mr. Secretary, you're looking at him right now."

Apparently Udall was too cold to refuse. I was hired on the spot as the architect for the Mall. This, added to the responsibilities of the Pennsylvania Avenue Commission, instantly widened my area of concern. I found it easy to contact anybody, see anybody, and do almost anything. Unpaid, running for no office and with a friendly press, there seemed to be no limit to the possibilities before me.

It was important to be in certain places at certain times. A good many important decisions are made before the office opens. Some of the biggest issues are settled at coffee before the boss goes into early morning meetings. Many of the definitive, creative ideas that run through men's minds are crystallized and pinned down between six o'clock in the evening and eight o'clock the next morning. The most creative work is done on the dark side of the clock.

Early in my tour of duty in Washington I got into the habit of dropping in on Stewart Udall, for instance, at about 7:30 A.M. for a cup of coffee and a chat with the girls and his personal secretary, Walter Pozen. Usually the boss's door would pop open and Stewart would stick out his head and say, "Nat, come on in — what's new?" On one of those early morning visits he handed me a highway drawing with some strange new roads wandering all over it down around the tidal basin. These roads wiped out a narrow park and raised havoc with the basin itself. "Go out into the grounds and tell me if it should be done," he said. "Three senators were in here about it last night."

The wind was blowing cold, wet rain in my face and the drawings were crumpled in the crosscurrents of the wind and water, but I knew that a lot more than drawings would be crumpled if the secretary stopped this one. There was a tunnel and a bridge and an intersection that were all out for bids, and contracts were about to be let by the District. When those contracts were let, then the roads I was looking at would have to be built. It was now or never.

The crisis lay with these park lands, which were irreplaceable. There was only one Washington, only one tidal basin. There must be some other way. Maybe the roads weren't necessary at all. If they were, why not under the basin instead of over or around it? Expensive? But what is the proper price for an irreplaceable thing? I folded the wet, battered blueprints, stuck them in the pocket of my raincoat and went back to see Stewart.

Stewart was backed by some strong, intelligent senators and stopped the bidding. Presidential appointees, like highway administrators, were beginning to pay a lot of attention when I talked about a tunnel under the basin. Six months earlier they would have thrown me out of the office without a hearing. The tunnel would be twenty-six hundred feet long. They had the money and they didn't need Congressional action. The bureau was a Midas.

The highway administrator authorized the one-hundred-million-dollar tunnel under the tidal basin, but the tunnel has not yet been built. A contract is only a piece of paper and phase two of that story is still to come.

But there was more than that to be done. There was a whole pattern of attack and opposition in Washington. The lines were drawn between the highway lobby, the generally proconcrete Public Works Committees and the highway engineers. They had positive plans and knew what they were fighting for, while we, the opposition, were always fighting a rear guard defensive battle, generally had no plans and were traditionally disorganized.

We came up against this combination of highway interests over the key design for the Capitol end of the Avenue: a reflecting basin of wide dimensions embracing the Grant Memorial and offering a double reflection of the Capitol.

For many years a leg of the Interstate Highway System had been planned to run underground across the Mall in front of the United States Capitol. Originally, old Sam Rayburn, to save some trees, had demanded that this sunken freeway swing in a great outward curve across the Mall in front of the Capitol. Dangerous and expensive, this curve sorely bothered the district engineer and the federal highway commissioner. I suggested to them that a six-and-a-half-acre reflecting pool could be made to serve as a sort of lid for this depressed eight-lane freeway. Since we on the Pennsylvania Avenue Commission had no appropriation for this great reflective feature, and no likelihood of getting any, I also suggested that if I could obtain approval of Congress to straighten the offending curved highway, perhaps we could have the savings to use for the reflecting basin.

I then discovered the little-known fact that the architect of the Capitol had the power to make this change with the approval of the Speaker of the House without formal legislation, so, loaded with rolls of drawings, I bearded Speaker McCormick in his den.

Speaker McCormick looked askance at the forbidding rolls and inquired who was for the straight road and the resulting pool. "Lady Bird." He brightened, waved the drawing aside and signed a scruffy little piece of paper now safely in the archives, to which had been added within an hour the signatures of Vice President Humphrey, the majority and minority leaders of the House and Senate and the architect of the Capitol. Upon being apprised of this great news, the district engineer, General Duke, and the highway commissioner, Rex Whiten, remarked, "But there's no such thing as a saving in government! That highway should have been straight to begin with." It would appear that these two gentlemen were trying to deny the savings now that the straight road seemed assured and I would lose the reflecting basin.

In a grieved tone I replied that I had assumed there was honor among thieves and reached for the signed drawing, starting to tear it to shreds before their eyes. Hastily repolishing their tarnished word, they agreed verbally to give us our three million dollars. But once bitten and no longer trusting, I quietly arranged that they give their public announcement as to the agreement at a TV news conference. This announcement, to sign and seal and set in perpetuity the reflecting pool and the straightened freeway, is on a tape which I still possess — the only contract document extant.

At the foot of the steps on the western front of the Capitol of the United States, half-hidden by shrubbery, is a large sculptural group executed in 1912 as a memorial to General Ulysses S. Grant, the general of the armies victorious for the Union at Appomattox in 1865. Made in three parts, the central one is a gigantic, monumental sculpture of an equestrian General Grant facing west toward the Lincoln Memorial. To his right and left, some thirty yards apart, are two sets of soldiers: one an artillery group in anguished action and the other the infantry, equally anguished and apparently shooting at each other. Surrounding the general are four very domesticated lions, sitting in rapt attention, unperturbed by the bullets which must be whizzing by, as the general sits silently staring to the west at Lincoln.

Our plan for the reflecting pool embraced this truly charming piece of Victorian sculpture, but grandson Ulysses S. Grant III objected to the water. To satisfy his legitimate concerns we met at the foot of his grandfather's statue as the sun set beyond the Washington and Lincoln memorials. The issue was quickly settled. The old man had spent a good bit of time at Vicksburg, hadn't he? And there was a river there, wasn't there? As a final check the grandson unrolled a 1901 Commission of Parks drawing showing the original design — and much to his embarrassment, there, colored in blue, was the reflecting pool to which he was objecting, drawn by his own hand sixty-nine years before and forgotten.

In 1972 the great pool was flooded to its brim, and a new architect for the Capitol wrote me:

I must say that the fantastic result of the reflecting pool on the West Front of the Capitol is something of which you can be very proud. I really believe that it is the greatest addition to the beauty in the vicinity of the Capitol that has occurred since the advent of the Olmsted terraces. I hope the future contains the opportunity for some small thing that I might do that would have one tenth of the impact of your influence on the Capitol City. If that should occur, I would consider that I had accomplished a great deal.

Cordially,

George M. White, F.A.I.A.
Architect of the Capitol

Incredible as it may seem, I discovered that no one had bothered to designate Pennsylvania Avenue, the White House or the Mall as an Official Historic Site. Corrected, this oversight about a site of such importance could accomplish for us in one fell swoop what we had been unable to do through ordinary diplomatic channels with the Interior Committee of the House. An Act of Congress — the National Historic Act — passed in 1931 had the prestige of forty years of long and honored usage, and

once the secretary had so designated the area as an Official Historic Site and the President had proclaimed it by executive order, there was little the Congress could do other than refuse to
appropriate funds for the maintenance of the area.

This aspect of it didn't bother me and I spelled out the plot
to the always sympathetic Stewart Udall. Late one evening he
gathered his co-conspirators together in his great high-ceilinged,
fire-lit office. Circling my large drawing spread out on the carpet
in front of the fire were Attorney General Katzenbach, HUD
Secretary Bob Weaver, DOT's Alan Boyd, Supreme Court Justice
Arthur Goldberg, Charles Horsky and Pat Moynihan. Following
the changing views of the assembled ad hoc planners, I marked
out with a piece of red chalk in one hand and a blackboard eraser
in the other a comprehensive area of some six hundred and fifty
acres, the area we desired as a National Historic Site. The executive order followed shortly. The President then proceeded to
create a Temporary Pennsylvania Avenue Commission, and we
were off and running.

I was aware that time moves slowly in Washington; that
L'Enfant wandered through the halls of Congress for years after
being fired. I knew that the grandiose Burnham plan in 1902
had, undoubtedly for the best, been shelved. There was merit in
delay.

I took every step I could to give the Avenue permanence and
a history. One was the engineering of a major exhibition
launched jointly with the Library of Congress. The librarian
graciously dug out of the vaults original drawings by L'Enfant,
Downing, Burnham and Olmsted, never shown in public before.
The appearance of Mary Cable's book *The Avenue of the Presidents* was an encouraging event. When Nixon reached the White
House Daniel Patrick Moynihan, counselor to the President, arranged that I meet Presidential counselor Peter Flanigan, who
would determine whether I should remain as chairman. He took
one look at me and said, "My God! You did my father's bank!"

How could I have known that Peter Flanigan was the son of Hap Flanigan, for whom we had done the glass lantern building for the Manufacturers Trust on Fifth Avenue in New York? I remained chairman of the Pennsylvania Avenue Commission.

President Nixon may have had good and sufficient reasons for appointing Daniel Patrick Moynihan as Presidential adviser, but from my point of view there was only one: to insure full support for the Avenue.

Late one day the happy thought came to me that it was Herbert Hoover who had started the whole thing on Pennsylvania Avenue. So, during a forty-five-minute presentation to President Nixon we stressed that happy recollection and suggested that Nixon could complete the work on the other side of the Avenue that Hoover had begun. He could be his own private "Sidewalk Superintendent" and walk down from the White House every morning to see the Avenue grow.

In 1972, as the second session of the 92nd Congress was nearing its end, even the formidable combination of President Nixon, Peter Flanigan and Daniel Patrick Moynihan had not been able to bring about the passage of the Pennsylvania Avenue bill. With but two days left for Congress to pass bills, with forty much more urgent ones ahead of us on the calendar and furious wrangles flaring up in both chambers over far more important matters using up valuable time, everything looked dark indeed.

Finally, at 6:21 P.M., Tuesday evening, October 17, 1972, the House passed the Pennsylvania Avenue bill, but it was not the bill the Senate was prepared to approve. At this moment in time Peter Flanigan and the White House staff made a final effort and pleaded with the House Interior Committee to pass another bill, modified to conform with the administration's ideas. This they refused to do, but did pass a bill with half the objectionable amendments removed, although still different enough to make the concurrence of the Senate unlikely.

243

The last night before adjournment came, and David Childs and I were frantic in our feeling of helplessness. At eleven o'clock that night we went to the Senate chamber, sat in the family circle, and listened to two score or more senators discuss the debt ceiling involving some two hundred and fifty billion dollars or more, when suddenly I spied Senator Bible sitting there. I had an idea.

Next morning at nine o'clock I was at Senator Bible's door. Just half an hour before the Senate would reconvene for its last session, I reached him in his office and asked if the bill was dead. He said no, and that he might have some good news for me at the end of the day. I started to point out to him the importance of having the bill passed this year when he stopped me in the middle of a sentence. "Young man," he said, "you better get out of here while you are still ahead."

In less than half an hour the word came that through Senator Bible's good efforts the Senate had passed a bill identical with the latest House version, and that both had been sent to the President for signature. The working machinery for the reconstruction of the central core of Washington, epitomized by Pennsylvania Avenue, was now on its way to becoming a fact.

Perhaps the Andrew Jackson policy of "throw the rascals out and then put new rascals in" is sound, but my ten years under three Presidents had brought into focus for me one hell of a lot of American history. All through those years my real collaborators, friends and advisers were ghosts turned flesh and blood — the triad of George Washington, L'Enfant and Thomas Jefferson; crotchety Andrew Jackson and his misplaced Treasury building; the surprisingly effective short-term Chester Arthur and his landscape architect Andrew Jackson Downing, whose death when Fulton's steamship blew up was the only thing that saved the Mall from becoming an English garden; Teddy Roosevelt, Daniel Burnham and Frederick Law Olmsted needing only Roman togas to crown their misdirected, compulsive drive for an Augustinian Roman plan.

I learned the inverted values and reinforcing strengths of reverses, the teasing stimulant of frustration, and the gamesmanship involved in stirring together luck, contiguity and delays, and brewing therefrom a strong draft. I gained some sense of the difference between great names misused, great people misplaced and performance in high office missed entirely.

And the Avenue is growing.

5

Baltimore

THIS IS A STORY of a battle between entrenched bureaucracy, rich in dollars, and the faceless masses of people. The Federal Bureau of Public Roads, holding powerful tools and using money as the carrot on the end of its stick, has supported each State Road Commission in what generally has been an inexorable march through whatever stood in the way — tree, stream, home, village, it made no difference — until they came to Baltimore.

Three-hundred-and-fifty-year-old Baltimore, granted by King George I to Lord Baltimore as a haven for his repressed Catholics, is known as the Queen City and a great port. It is rich and colorful. Bubbling over with crimes and vices, teeming with dens of iniquity, dangerous and fascinating, Baltimore is a stage-set sort of city. It was the inventor of the clipper ship, creator of the Tom Thumb, the first steam engine on the B&O, birthplace of the B&O Railroad. Over weekends I wandered through the streets lined with ancient, hand-fashioned, small-scale architecture: monuments, house fronts, big trees, old forts — a many-faceted display. On the top of a Doric column stands the first monument to George Washington. Marylanders were an independent lot. They had instructed their delegates to the first

Congressional Congress to vote no. They distrusted the king, England and the new democracy; and in 1965 they were still of the same general opinion about practically all current events. Now there was a new element they rightly should distrust: the burgeoning bureaucracy of freeway construction which had cast its tentacles of concrete around the fragile precincts of Baltimore's inner city. The Baltimorean didn't understand exactly what was wrong but rightly sensed that his environment was threatened and proceeded to rebel.

This was the situation when the telephone rang. It was Baltimore-based Archibald Rogers, F.A.I.A., who seemed to be determined to involve me. I pictured Rogers, with his tiny, ever-fresh orchid in a vial clamped to his coat lapel, as he was eloquently trying to induce me to take the plunge into this murky mess. I realized that had he chosen to perform this role himself, his tiny orchid could never have survived.

The question posed when he asked me to head up a Concept Team of professionals was whether the sacred, central core of Baltimore could be saved and still have a compatible freeway system. Could both be accomplished without producing anything more than added chaos? The answer, we both knew, was — short of a miracle — no. In fact, hiring me might be an acute case of wishful thinking on the part of Maryland and certain federal agencies. But with that kind of an investment in fees and that kind of commitment in the taking of rights of way, somehow this misbegotten creature, the road system already worked out before the call, could not be abandoned, must be made to work. But at what cost? Not just in dollars, but in the irreparable destruction of the Baltimoreans' own habitat?

Engineers use strange annotations for road systems, and this result of ten years of effort by the Maryland Roads Commission was called the "10D system." Its heart was the twenty-six miles of freeway already designed which, at the going rate, would represent in dollars at least three quarters of a billion. But if

247

the environmental impact involved in this system, and the joint development including playgrounds, schools, shopping centers and additional housing, were added, the total would run much, much more.

Although money is the measuring stick used by almost everyone, here it really had little to do with the gut issues — quite the opposite. In this case, if the 10D road system were built through Baltimore as designed, the environment of the city would be destroyed forever, wiped out, erased. The intangible values involved were beyond calculation, except to say that they were what Marylanders had fought for since Revolutionary days.

Our mandate, in the form of "givens" set up by the federal and state agencies, called for this freeway system to run through the heart of Baltimore. Under existing law, the 90 per cent subsidy furnished by the feds could only be obtained if the matching interstate systems between Florida and New York City were connected. This single stipulation forced over 60 per cent of the through traffic — which didn't want to go through Baltimore at all — to pass through the heart of that city. This arbitrary ruling, easily changed by the flick of an official pen, would, if unchanged, wreck the heart of Baltimore, a potential disaster which seemed to concern the federal and state bureaucratic wielders of that pen not at all. In desperation I inquired of Federal Administrator Lowell Bridwell if there was anything in the Constitution of the United States that prevented federal officials from solving a crisis before it arose; or whether, under law, they had to wait until one was created. After due deliberation, Bridwell finally flicked that pen, released the bottleneck, and in effect created a new era in highway concepts. When this was done — quite a long while after we started to work — more than half of our traffic problems in Baltimore immediately disappeared. Why, oh why, couldn't someone have asked that that pen be flicked ten years earlier?

Unlike his predecessors, usually appointed through the efforts of the concrete and highway lobbies, Lowell Bridwell had been a newspaper reporter with a muckraking background and hailed from Columbus, Ohio. The fact that he cooperated with the Concept Team seemed to irritate the chairman and the director of the Maryland State Roads Commission no end. It would appear that officials in such capacity as the chairman of the Maryland State Board were unwilling to drop one strand of the strings of job-giving patronage or share any of the influence that might accrue in the decision making at high federal levels. My interference was resented, and I was forbidden in writing to even visit the federal-related authorities. I ignored this and proceeded to carry on as before. The risks? Contract termination, perhaps, but the goals were worth the risk. The press, locally and nationally, were watching, and the advocate planners were on the alert. The Concept Team representatives themselves were stalking the bureaucratic jungle with predation in mind, while the bureaucratic predators were stalking us. We worked and waited for the inevitable showdown.

I saw the problem as one of dealing with a living organism: the city and environs of Baltimore. I saw it as one of lacing the tubes of traffic through the flesh and bones, the nerves and muscles, without disturbing the living organism too much. I felt that in creating the Concept Team an enormous stride had been taken toward recognizing the interrelationship between a transportation system and the communities through which such a system must pass. I was impressed with the fact that the sovereign state of Maryland was leading the way; it was not the first time that Maryland had done so. She had forced several of the original thirteen colonies to agree to cede their colonial holdings to the newborn United States as public domain. She had required this concession on the part of the colonies before she would ratify the Articles of Confederation in 1781 prior to the establishment of the Constitution. This first act of prescience guaranteed the natural growth of a continental power; and to me

249

this second act of instituting a Concept Team might be another landmark in showing the way toward a balanced treaty of peace between man, his mobility and his sedentary establishments.

I knew of no such effort having been made in the United States before. The Concept Team would bring multiple benefits to Baltimore through making the right-of-way alignment become an instrument of corrective surgery for good instead of bad. That something useful could come from the highway engineers and the bulldozers and the great ribbons of concrete was unheard of. But present conditions of the proposed right of way were deplorable. Untouched because they were said to be tax-producing, industrial areas were producing more pollution than taxes and were hosts to slums and crime. We would use highway engineers and bulldozers constructively as drastic cleaning-out agencies. Only in this way could such cancerous growth existing in many of the pockets of industry in Baltimore be dislodged.

As architect-chairman of the Concept Team I felt comfortable, since the architect is historically oriented toward *place* in contrast to mobility, supplying habitat for sedentary civilizations rather than nomadic ones. Today in dealing with Americans who are half nomad and half cliff dweller, this precarious balance can only be maintained by someone sensitive to both.

There were some nine hundred thousand people within the city of Baltimore, over 45 per cent of whom were black or brown; and in opposition were federal and state professionals — compact, organized, motivated. They knew exactly what they wanted and had no intention of being blocked by the infant Concept Team. The local newspapers were another element to be taken into account. The press was forever looking for the crack in the unity of the Concept Team, but no such crack was ever found. With straight face and solemn mien I stressed our perfect agreement; and although there wasn't a reporter in the group who didn't know differently, not one could prove it. The press, prying into every nook and corner, was a constant prod keeping us all on our toes. Without the press we would never have made it.

The Concept Team included the private engineering firm which had worked on the original scheme, J. E. Greiner and Company. Competent, powerful, they accordingly used this know-how as a sharp tool which could cut either way. We intended that it cut for the benefit of the Concept Team. Working together smoothly, we reached a conclusion based on pure engineering: that the original scheme would, "when open to service, be a disaster."

As these words rang the death knell to the 10D scheme, and since both nature and engineers abhor a vacuum, an alternate proposal was necessary, called "3C." This scheme by-passed the inner city and provided a simple, direct solution. Conceived in less than a month's time, it seemed as simple as Einstein's theory of relativity, and was almost as complicated.

The 3C scheme was conceived by one man, as much as any idea that large can be. Norman Klein was that man — wide-eyed dreamer, liberal advocate planner for the minorities, at the time about forty-eight years old and an associate partner, follower in the great tradition of Skid, Bunshaft and Hartmann as an M.I.T. graduate in architecture and a winner of the Rotch Traveling Scholarship. Klein came to San Francisco late — about 1960 — and concentrated on the science or art of people-moving, mass transportation and such, and therefore was a natural for a key role in the innovative, creative side of Baltimore. A motivated reformer leaning toward the social rather than the architectural, Norm Klein came up with the 3C solution at a time in the Baltimore schedule when there didn't seem to be a prayer of its ever going through, violating as it did every codicil of our contract and threatening to destroy every "given." Thus subtly the unattainable became the goal, having once been posed, and finally the great day came. The 3C scheme became that goal accomplished.

But not before I subjected the scheme to another even more telling check. I submitted the whole idea to Michael Rapuano, my old friend and Cornell classmate. I knew that his judgment would be sound. His advice: either force through the 3C scheme or resign. Although Mike never officially appeared on the scene, it was his moral support that gave me the courage to force the issue.

The 3C plan by-passed the black community of Rosemont, eliminated the crossing of the inner harbor and saved the historically important Federal Hill. Each of these three elements was a victory of design in itself, but most important was Rosemont. Stable, with a population numbering some seventy-five hundred blacks, handsome with its lovely tree-lined winding streets dating from 1903, white marble steps gleaming in the Maryland sun, its row houses were reminiscent of Bath, England. All set in graceful curving patterns of streets, the houses with richly molded façades complimenting the heavy shadows cast by the chestnut trees — all this was to have been blasted out by bulldozers in order to make way for a freeway forbidden by law to go through a cemetery next door. The cemetery was untouchable, while living neighborhoods were not. Only the federal government could change all this. Risking the wrath of the Maryland dead, the federal law was modified to meet the needs of the living. The freeway would go through the cemetery and by-pass Rosemont.

The second item, the elimination of a fourteen-lane crossing of the inner harbor, removed the need for a monster bridge. Using innovative architects and imaginative engineers, false perspective drawings and tricked-out models, proponents of the bridge had gone to strange lengths to produce a mind-boggling design structure which we demolished by a simple comment. "It looks like a spring hat stuck with hat pins." Ridicule succeeded where scientific double talk had failed, and Federal Hill, a Revolutionary fort, was saved because the bridge was not built — the domino theory in reverse.

In a fairy tale, the happy ending of this story would be discarded as being too fanciful. The idea that we could come up with a workable solution approved by the engineers which would eliminate all crossing of the harbor seemed beyond comprehension — but there it was. Boulevards were introduced instead of freeways, and a by-pass run through the very area where a freeway would be most needed, produced a near perfect, scientifically sound, aesthetically desirable solution. But our fairy tale was still just a fairy tale. Although the advocate planning groups kept the heat on everybody, popular pressures had so far failed to save Rosemont, the harbor and Federal Hill.

At this point I decided the time had come for the showdown. I chose the annual meeting of Greater Baltimore's Citizens Planning and Housing Association as the forum and planned a spectacular. My secret was well kept. Mayor D'Alesandro innocently agreed to introduce me and the speakers' table was lined with city council, state and federal officials. Over seven hundred and fifty people jammed the hall, with standing room only. I withheld my prepared address from the press until one minute before I rose to face my audience.

Recalling the words of a wise old Catholic priest I knew who admonished his flock to "follow the straight and narrow path between right and wrong," I suggested that, like the gentleman in Disraeli's novel, I was "a person distinguished for ignorance, having but one idea and that one wrong" — that idea being that the ordinary citizen was reasonable if given sufficient information. Freeways, I said, must go under or around, never through the fragile fabric of the city. Knowing that Baltimore had managed to survive three hundred years of changing technology and social order, I doubted that the modern Baltimorean would put up with anything as new and unseasoned as the intrusion of the forty-year-old American highway and the seventy-year-old family automobile. The automobile had always been a dangerous thing. Even when there were only four gasoline motor cars in the United States in 1895, the two that were in St. Louis managed to collide with such impact as to injure both drivers, one seriously. And statistics showed that over one quarter of the cars manufactured today ended up with blood on them. It wasn't just the highway we were up against; it was the control and limitation of permissive license. I wondered how they in Baltimore were supposed to know what was right and what was wrong when they had been told different things since 1939. How, in 1968, we — another group of experts — had come along and why should they believe us? They were entitled to know whether or not they had a good or bad system. "Stripped of all verbal garbage, the Urban Design Concept Team is unanimous that the 10D system fails as an efficient transportation system." If this system were opened to the public it would produce an impossible traffic situation and would be completely outdated, beyond capacity, from the day it was opened.

I pointed out that these negative findings obliged us to report a constructive solution and described our new proposal. It would take less land, make fewer intrusions, cost less money and could be built more quickly.

The black, the Polish, the Lithuanian, the Catholic, the Protestant and the Jew, the rich and the poor, the conservationists and the minority leaders who were present there climbed onto their chairs with excitement and the ovation lasted quite a while. This was a classic example of advocate planning at work. They were on their chairs because they had been given new hope. It was our job to see that they were not disappointed.

Next morning the papers responded. From the Baltimore *Sun*, dated October 1, 1968:

> In his address to the Citizens Planning and Housing Association he even managed to convince City Council President Schaefer that

current plans for an east-west expressway through the city are a dreadful mistake.

In Mr. Owings' analogy, Baltimore's expressway mess has been like the Vietnam war in that the city has got itself ever more deeply committed to the wrong course without knowing how to extract itself. Put in this context, William Donald Schaefer has been the chief hawk, insisting that the City Council adhere to the present expressway course and give no ground to detractors. The ruinous effects that Mr. Owings cited left the City Council President's faith shaken and no longer convinced that the expressway was needed.

The answer has to lie in a new set of plans which will serve traffic needs without demolishing urban values and which will be financially feasible for the city and federal government. Mr. Owings promises that his design team will have such plans in about two weeks, at which time the local equivalent of the Paris peace talks can begin in earnest.

About this time Daniel Patrick Moynihan told me a story from a time when Eisenhower was taken around the White House by Truman. Truman was outgoing and Eisenhower was incoming. Finally they came to the Oval Room and Truman's Presidential desk. Truman pointed to the desk and said, "Here is where you will make your great decisions. You will call on your aides, you will sign papers and send out orders for action. These orders for action will be passed from desk to desk, department to department and bureau to bureau, and finally nothing will happen."

In planning, often the best thing that can happen is nothing. Our victory in Baltimore, contributed to and shared by all joint members of the Concept Team, was the basic fact that the past mistakes were cleared away and a master plan for a superb solution to the city's transportation was substituted.

The smoke has cleared now. Most of the actors have gone on to other fields. There is a new mayor — happily Mayor William D. Shaefer, whom I have swayed a bit in our direction. The shadow of the past threats has been removed and a people-supported plan for the future offers wide scope to environmentalists and commercial interests alike. There seem to be few clouds on the horizon.

Externally, as chairman I served as a visible rallying point for the diverse interests coalescing at this point. Within, I was a mediator and unifier for the four member firms on the Concept Team, knowing that the opposition could not rule if we all stuck together. SOM had put its heart into it on the side of the environment and had provided the logistical support in all matters beyond the engineering competence of the other member firms. The Baltimore job was a crusade beyond all tangible things. It was a song of action. It was truly the story of *the spaces in between.*

6

Oh! To Be Eaten by a Lion!

S TANDING ON THE THIN EDGE of the present, behind me civilizations — none very old — around me glimpses of heaven on
earth. I was in Africa's great Rift Valley, the past in the present
and, hopefully, the future in the past. There I learned that it
would be an honor to be eaten by a lion.

Each of the thirty-one days spent in East Africa's Kenya and
Tanzania, in the open, under tent, surrounded by and mingling
with free wild animals and birds was, for me, a sort of layman's
"forty days of wandering in the wilderness," a living wilderness.
Through each day's happenings I identified and consolidated a
strange new philosophy from which I moved into a broader religious experience — a rich, colorful, action-filled polytheistic
faith.

Margaret had long had her heart set on going to Africa —
perhaps for the same reason she married me in the first place:
her interest in rare and endangered species. She wanted to see
the animals before they were all gone. I had not been so sure
I did.

Our safari plans had been carefully laid. Paul Brooks contributed his secret special guide, Robert Lowis; and some kind of
an instinctive assurance that Evelyn and Amyas Ames would

prove to be the perfect companions led us to invite them. Like a stern, gentle Moses, Robert Lowis guided four subdued and humble neophytes through the Garden of Eden.

There were just thirty-one days, each standing clear like tall poplars on a country lane, each marking a distinct kind of exaltation. I discovered some rather startling things about myself through this procedure: I adjudged myself crude, unfinished, transitory, way down the line in the evolutionary process. A new light was shed on Africa. The life on the Mara River, complete with life through death, is a polished, sophisticated cycle evidencing there the deep tissue demand involved in all mankind, and animal too, in a love affair with death. Life, death, life. Each creature — the slender impala, the imposing elephant, the floating giraffe, the smiling Masai — all were in balance in the world of ever-changing unchange.

"It is a world and a life from which one comes back changed," Evelyn Ames was to write of this experience. Her moving book, *A Glimpse of Eden,* was testimony on this score. No matter what is told about it, it remains an area of the unknown. Our trip to Africa became a spiritual transformation, a religious conversion. Instincts, emotions and religion, never separated, were arising again, merged with the only thing I knew: architecture. Just as it had been with my first view of Chartres and Notre Dame, the Virgin and the Son, when the lightning had struck, so the lightning struck again in Africa. Suddenly it became important for me to design for a world nested in "ecology." What all this meant to me was eloquently spelled out in Margaret's probing observations written by her on that African safari and titled "Nerve Song":

An intricate rhythm, not instantly comprehended, touches all wildlife in Africa — a harmony, but not a guarantee. We witnessed again and again the formation of order, the interjection of uncer-

tainty and fear, the clash, the climax, the return to order — a sheet of music in which small confusions were but elaborations of the great design.

Never will I lose the memory of the birds' superb music along the Mara River — a clear note of sunshine, liquid beauty, glory! At dawn the first bird song came as a reaffirmation of another day — a bright, supporting, comforting renewal of life after the dark night sounds of predator and prey. It came as the lions were seeking reunion with one another by great throaty rumbles. It came as white follows black, purer and more glistening than before.

Game trails over the plains or converging on a water hole illustrate decisions made by the moving herds. This path or that path — a luxury of alternatives, but the intuitive selection and timing often means life or death. Each day and night, each hour of the day and night, death is waiting; death is near. Each animal is keyed to this tightly strung web and loses its individual sensitivity to it only when a herd stampedes.

The sky is turning copper now on the Uaso Nyiro River, sharpening a silhouette of two vultures hunched on a bare limb. A covey of vulturine guinea fowl sift out of the undergrowth near the water's edge. Once again an order takes place: the approach to the river for a few at a time to drink, the watchful waiting for each to take a turn, holding their heads like embellished crooks inset with burning ruby eyes. A luminous blue, taffy-brown and slate gray, they sweep up the bank and are propelled forward again for the intuitive procedure.

A hawk is wheeling overhead. Circling a tree, he reappears suddenly at an acute angle, dropping among the guinea fowl like an explosion. Out of the confusion, only the hawk remains. Stretching his wings, he rises slowly up through the narrow corridor of the river. On the earth lies a feather.

I slip off the tree trunk to claim it. Eight inches of exquisite understatement — warm in charcoal brown, pierced by a white quill with opposing elements of the design on either side. It is the symbol of life in Africa, these opposites paralleling one another. Three steady, delicate lines march up the quill on the left: birth, life, death; while on the right the staccato pulse of life, uneven, nervous and varied, lies in four rows of dots.

So here is the rhythmic harmony — but, as this fallen feather indicates, without a guarantee. Give one a guarantee and vitality stagnates. The nerve song of Africa, found in this unexpected pattern, hidden beneath the vestments of the handsome vulturine guinea fowl, will be the tangible record of the journey I shall take home.

Turning it in my fingers I too must accept the opposites in the rhythm as a part of the full harmony. I too must not ask for the guarantee. I look upon the feather with fresh insight. Is it my life?

We reacted differently to the same experiences. Africa flowed over Margaret, I sought confrontation — preferably with a lion. Of course it had to be a free-ranging, wild lion pursuing its own role in the biota of the African plains before I would consent to being eaten by one, but it is satisfying to discover in one fell swoop that one can reach an agreeable reconciliation with the idea of death and decide on how one wants to accomplish this inevitable termination. I would insist on satisfying the king of the beasts' own hunger and provide a bit of sustenance for his young as well. Having determined this, then life can assume the basis of any good design with a well-planned beginning and an end.

From a reluctant follower on this safari, thinking my interest lay in the habits and habitats of people — a people mostly without a sense of humor or appreciation of nature — as a convert to nature I soon became an avid reformer, dreaming dreams about a possible utopia for these dull, white egomaniacs who, although in the minority, still held the switch to the world's generator.

Assuming the present rate of change, I allowed myself the luxury of projecting a mental picture of the year 2200. Then we

260

would ride the range, avoiding power lines, dams, reservoirs, highways, the sprayed-out dead land and the solid layer of 1080 and DDT — and their newer equivalents. Across the silent desert, empty of animal and bird, with air and land thoroughly polluted, we rode on our ponies, since there was no fuel left for even the tote goat. All those automobiles had finally jammed up all together in one monstrous glacier slowly moving toward the seas. Mechanical mobility had been wiped out and those products would never extricate themselves again. Very stupid creatures, we are like the pterodactyl — as if we were eighteen feet long, mostly tail, and were eating ourselves up beginning at the tail end. Pain and all, that was us; and along with the tail we are eating all three of our easily identifiable standard forms of existence: body, soul and habitat.

With this grim vision before us, what harm in dreaming of a new faith based upon reverence for natural phenomena where man is counted as only one — and very far down on the totem pole; where ego will become vestigial and humility will be the growth that smothers it. Rhythm will be the general of the armies of all things, as it always has been since time immemorial, finally triumphant. The rhythm of the dance will survive and burgeon, almost unchanged, and the job of creating meaningful leisure will never enter anyone's head — it will be there already because we will have let our children alone from birth. They will have been let alone to paint and draw what they see — not what we tell them to see. This will be our common language.

The Katchina of the Hopi, the ruins of the Casa Bonita at Chaco Canyon and the young people of today are pinpoints of light against the backdrop of a great country, all of which involves land, people, animals and birds — and the experience is expressed in Margaret's "Nerve Song," which puts words to my song of action.

I place that month and a day spent on safari in Africa as a

time of revelation — a revelation strangely dual to the world of the Hopi. Animism, being worldwide, filled out the background for Hopi culture, Hopi religion. Somehow the animals of Africa and the living culture of the ancient Hopi supplemented and strengthened each other.

7

Quantum Leaps

I was glad that Skid lived to see SOM's quality of design reach a kind of aesthetic plateau of style, commodity and classic beauty, a condition which Skid was apt to compare with Periclean Athens just before it fell. He never dreamed of the quantum leaps the firm would make, sometimes across deep valleys, sometimes scaling high peaks. This was the situation in 1966.

Aware and proud, the younger partners thought it appropriate that this interesting growth pattern should be charted. They prepared two great cyclical diagrams on the occasion of SOM's thirtieth birthday. The subject of one chart was "People," a roster showing the gathering together of the partners and associates, their longevity and their advancement through the hierarchy of the firm. The long chart showed that SOM, gaining in momentum, reached its present strength in numbers and continuity in the middle 1960s.

The second chart of "Architecture" graphically illustrated only the very rarest of the rare, the projects these young partners thought best represented their concept of SOM. Those chosen from the completed works of the first fifteen years of the firm's existence were very few indeed: the New York World's Fair in 1939, Oak Ridge, the Terrace Plaza Hotel, the New York

University Medical Center and the Brooklyn Veterans' Hospital. But from the architectural chart it would appear that beginning in 1951, when these young men had begun to make their own fruitful contributions, a profusion of elegant stuff began to bloom. In this second fifteen-year period there were over forty projects, some twelve of which had received the American Institute of Architects' First Honor Award — admittedly a dubious measuring stick of the value of the work but the only intraprofessional one available. Of course such charts told less than half the story. Okinawa and the Air Force Academy and many others had never been submitted to anyone for award consideration.

Each name on the "People" chart marked a kind of tree ring, many in numbers and giving good accounts of the deep roots put down in the early years when Skid and I were making our investment in men. In those days, much effort went into training and conditioning of both client and colleague. These roots were in firmer ground, driven deep. Our philosophy in a good many ways and by a good many structures had proven out. We had done much to re-establish the plaza in the cities. Some of our buildings had set trends — Lever House, Chase Manhattan and Crown Zellerbach — and proven the validity of group practice among "people" and for "architecture." Life had been a veritable dance over fire and water. We could feel inside the developing rhythm of growth. We molded new materials and created new forms. We were involved with the habitat of man, vibrantly — the charts said so. We were even a step ahead in the emergence of some sort of overall planning discipline. We might — just possibly — be getting an idea of just what the hell it was all about.

The "People" chart, with seventy-five tree rings, included just one woman: Natalie de Blois. Long, lean, quizzical, she seemed fit to handle all comers. Handsome, her dark, straight eyes invited no nonsense. Her mind and hands worked marvels in design — and only she and God would ever know just how many great solutions, with the imprimatur of one of the male heroes of SOM, owed much more to her than was attributed by either SOM or the client.

From Columbia University she worked with several facile New York architects until Gordon Bunshaft and Bill Brown discovered her. From that time on she was the basic design coordinator on the Terrace Plaza Hotel, Lever House, and the Pepsi Cola Building. As a woman is wont to do — especially a handsome one — she married; and the conflict of career and home came into play, but not before four children and a year abroad on a Fulbright Scholarship had run their successful course. Without ever missing a beat in the rhythm of her all-out contribution to SOM, she asked for a change of offices to Chicago, where her divorced husband was and the children could be shared. And there she still is, carrying the full load of one major design job after another, alone among all those men until later — much later — Pat Swan became the second woman.

Among the rings there was thirty-seven-year-old Myron Goldsmith, who first came down from some Old Testament cloud in 1955 to help us design airplane hangers for United Air Lines, and later to engineer a thin-shell, clear-span structure to house the Olympic winter games in Squaw Valley. A Jew whose gentleness pervaded body and spirit, his full sun face surrounded by an aurora of encircling hair, he had the air of a young Einstein.

Myron often invented new solutions to old space problems, like the cross-braced, fifteen-thousand-seat drum he did for the Portland, Oregon, coliseum.

In construction, the triangle is much stronger than the post and lintel. The triangle is all bracing and doesn't need the intricate bracing added at every right angle. Visible cross bracing is common in bridges but hitherto hidden in buildings. This diagonal cross-bracing system was used on the Oakland, California, coliseum and then, on a much grander scale, on the Alcoa Building in San Francisco, and finally, with even broader strokes, in "Big John," the John Hancock Center in Chicago.

Quiet, meticulous, Myron was our first engineer partner. Within our partnership — a body neither monolithic nor homogeneous nor physically connected — each new entity falls into orbit like a satellite around the IDEA, the idea which is in essence the corpus of SOM. Myron helped provide this nucleus. Although the IDEA has developed mass — mass in history, personnel, and a collection of mind-boggling accomplishments in buildings and complexes of buildings — there is, of course, that sacred mortuary vault filled with the dream children that were never built, never approved, fallen by the wayside: the veterans' mental hospital at Toledo, the Squaw Valley dome, the first idea for the Mauna Kea and dozens of others — sad and poignant memories.

Bruce Graham was one of the strongest personalities ever to surface in SOM. Born in La Combré, Bogotá, Colombia, in 1925, an employee of the Chicago office since 1951, Spanish-Irish, spare, dominating anything he touched and strong in every department, he was not under that banyan tree. It was not until 1960, at the age of thirty-five, that he was elected a general partner.

Graham's abrasive power drive, harnessing the imagination, habitat needs and money of the Establishment, unhinged the calm SOM never really had anyway, especially in Chicago. Watching with concern as one head of our Hydra-headed monster seemed bound on growing out of all proportion to the rest, I have sought containment without damaging the earth-strong power. In 1972, at forty-seven, Graham epitomizes steam and SOM a generator that I can only hope we have built strong enough to stand the strain.

In the San Francisco office, his star rising sharply in a short, spectacular trajectory, was Edward Charles Bassett. Chuck was tweedy, informal, a creative designer of humane proportions

266

who had moved from glass and stainless steel to natural teak and rich materials, creating warm, comfortable architecture. Early on, Bunshaft happened to see in model form an example of Bassett's best, a little jewel of a building. It was also our first major commission for the John Hancock people, non-Bauhaus, fashioned of granite and bronze, a kind of contemporary Florentine palace. Bunshaft queried Bassett: "Is this your design?" "Yes," answered Bassett. "Then you have no future in this firm." It was only a year later, I believe, not too long after this beautiful structure was finished, that Bunshaft proposed Bassett for partnership within our august brotherhood.

Six-foot-two Chuck Bassett added a necessary element to the total SOM picture and established San Francisco as an office to be reckoned with. Known in the trade as the "young" office, it was the one where students tried to get hired. The State Department of the United States chose Chuck and the San Francisco office to do the United States embassy in Moscow, passing over the New York and Chicago offices to do so — an assignment which would certainly call upon everything Bassett had in warmth, humanity and richness. And following closely was twenty-eight-year-old Marc Goldstein, already sparkling, with promises of much, much more.

Another more softly glowing star in that same office was Walter Costa, who seemed destined to take the place of John Barney Rodgers — as loquacious as Rodgers was taciturn. Wally fitted into a specific function, part of which was to keep the more scintillating satellites in their proper orbits.

There was Santa Fe–born David Hughes of the New York office, six feet two and a half inches of elegance, and his equally elegant wife and their eight tall, equally handsome children. David Hughes was a square and the leader of our own young Establishment. Hughes dealt in big strokes, was fascinated with "international projects." Not easily pinned down on details or practical aspects, he preferred in eloquent language to envision enormous complexes of many city blocks in far distant places such as Johannesburg, for example. There he had projected office buildings, hotels, shopping centers, all clustered together under the sponsorship of beer and diamonds, making it sound quite safe.

An ever-changing, joined body of partners thus developed. Distinguishable even in their unity as separate, they jointly created a miracle of renewal and have each in his own way progressively helped reform the history of SOM through the years. Around them has sprung up a fast-growing body of apocrypha, legend and myth as each new partner becomes inextricably enmeshed in the SOM mystique.

During the formative years from 1936 to 1946, there were John Merrill, Skid and I. Between 1946 and 1956 we took in ten partners and lost two. As we and the firm grew older the average age of the partners dropped from fifty-eight to fifty. In the ensuing ten years the bright young faces of another generation began to appear. John O. Merrill, Jr., became a partner and Louis Skidmore, Jr., an associate partner. The ten years from 1956 to 1966 marked extraordinary economic successes and peaking, and some of us remembered that peaking was followed often by decline. As more new brothers joined, the autonomous brotherhood ran ever so smoothly, and by 1968 there were twenty-one of us all told. Most of the new partners had come so fast that I saw more young strangers around than familiar faces. In 1972 there remained only four of our original group — Gordon Bunshaft, Walter Severinghaus, William Hartmann, and myself — and the average age had dropped to forty-eight years of age, a fact of which I was proud.

One trademark of our profession is "great architecture designed by great architects," and by the early 1960s I felt that SOM could claim five of the dozen or so famous names generally acclaimed as such in the United States. A substantial part of the success of each of these five could be attributed to the workings of our own system — Gordon Bunshaft, Walter Netsch, Bruce Graham, Charles Bassett and Myron Goldsmith, their geniuses surfacing from a neutral start within our firm. Might this be proof that there were operating here the benign influences of a natural law? If so, perhaps this was a way to bring to the surface the genius badly needed throughout the world in many fields besides architecture and planning. I like to think that there exists within the bosom of all men, lying dormant like kernels of wheat in the Egyptian tombs, seeds of genius needing only soil and water and a benign climate to bring them to fruition. Perhaps we at SOM had inadvertently developed such a climate, and while we could not claim to be geniuses at finding people, perhaps we had been able to provide the natural climate with soil, water, sun and shade necessary to bring out the genius in the people we had.

I have always liked the working press. They have overlooked my boners and pushed my projects from the beginning. But the climax to my exposure to the press came in 1968 when I met the chief of the San Francisco *Time* bureau, Judson Gooding, and established a permanent personal relationship. Gooding has since gone on to another position — an editorship on *Fortune* magazine — but his guidance has continued, available only from a professional turned friend. He first called me for an interview, I found out later, to determine whether I or SOM could qualify for a much coveted *Time* cover story. I had never been warned about what was involved in a cover story for *Time*. Looked upon as a great honor, much of it is actually trauma-producing. The publicity is beneficial but is balanced by an incredible amount of personal inconvenience — sometimes embarrassment. Fortunately, my psychiatric probe was the same Judson Gooding. I had to reduce to words, single words put together in sentences, the jumbled, tangled mass of my feelings, hang-ups, prejudices, myths. The first real sense I ever made of SOM and my life in it, Gooding brought out of me. For this I am grateful. There were near disasters, as when managing editor Henry Anatole Grunwald showed me samples of the work of my portraitist, who seemed to specialize in decomposing bodies. One, bound and captive in a box, still burns in my mind's eye.

Gooding and I holed up at Big Sur for a seventy-two-hour stint, unwinding the story of the tangled past. Photographers appeared — not one or two, but droves. Finally, putting all this behind us and thinking the project finished, Margaret and I went off on a long-planned rowboat trip down the rapids of the Colorado River. Drawing a sigh of relief, safely tucked in our own small wooden boat with a party of selected fellow adventurers, we discovered that the man in the next boat was there to photograph us "in the wilds." *Time,* we decided, could not be faulted for lack of thoroughness.

Then followed a six-month period when the cover story was postponed each week by a newly arising crisis. Finally, when the threatened invasion of Czechoslovakia hadn't reached its peak on the final Saturday night before August 2, word came that the presses were rolling. No one knew even then what was on that cover or in that story. Monday morning revealed that the planned desiccated portrait had dissolved into what must have been the smallest photograph ever placed on the cover of *Time.* The story inside irritated each partner sufficiently to cut out normal communication for months, and it was obvious that the postponement had developed uncertainty even for *Time,* which had suffered editorial stresses.

My *Time* article — and most publicity about architecture — features a dozen famous names and totally disregards the thirty thousand–odd registered architects who do the work in America. This is no fault of the press. They need a handle to their stories, an identifiable individual. They need a hero or a villain — they can't talk about the faceless masses. But also, the great masters of architecture throughout the ages and today were and are generally masters of self-publicization, such as Mies van der Rohe, whose "Less is more" and "God is in the details" are quotable and memorable and almost alone would have gained him immortality. A teacher like Walter Gropius, founder of the Bauhaus, a pioneer in contemporary group practice, was articulate, precise and dramatic. Yamasaki is clearly identified by his multiple-arched structures, just as Patton had been with his pistols; and Paul Rudolph by his nervous cookie-cutter shapes which he strives to establish as a new architectural idiom. There is a gaunt, esoteric face of Philip Johnson: fragile, brittle, a loner, whose own house in Connecticut and his New Harmony, Indiana, memorial seem to me to have established some pleasant American trends. There is I. Ming Pei, American-born Chinese, whose structures come as close as any to being carved out of solid substance, his Washington National Gallery promising to add to Pennsylvania Avenue its first really good contemporary structure. There is the talented Edward Durell Stone who, it is said, had kicked the alcohol and earned the quip: "It was but a step from the bar to the grill." Stone has been castigated on one hand and praised on the other. The Carmel-Monterey Community Hospital is a true masterpiece where architecture and the environment have been ideally combined. But he has also done some very bad designs. (At seventy-one he appears to me to be dispensing corn in gilded carmine wrappings, such as his new Washington Kennedy Cultural Center. With great humor and a straight face, and with extraordinary talent, he has been quoted as saying that he wants to give the Establishment "what they want, good or bad.")

Each of those featured architects has his own trademark, his own way of not only capturing the essential quality of architec ture as he sees it, but also gaining the essential quality of pub' relations and national business-getting fame. One might how much concern has been given to the essential qual' good architecture: Humility informed by grace and imbu' respect for neighbors. Not enough, I fear.

But was I talking, as my hippie friends were inclir

like a man over thirty if I suggested that this array of "the best the era had to offer" wasn't so much? That it couldn't come within shouting distance of the creators of the Chicago Prairie School and Louis Henri Sullivan?

"The tall office building," now called a skyscraper, seems to me to be the single most significant symbol of this specialized time of ours in the twentieth century, and the contemporary designs for them are essentially "tailings" as compared to the nuggets of solid gold which were produced by Le Baron Jenney, Root and Sullivan in Chicago in the late 1890s.

The skyscraper was invented in 1887 largely through the creative genius of three men: Major Le Baron Jenney, who invented the steel frame; Louis Henri Sullivan, philosopher and architect, who died in disillusionment alone and unsung in an attic closet; and John Wellborn Root, an architectural genius dead of pneumonia at forty-two at the crossroads of his fate, his death blocking the one clear road to an indigenous architecture. The skyscraper they developed combined for the first time the elements of steel frame, elevators, cast iron pipe for plumbing, the Edison light bulb and, strangely significant, sheet glass, which has turned out to be an external prefabrication material never since excelled. Their product met the demand of an old idea: high-density cities. Now, nearly a hundred years later, there has been hardly a new idea added to their solution, though
e concept has still not been expanded to its engineering limits.
ik Lloyd Wright's mile-high office building design proposed
5, while treated as a whimsy by many, is no whimsy at all.
Sullivan believed that all science is sterile until it rises
inacle of an art and he believed we are under the
as a profession, of science. Sullivan, like Whitman,
iginal force influencing the beginnings — in which
ticipating — in America. Sullivan believed that
2ictum or superstition or habit should stand in
rchitecture *fit its function*. Today he would

question not the *design* so much as the *function* of our contemporary work. Sullivan was the only individual I know of who developed a system of ornament altogether excellent in design; organic ornament growing out of his buildings and an integral part of them.

One of Skid's last acts before he died was to send me for Christmas, 1960, a copy of Louis Henri Sullivan's *Autobiography of an Idea,* and Skid wrote: "Nat, you may not like his architecture but he could write." Actually, through the distillation process which has gone on for some fifty-odd years now, I have come to the inescapable conclusion that I am awed by both his architecture and his writing. Frank Lloyd Wright referred to him as "the master," and with all his glory never cast a shadow over the genius of Sullivan.

8

Four Miracles

Four miracles: a hawk's vision, a hummingbird's will, a yucca's peak and a spider's craftsmanship.

> *Plants absorb energy from the sun. This energy flows through a circuit called a biota which may be represented by a pyramid consisting of layers. The bottom layer is the soil. A plant layer rests upon the soil, an insect layer upon the plants, a bird and rodent layer upon the insects, and so on up through various animal groups to the apex layer, which consists of the larger carnivores.*
> Aldo Leopold, from *Sand County Almanac*

A harsh thrust of sound like pebbles forced through a nozzle sprayed over me as a red-tailed hawk reared into a stall above my head, talons down. I was partway up the path at Wild Bird with Nikki, our black male peke, when this powerful presence exploded over me, then plunged out and down to the sea edge. The big bird poured out another urgent rasp and described a perfect parabolic arch to meet the rising eastern hills head on, his shadow preceding him into eternity. Nikki lifted up his head, unaware of the harrowing journey just missed beneath the talons of that bird.

For an instant I was caught up, shaken loose into a new dimension. I was left to confront the question: for what purpose was I here? What return could I offer for the rich experiences of my life? In the separate world of Big Sur, suspended between sea, granite and sky, I would try to isolate the naked facts and to make from the tumbled skein of my life a thoughtful pattern to give new play to my unquenchable country boy idealism.

I know nothing of why I am on this earth or where I am going when I die. No one can tell me where the earth is, or the history of the moon. In this know-nothing atmosphere I believe in miracles — happenings beyond my comprehension or control.

In this last chapter I deal with four miracles: allegorical, but also factual; happenings seen with my own eyes. They symbolize my faith. Each illustrates a tool. The high-soaring, wide view of the hawk gives clear judgment, with high perspective, on the Earth and on the Being and on the Everything-Else-But-Me. The hawk I describe lives nearby in the infinity of his universe. From our relationship based on respect, I draw strength and power. Only a dead Owings or a dead hawk can end this relationship.

The story of the hummingbird has to do with the breaking of barriers. The hummingbird seeks the light and naturally turns toward the light. When man places a barrier between him and that light, the hummingbird cannot break it; the bird is unable to change his approach. In nature there is no barrier in his way and man-made ones must be removed by man or the bird will perish. He cannot change his approach — man can.

The third miracle has to do with the peaking of the yucca plant. The miracle of rising to a heroic climax often followed by death is common to all nature. This mystical power teaches us that peaking is natural. There are limitations of growth. In nature nothing stands still. Man alone can create averages. Mediocrity does not exist in nature.

And the fourth miracle — the spider — all-encompassing as a constructor. His competence is my ideal as a builder, large or small; an ideal I can strive for but never reach.

Perhaps Montaigne explained why miracles appeal. "Nothing is so firmly believed," he said, "as what we least know."

In my unnatural man-made world the harsh sound of human complaint reaches a crescendo, each fellow pressing his neighbor. The air crackles with it on every side from everyone, condemning man's own failure. Government is failing the people; the people are failing the government. Cities have failed; they are filthy traps, unfit for humans to live in, everyone says. And while this is being said, more of the so-called underprivileged move in, or out — whites, blacks, browns — from city to suburbs and back again. Man adds power plants and is surprised when black smoke pours out of the smoke stacks. Power plants are much needed, people say, to meet the power shortage. These are the people who usually tend to leave their lights on all night.

This is the man-made scene that irritates the same man's eye, ear and olfactory senses. How and what can a young man or woman do who cares enough to remedy this situation? What kind of education does one seek? Where does one find an answer? At whose feet can one sit to learn? What textbooks can one use?

When eager and optimistic minds pose these questions, how can they be answered? It takes a hawk's view. With the hawk's vision I gain the needed dimensions, see the big view and gain perspective to combat the mechanical mind-shredders in whose hands most of us are today. These technicians squeeze a button or two and their computers respond with a flood that swamps the printed page with arguments valid only if taken piecemeal and out of context with the total environment. Taken together, false. Power shortages can be proved if sufficient false assumptions are used and thus the need for an Alaska pipeline can be established — but only if the ecology of the total Alaskan subcontinent is

276

ignored. The technique of misstatement by faceless men in formidable public and private agencies comes at us fast, and is highly organized and in such polished granitic form that few dare try to catch hold. Endless theories of new forms of management are put forward, are tried, fade, fail and die — all designed to gain time, to confuse. When one is transposed in spirit to the high point of the hawk's perfect parabolic flight the fallacies show — hollow, lifeless.

In my field of planning for me and my family and all the other collective families totaling up to a mind-boggling two hundred million just in the United States, how impertinent to offer suggestions on how to reorder cities or how to preserve open space, or how to advise government on new laws. How can one make efforts to manage people when he cannot manage himself?

As Montaigne cried: "Man is certainly stark mad. He cannot make a worm and yet he is making gods by the dozens." But still, one might ask, to put it as baldly as possible: what relationship is there between a hawk attacking a peke and the planning of cities? The answer is just as bald. Where else to look except to the gravity-free, independent force sweeping out of the heavens, on a mission of its own choosing, for inspiration and courage to tackle the little burrowings of man down there on earth? From that great height the details disappear and the firm outline of a grand design just might be emerging!

I see stark urban contradictions. I see two islands of humanity — one wrecked and ravaged, jammed with tenements — and I smell the greasy, sweaty, sooty air clouded over the masses of the dispossessed; on the other island I see the cluster of varying shapes and sizes standing like empty boxes in Sunday emptiness, dressed in granite, marble, stainless steel and glass, surrounded by bare plazas with stiffly paneled pools of water, and hothouse flowers. Everything is cold, lonely, empty. And around these islands of the poor and the established standing together, side by side, an enveloping endless wash of gray urbanity extends as far as my eye can see.

So, back to earth, a man again — but shaken loose into a new dimension where the naked truth of those two mismatched islands is plain. Our city is in extremis. One incident of seemingly unsolvable despair sums the crisis up for me and reaffirms my determination as a trained constructionist to commit my strength and spirit.

Early one morning in San Francisco when the streets were filled with office workers, there emerged from the gloom of the Mission District a slender, Afro-haired youth who crossed into the sunlight of Market Street, a street which marks the edge of the business district. Squeezing the trigger of an automatic rifle he sprayed bullets indiscriminately, severely wounding two strolling policemen, one of whom later died. The youth, it was learned, lived at home with his mother, his white wife and three-week-old baby. His utter revolt against the system appeared to have pushed him over the brink of sanity. He simply returned home, where they found him, his emotions and his bullets spent.

Consider this tiny act of violence, so small compared to all the violence, legal and illegal, occurring each day. Abandoned and neglected, this man had struck out blindly. Now society would give him the attention withheld from him before. Society, in fact, would now spend vast sums of money and energy upon the investigation and trial of a man who could no longer serve the system — a man running toward the light, toward the Establishment, blasting out his complaints in gunfire. His actions told me something I had overlooked. I would try to help the others of his kind to live within a tolerable habitat. But there were barriers to be removed and I returned to the sanctuary of Wild Bird, where I had first gained my new vision from the air, to find another miracle to help me on my way.

There, at Wild Bird in Big Sur, the tiniest of our feathered friends, the *Calypte anna,* with its needle-like bill for sipping

278

honey and wings which beat so rapidly that they blurred like fluffs of gauze, having sought out honey, zoomed against the undersurface of our living room's skylight in search of escape. The little bird's instincts drove him to rise upward toward the sky, where he seemed determined to crush out his life. Blocked by the artificial barrier, his strength was ebbing fast. No inducement we could offer would bring him to try another avenue of escape. Finally, with pole and net and honey we at last set him free; released that tiny bird. How often I too have battered blindly against barriers when all around me were open avenues to freedom that I'd never dreamed of trying. Now, perhaps, I could better perceive some of those open avenues by which I could circumvent those barriers.

I must now examine those barriers damming up those urban islands of despair that grow in every city in the land, mostly in abandoned white neighborhoods where most efforts to superimpose governmental plans on the people have failed. And in the corporate island the benign, virtuous but vacuous efforts made had followed conventional guidelines toward a garden city and a life style much like the one SOM had set years ago in Lever House. *Calypte anna,* I knew, would never understand the lesson of our skylight. Perhaps by using planning equivalents to "pole, net and honey" I could find solutions for man's upward urges, remove the barriers and provide alternative avenues of escape in these two areas of our concern — the one where trapped and fast eroding human chaos burgeoned and the other where human life was needed to fill the empty grandeur.

One thing was certain. There would be no valid solution without taking into account the blacks and Puerto Ricans and Chicanos, who in spite of the designation minority races were in the majority — 85 per cent in most city cores, and growing. The master white Judaic-Christians were in the minority. The middle- and upper-income suburban class, scurrying back and forth along the traffic arteries, by-passed not only the dark islands of despair but also the naked truth, which they refused to face on their journey from citadel to gray suburbia. So long as suburbia had its way, there would be no barriers removed.

So far we had failed; failed because of the lethargy of the average American who, once in the sanctuary of suburbia, tended to pull the quilt tight over eyes, ears and nose, repeat his "forgive us our trepasses as we forgive those who trespass against us," and fall into a peaceful sleep, to dream of another car and a larger garage in a farther-out suburb floating just beyond his reach.

Neither of those islands had been there in that physical condition very long. Those islands reflected in part the living history of the people and were malleable if vigorously attacked, could be changed. For a valid solution the principles of self-renewal must be incorporated. Machine production must be subordinated. Man's creativity must be re-established through the revitalization of the utility of his hands — and this is where the miracles begin. My former neighbor Henry Miller wrote: "In instinct, not intellect, lies genius; and the task of genius is to keep the miracle alive — to live always in the miracle, to make the miracle more and more miraculous, to live only miraculously, to think only miraculously and die miraculously."

Earthbound, gazing from my window at Wild Bird, I recognize such a miracle of life and death. A yucca plant growing on the cliff for some seven years had commenced as a simple ball of spiny green clinging to the dry, broken rock. Suddenly on this particular spring day I noticed a huge, asparagus-like tip issuing from the heart of the plant. Within thirty days the stalk had grown to an eight-foot height — almost four inches a day. Then the great spear blossomed. Where did that energy and substance come from? Where had it been hidden? What triggered the growth that hastened it toward fulfillment and death? When the creamy-colored blossoms appeared, a moth came to fertilize the seed. Here I gained a glimpse of the secret of renewal of our cities. Just as the yucca peaked and died, so have our cities: burgeoning in the nineteenth century, peaking in 1929, and now dead or dying, ready for renewal. Let the new seeds spring up in the compost of the past. Yuccas have long been growing from the wind-cast seed, reaching their mystical time of fruition and death. We accept miracles as commonplace until a special circumstance arises that points out an example of how to meet a definite need, offering — perhaps — a solution.

The phenomenon of peaking is common enough. Cultures, tribes, nations and societies have peaked: the Incas, the Egyptians, the Romans. Could not our two islands have reached peaks and died and needed a moth to fertilize the seed to create new life to help solve the problems of the urban scene?

The achievements of two young blacks show promise of great success. Like the miraculous yucca, Bob Nash surfaced within these islands of despair and within the planning profession and the Establishment. Almost unknown, he had suddenly appeared through service in the American Institute of Architects, crossing that invisible line into the arena where he could be heard by all sides. And there was young Taylor Culver, black and tall as a skyscraper, who had led the student revolt at an American Institute of Architects' convention and beguiled the delegates into pledging him fifteen million dollars to mount his student aid program, without a sou to back it up.

Together these two men, working within the white hierarchy, planted the seeds of community design centers in eighty-six cities — places where the professionals can help the poor to help themselves; where dependable solutions are offered for leaky plumbing and tricky contracts. Down payments and leases on apartments are checked, and advice is offered on "do-it-yourself" building in the city. These seeds of offered aid have taken root and sprung up and grown rapidly throughout the land. Self-remodeled homes carrying a sense of ownership pride with taste and cleanliness are visible proof that this crusade is growing.

Barriers are falling in downtown areas. Clean, habitable dwellings are re-establishing a dignity and a kind of recycling of human beings is in evidence.

In the empty enclave of the Establishment obsolescence is more in evidence than despair. This empty enclave is the terminus of the suburban traffic artery, receiving each morning the time-consuming migrations come there for the eight-hour day of business five days a week. Those enclaves stand empty all the remaining hours of the days and nights, empty and silent in these islands, and need the hand and heart and footprint of the individual again. People must be brought back in order to bring back life beyond the working hours. So simple, so obvious — so impossible? The gray, faceless anonymity of each tiny, identical section in the huge beehive of the modern office building is no suitable habitat for man for even part of the day. Can we introduce below, on the plaza, gaiety, spontaneity, excitement and human interest — to make up somewhat for the inadequacies within?

Standing on the plaza where the big bank is, I wondered what the Italian grape-grower who had founded the world's greatest banking institution would think about the polished granite, stone and glass. What has this to do with people, he might ask. Would he regret the failure to plant a vineyard in the open space where the great paving is?

How can SOM get with it to justify our continued existence into the year 2000? We are replete with gold medals, our bank account burgeons and our economic growth is embarrassingly expansive. But all of this plenitude cannot obscure from my hawk's view what is needed to correct our dismal failure with the slum, the business district and the suburb — which are in fact all combined, all tied together as one ecological unit. There can be no individual solution, the false promises of the mechanical mind-shredders to the contrary. We must tackle these problems as a whole. Let's help commerce and industry to get it all together. There is still time to find some tools as yet unknown or at least untried by us. Cities are living organisms, with their own life cycles. There are planning secrets hidden there, wrapped up inside like packaged seeds in peaking yucca plants. Where all else has failed, let's regroup in nature and add to our architects' competence the miracles of nature's limitless variety of structures.

At Wild Bird there is another necessary miracle which can be seen any early morning while the fog still clings: marked out in tiny drops of moisture is every strand of the intricate web of a Big Sur spider anchored among the spikes of the giant agave plants. Successfully completed without scaffolding, fashioned by the tiny empire builder's own gut-spun cable, capable of taking the highest tensile stresses per cross section known to the scientific world, this web is a Brooklyn Bridge flung across voids of the Grand Canyon to the scale of a thousandth of an inch per foot. The concentric fabric is braced and gusseted, freely improvised, the keen eyes of the spider engineer meeting the need for wind currents, using leaf or branch for anchor. Every effort is directed toward the main show: a giant radar screen fans out from the central crossing of the lines where our spider, in bejeweled Medieval fustian, stands ready, prepared for whatever fate will bring. A buzzing fly caught in a strand or a sudden rip from a dropped twig tests the resilience of the web and the cunning of its design.

The spider engineer is at once the designer, material supplier, constructor, owner, user, landlord and tenant, yet remains dependent upon an environment over which he has no control. But we, *Homo sapiens,* tool users, were busy ravaging not only this environment but all environments, and it would seem that all efforts, all ingenuity put into the partner-building of SOM — to mention only a small segment of the problem — had gone for nought. Where was our basic concept of anonymous Gothic builders? Were we guilty too of a monocultural approach failing to meet the requirements of diversity of habitat as the keystone of successful planning?

One very visible part of the reason for despair, which with my new vision I saw all too clearly, was the question of the hundred-story-tall office building as a valid module of the city's fabric. Such buildings, sucking up the vitality of the city into the vacuum created by the vast empty spaces in their own great tall shafts, with seemingly endless capacity, seemed to place corporate America in a hazardous position. Living on natural resources nearing the point of exhaustion, they might well prove an entity poorly equipped to withstand the shattering reverses which nature evidences in growth, peaking and death and which would seem to be inevitable.

Then suddenly, like a shower of meteorites appearing on the dark horizon, came evidence that the age of miracles was very much alive. Walter Severinghaus' voice came strong across the continent: "Nat, we've been given a great planning job in New York City. The trustees of the Cornell Medical Center and the Rockefeller Research Hospital are joining together to work out the development of a major chunk of Manhattan along the East River. They hope to create the largest and most important, the most beautifully oriented, environmentally conditioned hospital in the world. Nat, we were chosen for this, and our competition were firms with much less of the weight of the past upon their shoulders. The planning department of New York City and Mayor Lindsay will be involved. We'll need all the help we can get from our Washington planning office — we need planners because the job is overall, long term, and involves the city."

It seemed that, like a great underground river suddenly surfacing again, SOM was demonstrating the capacities needed and was being given the opportunity to produce in the new era.

Days later a phone call from Walter Netsch reached me at Big Sur. I found him tackling one of the toughest sections of St. Louis in a total effort to resolve the repressions of a depressed area; to mount an on-site self-renewal of the blacks in the central core. I heard him say all this in a voice filled with excitement and emotion. "But, Nat, this job cannot be charged on a commercial basis. How can we accomplish it within the fabric of SOM?" "We will discuss this as a research project when the partners next meet," I told Walter. And at that meeting I heard them say, the partners, "We wish to give, not take, fees here. Profits from conventional work will be reinvested in such sensitive areas."

Then the sun breaks through the rain clouds of the Pacific Northwest. Our senior partner in Portland, Oregon, David Pugh, is carrying on an involved program, weaving a highway through the fragile fabric of that area. This must be done gently, making transportation an asset, not a degradation, to the warp and the woof of the city.

It was during this period that Chuck Bassett and the Weyerhaeuser people in Tacoma, Washington, created something new under the sun. They turned a needed thirty-four-story skyscraper on its side and made the roofs into a series of horizontal terraces, each surface converted into a park: wooded, shrubbed and flowered, five terraces in all facing outward toward a man-made lake reflecting color, light and motion for the people working there.

It was clear that there was some young blood flowing in the old veins. In the Washington, D.C., office there could be found in the back room a clutch of minority groups, the Afro haircut, the uncut hair, the beards and sideburns. We even had a new brand of enthusiasm and commitment led by Walter Netsch with Norman Klein, Peter Hopkinson, John Galston and David Childs. Their solid enthusiasm reminds me of the early days of SOM, when the office was vibrant with concern. The names in this group will change, but the concern will not.

Yes, I began to believe that there was a "turnabout." My fear for what SOM might do had been changed to confidence in what its strength would add. There was still no basis to hope for quick solutions. The hawk, the hummingbird, the yucca and the spider pointed only to slow, steady growth. Couched in humility, keyed to the pace of natural forces, we play our minor role in rhythmic counterpoint. Then, like the spider, secure in our natural setting, we can do our part as builders should.

Perhaps a central theme of what I have learned in my life is that the city is here, stronger and more vibrant and more meaningful than any of the complexes which have been spun over it like a web, misleading the casual student. If the promised reduction in "slave labor" through the use of cybernetics and the computer actually happens, then we must find new and humane solutions to the otherwise brutal, soulless, antiseptic spaces offered now in our modern office buildings for human employment. We must find a modern equivalent to cottage industry to occupy the hands of modern cliff dwellers otherwise left idle from a four-day week. I look forward to new shapes for cities: low-rise, high-density habitat, stratified according to the specific gravities of its functions. Since large cities with diverse demands are already a miracle of functioning, I look forward to new miracles to meet the ever-growing complexities as the population rises and the cities grow. Man must be kept to his narrow slice of the ecosystem; and, through the blessings of communication — man's greatest miracle to date — a workable formula can be developed for a working environment.

I feel called upon to go back to the roots of mankind; roots which have not fed on a system of formulas and exactitudes but which have survived through a living corpus of myth, fable, miracle and witchcraft. I also believe that science will never take the place of witchcraft. We will find our way because of a desire to create, and joie de vivre will move us rather than threats of death or extinction. What we do must be done for love, not fear.

286

Index

Index

289

Index

293

Railroads, electric, in Indiana, 13
Rain dances, 218
Raleigh Hills Hospital, 199
Rancho de Taos Church, 225
Rand, Sally, 53–54
Rapuana, Michael, 103–4, 146, 252
Rayburn, Sam, 239
Rebori, Andy, 53–54
Religion, and catastrophe, 218
Rexroth, Kenneth, 189
Richardson, Ambrose, 65, 67, 114, 178
Rift Valley, 257–62
Rijkens, Paul, 108
Roberts, Isabel and Laurence, 146
Robertson, Senator A. Willis, 157
Rocha, Father, 224, 227
Rockefeller, David, 164, 168, 169
Rockefeller, Laurence, 169–72
Rockefeller, Peggy, 164, 168
Rockefeller, Winthrop, 169
Rockefeller Center, 46
Rockefeller Research Hospital, 284
Rodgers, John Barney, 137, 174, 177, 267
Rogers, Archibald, 247
Rome, 146–47
Roosevelt, Franklin Delano, 80–81
Roosevelt, Nicholas, 190, 202
Roosevelt, Theodore, 244
Root, John Wellborn, 45, 53, 272
Rosemont, Maryland, 252
Rudolph, Paul, 271
Ryukyu Islands, 129–30, 133–34. See also Okinawa

Saarinen, Aline, 108
Saigon, 64
Saint Bartholomew's Church, 109
Saint Peter's Cathedral, 147
Saint Thomas Church, 37–38
Sampsell, Marshall Grosscup, 70, 72, 97, 119
Sand County Almanac, 274

San Francisco, police attacked in, 278
San Francisco Peaks, 219
San José de Gracia, Church of, 222–28
Scenic Roads Commission, 209
Schaefer, William Donald, 254–55
Science, 195–96, 272, 286
Seagram's Building, 110
Sea lions, 192–93
Sea otters, 207–8
Sears Roebuck, 82
Severinghaus, Walter: role in New York SOM office, 73–74, 76; character, 74; and prefabricated housing, 80; and Ford executive office building, 127; and air bases in Morocco, 135; and Chase Manhattan Bank, 165–66, 168; and Skidmore's retirement, 174; role in SOM, 100, 179, 268; and East River project, 284
Seymour, Professor "Uncle Joe," 30, 31
Shaw, Alfred Phillip, 151
Siam, Crown Prince of, 58
"Sidewalks in the Sky," 114. See also New York Life Insurance Company project
Singer Building, 162
Sipchen, Bob, 52
Site plans, 88, 89
Skidmore, Louis: in Paris, 38; and Eloise Owings, 38, 39, 43; in World War I, 40–41; wins Rotch Fellowship, 41; meets Owings, 41–42; marriage, 43; and Chicago World's Fair, 46–60; as planner, 47; takes over SOM New York office, 72–73; ulcers of, 72–73, 77, 100, 136; and New York World's Fair, 76–77; shyness of, 77, 100; and alcohol, 77; and H. Heinz, 78; hometown of, 87; and Oak